THE CARIBBEAN

DIVING GUIDE

SWAN·HILL
PRESS

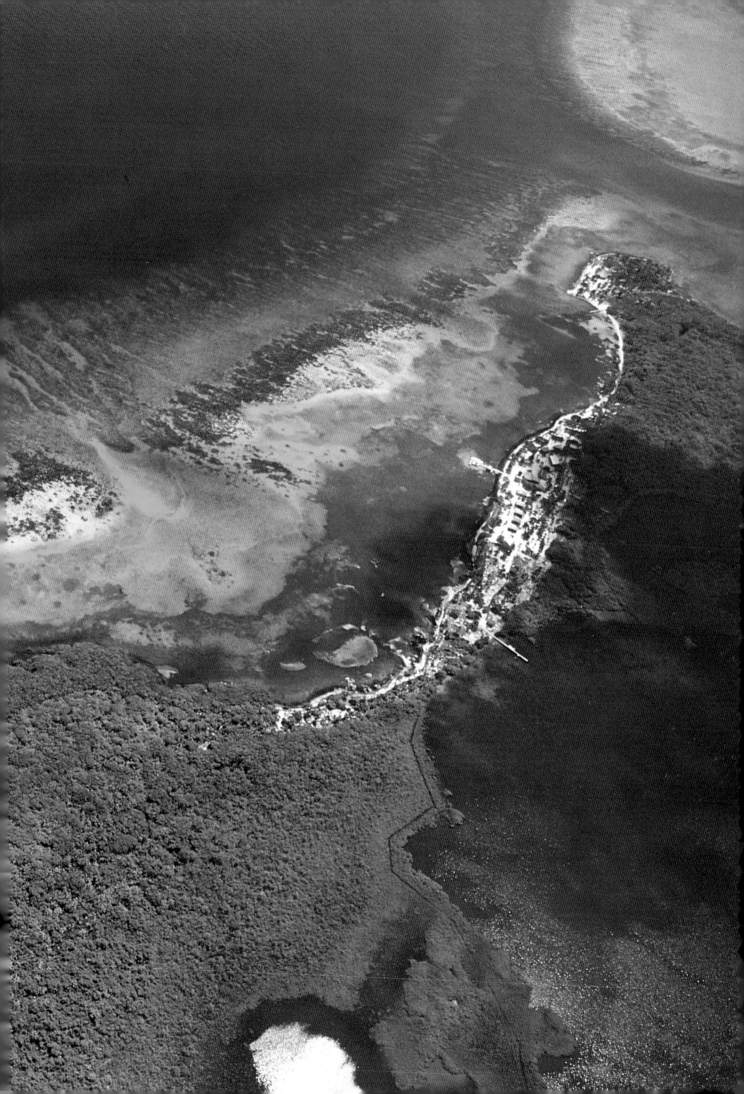

UNITED STATES
OF AMERICA

FLORIDA

MIAMI

1-2-3 · *Grand Bahama*

BAHAMAS

Turks and Caicois

GULF OF MEXICO

Florida Keys · ▼ 4-5-6

HAVANA

CUBA

10-11-12

▼ 7 · ▼ 8

Isla de la Juventus

9 ▼

HAITI

MEXICO CITY

BAHIA DE CAMPECHE

Cozumel Island

Cayman Islands

JAMAICA

13-14-15-16

MEXICO

BELIZE

▼ 17-18-19

20-21-22
▼

GUATEMALA

HONDURAS

CARIBBEAN SEA

NICARAGUA

COSTA RICA

PANAMA

COLOMBIA

© 1996 White Star S.r.l.
Via Candido Sassone, 24 - Vercelli, Italy.

First Published in the UK in 1996 by Swan Hill Press,
an imprint of Airlife Publishing Ltd.

British Library
Cataloguing in Publication Data
A catalogue record for this book is available from
the British Library

ISBN 1 85310 811 1

Printed in Italy by Milano Stampa (Cuneo)
in the month of September 1996
Colour separation by Clichè Offset (Milano)

SWAN HILL PRESS
an imprint of Airlife Publishing Ltd.
101 Longden Road,
Shrewsbury SY3 9EB, England

1 *The grey angelfish (Pomacanthus arcuatus) is of the most rapresentative symbols of Caribbean seabeds.*

2-3 *The incredible colours that can be admired in this photograph belong to the Belize coast.*

THE CARIBBEAN

DIVING GUIDE

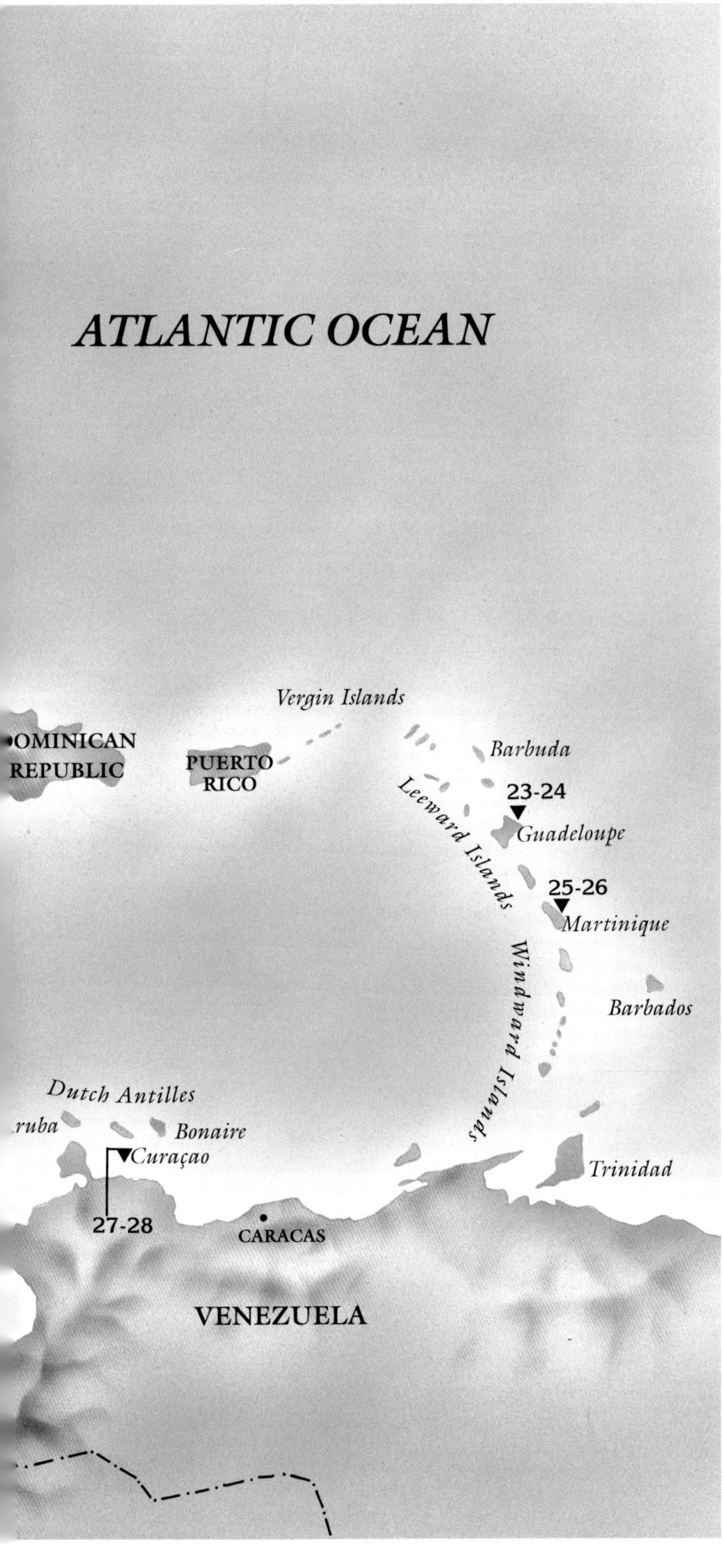

ATLANTIC OCEAN

Vergin Islands

OMINICAN REPUBLIC

PUERTO RICO

Barbuda

Leeward Islands

23-24
▼
Guadeloupe

25-26
▼
Martinique

Windward Islands

Barbados

Dutch Antilles

ruba *Bonaire*
▼*Curaçao*

27-28

• CARACAS

VENEZUELA

Trinidad

Contents

Texts and photographs
Kurt Amsler
Daniel Deflorin
Eleonora De Sabata
Andrea Ferrari
John Neuschwander

Biological files
Angelo Mojetta

Editorial supervision
Valeria Manferto De Fabianis
Laura Accomazzo

Layout
Patrizia Balocco
Clara Zanotti

Translation
Jane Elizabeth Glover

Illustrations of the dives
Cristina Franco

Illustrations of the fish
Monica Falcone

INTRODUCTION

To most people this part of the Atlantic, which stretches from 110 to 180 degrees longtitude West and 30 to 10 degrees latitude North is known as the Caribbean. The name was coined by the European conquerors, who borrowed it from the primitive natives, the Caribs. The islands in this corner of the earth, who maintained that it was their territory on which Christopher Columbus had first set foot, had no hesitation in accepting the name of Caribbean archipelago when this seemed economically advantageous. However, from the geographical point of view, its borders are strictly defined: the Caribbean Sea is bordered in the north by Cuba, in the east by the Antilles, in the south by Colombia and Venezuela and in the west by Central America, more precisely Belize, Honduras and Nicaragua. North of Cuba, lying like a sickle in the sea, and of the Yucatan peninsula, the Gulf of Mexico starts.

The Bahamas are away to the north east in the Atlantic.

The whole of the western Atlantic offers scuba divers exceptional landscapes characterised by sub-tropical flora and fauna.

This is mainly due to a warm current originating in the equatorial current which turns west before the trade-wind latitudes, pushing enormous masses of water against the West Indian islands.

One part of it is diverted north towards the Bahamas, while the greater part flows between Cuba and mainland of Central America. Blocked by this and by the Gulf of Mexico, the warm current is diverted strongly to the west where it enters the Atlantic, between Cuba and Florida, as the Gulf Stream.

The Caribbean Sea and the waters to the north of it are not coral seas like the Indian Ocean and the Pacific.

Although the temperature of the water never falls below 20 degrees, coral barriers or atolls are not formed as there are no corals to create them.

The ocean floor is a bizarre region formed by limestone and lava and characterised by an infinity of chasms and caves.

The entire landscape was formed during and after the Ice Ages. At that time the sea bed was hundreds of metres higher and atmospheric agents, including violent floods, seismic activity and vulcanic eruptions gave birth to what is now the sea bed.

All over the Caribbean you can dive and find underwater caves which contain stalagtites and stalagmites: unequivocable proof of their formation. A great variety of flora and fauna now flourishes on this ancient foundation. Coloured sponges of infinitely varied shapes are a characteristic feature of this underwater world. They are found at all the depths which can be reached by divers and some are so large that a person could get inside them.

The soft corals and the sea fan corals are unique. Some are very similar to the gorgonians of the Mediterranean Sea or other types of tropical corals, but most of them are endemic, peculiar to this area. Surprisingly they have not evolved

A - The history and evolution of the Caribbean coral sea beds are quite different from those of the Indo-Pacific, but they too provide exceptional underwater views.

B - The action of waves and currents continues to modify the coastline and influence the appearance of the underwater reefs. This photograph shows the coral reef of Guadeloupe.

C - A blue stain opens up amongst the reefs. This is the classic sign of the presence of a blue hole, a gigantic cavern whose roof has collapsed, opening up a chasm in the sea.

D - Many Caribbean islands have lush vegetation which, thanks to regular rainfall, often goes right down to the edge of the sea.

E - It is common when going from one dive site to another to be accompanied by elegant dolphins, jumping and spinning acrobatically in the waves.

F - The big rays are common on sandy bottoms and they are the main attraction for divers at Stingray City on Grand Cayman.

E

F

G

H

G - A huge black grouper (Mycteroperca bonaci) *surprised against an unusual background which highlights its colour and size.*

H - To ensure safe diving, dive sites are often marked by buoys and other markers. However, a dive master is in charge of all dives.

in the deeper regions, but seem to prefer the sea bed at depths which go from 3 to 20 metres. For divers swimming above the areas covered with soft corals, waving in the halflight like bushes in the breeze, it is like being immersed in an enchanted world. In the shallower areas hard corals grow so close together that they form a kind of barrier - in this case the denomination "coral barrier" would not be out of place. There are huge elkhorn corals, branch corals, yellow fire corals, flat corals and brain corals. But the most spectacular underwater landscape in the Caribbean is found in the sheer walls, called drop-offs, where the reef plunges vertically to depths of 2,000 metres. This is where scuba divers will have the most exciting experiences of their lives. The rich variety of living creatures starts with the lower animal species, including snails, bivalves and worms, which are not much different from the corresponding

types living in other seas. The crustaceans, including crabs, prawns, shrimps and numerous lobsters, are more comon. The tiny, gaudy, reef fish light up the landscape, although their range of colours is not as rich as tropical fish. The most characteristic fish found in these waters are the angelfish. They reach up to 40 centimetres in length and are bigger than their relations living in other seas. There is the grey angelfish, the French angelfish and the queen angelfish with its splendid gold and blue colours. This is the only place in the world where you will find the Nassau

A - The big rock formations hanging downwards in the blue holes are the remains of huge stalactites formed when the cave was out of the water.

B - Many of the wrecks scattered over the seabeds of the Caribbean rapidly became compulsory dive sites. They are often decommissioned ships which have been expressly sunk.

C - The gorgonians are the predominant organisms on many of the Caribbean reefs. Use to the typical fan shapes seen in other seas, divers are amazed by the variety of shapes found among Caribbean gorgonians.

groupers. They grow to a considerable size and in busy dive sites they are as friendly as puppies. The huge sandy expanses guarantee ideal conditions for the stingrays to multiply.

This species lives prevalently on the sea bottom feeding on crabs and other small animals which it hunts in the sand.

Rays can have a wing span of more than a metre and have a long tail with a poisonous tip.

Despite this, they are absolutely harmless animals which only use their dangerous weapon for defence. What is more, they create one of the "Seven Wonders" of the underwater world: hundreds of them live in a lagoon on Grand Cayman, where they are an extraordinary attraction for all diving or snorkelling enthusiasts. In these reefs, where the sea bed drops sheer away into the void, the region is patrolled by large fish: there are manta rays and eagle rays, grey sharks, hammerheads, barracuda, enormous schools of jacks and the biggest fish of all,

B

C

A

D

the whale shark, is not uncommon in the Caribbean either.

From the Florida Keys to the southernmost Antilles, sport diving is very professionally organised. All the islands and coasts which have been opened up to tourism have efficiently equipped dive bases which work on American standards, provide modern equipment and guarantee a high level of safety.

The best diving areas in the region are, from north to south: Florida Keys, the Bahamas, the Yucatan with the island of Cozumel, Cuba,

D - Along with gorgonians and corals, the sponges are one of the most classic ingredients of diving in the tropical Atlantic bordering the American coastline.

E

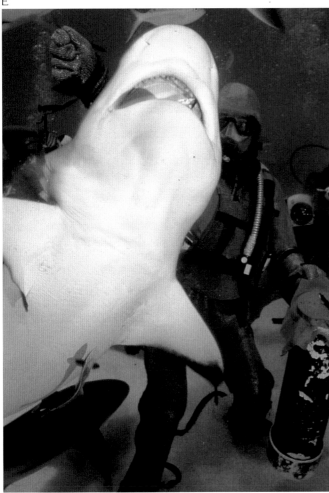

G - In this photograph can be observed a spotted goatfish (Pseudopeneus maculatus) *lying on the seabed.*

H - A palette of colours which illustrates the wealth of life forms and the variety of the Caribbean sea bed.

F

G.

H

E - *It is not uncommon to meet sharks in the Caribbean. In some places, like Shark Junction in the Bahamas, divers can watch sharks being fed.*

F - *Life on the sea bottom provides continual inspiration for enthusiastic underwater photographers.*

Turks and Caicos, the Cayman Islands, Belize, Honduras with the island of Guanaja, the Virgin Islands, the French Antilles and the Dutch Antilles, Bonaire and Curaçao.

The Caribbean archipelago exerts a particular allure on visitors, but one which cannot be explained by the extraordinary underwater landscape, the fantastic weather and the resort facilities alone.

I think that it is principally the inhabitants of this corner of the world, their outlook on life and their music. Their happiness and their taste for living are astonishing and immediately take tourists, frustrated and stressed-out by their daily routine, out of themselves.

In addition there are the thrilling stories of pirates, treasure hunters and buccaneers, part of a well-orchestrated advertising campaign. But they are still exciting and it is not unusual, after a drink or two in one of the innumerable "Buccaneers' Tavern" or "Pirates' Pub" for tourists to see the infamous Henry Morgan, no less, put in an appearance on the dock after midnight.

UNDERWATER PHOTOGRAPHY

The diverse underwater world of the Caribbean and the splendid colours of the fish and the coral tempt divers to immortalise this fantastic universe on film.

Many scuba divers have found that underwater photography adds a new dimension to their sport and is a wonderful addition to their holidays. With a camera in their hands divers pay closer attention to everything, in order to understand animal behaviour better and to live the underwater world in general more intensely. Looking at the photographs at home means reliving these thrilling dives and divers can show friends and acquaintances, not without pride, the fruit of their underwater adventures. Many divers have become fanatic underwater photographers. Many would like to start but do not have the courage, fearing that it is difficult to take good quality pictures with satisfactory colours underwater. This was certainly a well-founded fear several years ago, in view of the equipment available, but nowadays there are modern, easy-to-use underwater cameras on the market, which guarantee high-quality pictures.

The most popular cameras are the underwater ones, such as *Motormarine* and *Nikonos*. They are totally waterproof and so do not need any special underwater housing. Thus equipped the photographer will very quickly be able to take good quality pictures. Alternately, there are special underwater housings available for traditional automatic cameras. As for all the skills associated with diving, it is a good idea to follow an underwater photography course. Nowadays they are held all over the world in modern diving schools.

The waters of the Caribbean offer the best opportunities for underwater photography.

One of the most important factors for good results is the degree of transparency of the water.

There is in fact in every specific area of the Caribbean a season in which transparency is not optimal, but it is rare for it to be impossible to take photographs at all. Usually the photographer can almost always count on virtually ideal conditions. Sunlight plays a tremendously important role in underwater photography, but it would be a mistake to think that the use of a flash is superfluous in the presence of sunlight. This is a fundamental aspect, especially for wide-angle photographs.

The topography of the sea bed and the lie of the reef provide photographers with spendid subjects even in shallower waters. i.e. 5-30 metres. At these depths the sunlight shines through without any problems. Along with the colours provided by flash it ensures an even deeper blue background. Thanks to the light, transparent water no special film is required

A
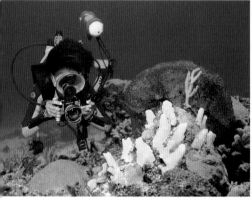

B

C

D

E

A - Here can be observed two angelfish, one of the main attractions for photographers.

B - The great variety of marine organisms provides underwater photographers with an infinite range of shots.

C - The fascinating worlds of macro photo let you admire this toadfish (Batrachoides gilberti).

D - The big yellow-orange sponges and the colonies of sea-plume gorgonians are a favourite subject in Caribbean waters.

E - The topography of the sea bottom and the reef provide plenty of splendid subjects for photographers at all depth bands. Even on wrecks can be observed splendid life forms.

and photographers can use normal speed films. The best results are obtained with 100 ASA.
As we have already mentioned, you do need a flash gun to get those breathtaking colours.
As the density of the water filters out different part of the colour spectrum at different depths - from 3-4 metres down even the most colourful fish and corals would come out a dull greeny-blue.
The opportunities for photography in the Caribbean are practically endless and the challenge for the enthusiastic photographer is an exciting one. Photographs of divers and shoals of fish on top of the reef are always spectacular ones.
When you dive to inspect one

F

of the wrecks described in this book, do not forget your camera. You need a wideangle lens for this kind of scenario, 20mm - 14 mm lens are particularly suitable.
With a normal lens the photographer would have to move too far away from the subject to get it in the frame. The sun's rays which, in the last analysis, project the image onto the film, would have to travel too far in the water and the results would be lacking in contrast, with greeny-blue colours.
Alongside the advantages of getting closer to the subject, these wideangle or fish-eye lenses deliver considerable depth of field over the entire photograph.
For smaller subjects such as

gorgonians, soft corals, tubular and barrel sponges and small fish, the ideal focal width is from 20-28mm. If the photographer keeps the distance at between 0.8 and 1.5 metres, the photographs will be very precise, rich in contrast and with true colours. 35-50mm wideangle lenses are recommended for individual fish, anemones, particulars of coral formation, small sponges and gorgonians. These lenses do not have a very high degree of precision so the photographer must take care to select an aperture between f8 and f11, which will make it possible to reduce the focal distance to less than a metre. No underwater photographer should ignore the fascinating world of macro and close-up photography.
There are innumerable numbers of invertebrate species which live close to, above or inside coral, including the vividly coloured sea slugs and worms, as well as prawns and crabs. Details of soft corals, anemones, sponges as well as all types of blennies and gobies make perfect macro subjects.
The technique for lighting subjects such as these, ranging in size from small to minimum, is extremely simple, as long as you have the right accessories. Depending on your camera you can use superimposed lenses, intermediate rings or special macro lenses.
A TTI flash gun guarantees perfect lighting for the photographer. In the tropics and in saltwater camera equipment needs looking after with particular care. After the dive the camera must not only be rinsed, it must be immersed in fresh water for ten minutes, which is the only way to eliminate the sand particles and the salt crystals from the 'O' rings and apertures.
To make sure that the camera and the flash are absolutely watertight the 'O' ring has to be checked every time the film is changed. To clean the 'O' ring from any deposits run it gently through your finger and thumb. This will also pick up any damage which has been done. The 'O' ring channel can be cleaned out with a paper tissue. Black neoprene 'O' rings must not be over-greased,

F - The transparency of the water is an important factor for good pictures.

G, H - On night dives the Caribbean sea bottom appears to be populated by

strange creatures like this giant basket star (Astrophyton muricatum), top, or this evanescent tuft of glassy encrustant organisms, hydroids perhaps, bottom.

G

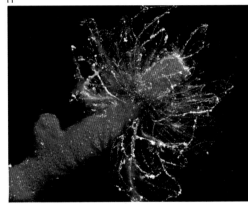

H

but the orange silicone ones must be well-greased to provide an efficient seal.
At the end of the holiday all photographic equipment must be immersed for half an hour in fresh water with one spoonful of vinegar for every litre of water.
This will get rid of all saline corrosions on the metallic components. After rinsing everything for a further hour in fresh water, dry carefully, grease the 'O' rings or, if you do not expect to use the camera for a long period of time, remove them so that they do not lose their shape.
During flights, other transfers and on the dive boat, it is best to carry your equipment in a rigid, padded, plastic case.
Do not forget to take enough film with you and also remember spare batteries, 'O' rings and everything you need for maintenance.

THE BAHAMAS

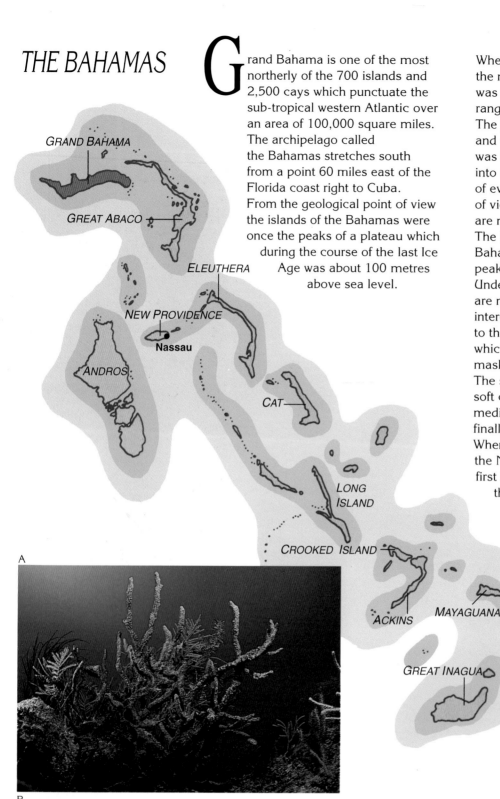

Grand Bahama is one of the most northerly of the 700 islands and 2,500 cays which punctuate the sub-tropical western Atlantic over an area of 100,000 square miles. The archipelago called the Bahamas stretches south from a point 60 miles east of the Florida coast right to Cuba. From the geological point of view the islands of the Bahamas were once the peaks of a plateau which during the course of the last Ice Age was about 100 metres above sea level.

When the water level rose following the melting of the ice, the plateau was submerged and an underwater range of mountains was formed. The powerful peaks became islands and what remained underwater was transformed over millennia into reefs rich in corals and fish of every kind. From the point of view of their scenery, the islands are not particularly interesting. The highest point in all the Bahamas is a 65-metre high peak on Cat Island.
Underwater, however, there are much more geologically-interesting sights and close to the coast there are shallow reefs which can be explored with just mask and fins.
The sea-bed, covered with soft corals, slopes down to the medium reefs, the deep reefs and, finally, to the drop-offs.
When Columbus reached the New World in 1492 he made his first landfall on what is now called the Bahamas.
The Spanish navigator Ponce de Leon was the first European to explore the island of Grand Bahama.
As was the case with the other islands, the Spanish showed no interest in Grand Bahama, considering it without resources worth exploiting and it was the English who colonised the Bahamas.
Piracy was for many years rife on the islands whose economy was based on such activities as fishing, sponge-fishing and, during the Prohibition period in the United States, rum smuggling.
Everything changed towards the middle of the Fifties when American financial backers negotiated a historic agreement with the English crown to promote tourism in the area in exchange for enormous tax concessions.
The agreement continued after 1973, the year in which the Bahamas became independent.

A - This sponge reminds the shape of a tree's branches.

B - The light of the flashgun clearly shows the colour of this longspined squirrelfish (Holocentrus rufus), caught out in the open next to the unusual branches of this candlestick gorgonian with large polyps.

DIVING ON GRAND BAHAMA

On Grand Bahama the reef topography falls, once again, into three sectors: shallow reef, medium reef and deep reef right up to the drop-off, otherwise known as the "edge of the ledge". Grand Bahama Island is 70 miles long by 8 miles wide and the reef which interests us lies along the southern coastline.

Less than a mile off the mainland the reef descends rapidly into the Northwest Providence Channel. To the east (East End) things are exactly the opposite: the shallow Little Bahama Bank separates Grand Bahama from the Abaco Islands. The coral bank of the Bahamas is famous amongst divers because it is possible to dive and swim amongst spotted dolphins in their wild state.

There are excellent provisions for all diving sports on Grand Bahama organised under the auspices of the Underwater Explorer Society. Fifty-seven permanent buoys mark the areas reserved for diving, which because of their distance from the coast can only be reached by boat. Most of the sites are between Silver Point to the west and Lucayan Waterways to the east.

They can all be reached by boat in relatively short times varying from 15 minutes to 1 hour, starting from the UNEXSO base.

The furthest, less popular, sites on the coral reef, such as Deadman's Reef or East End, need full-day trips.

The presence inland of many water-filled craters (known as sinkholes) provides opportunities to investigate enormous caves full of stalagtites and long, maze-like, tunnel complexes. There is a splendid grotto called Ben's Cave, after Ben Rose, who discovered it.

All diving in this sinkhole is regulated and organised by UNEXSO. Thanks to the Gulf Stream which runs close by, the temperature of the water never falls below 20 degrees Celsius and from May to September water temperatures are as high as 28 degrees.

There are no particularly strong currents in the most popular diving sites, although divers should watch

C

D

E   F

C - This close up shows the particular colouring of the body of a black grouper (Mycteroperca bonaci).

D - At Grand Bahama it is possible to have a close encounter with the joyful dolphins.

E - This curious coral formation of Dendrogyra cylindrus resembles a sculpture created by a modern artist.

F - In the Bahamas it is even possible meeting the cruel lords of the abyss: the sharks.

out for medium-strength currents, depending on the wind, the waves and the tides. Such currents do not create any problems however, as there are buoys marking entry and exit points. The underwater world of Grand Bahama is no different from other areas of the Caribbean, but the island does have two spectacular attractions of its own: Shark Junction and The Dolphin

Experience. UNEXSO was behind the introduction of scuba diving both in the company of Caribbean reef sharks and of bottlenose dolphins, which attracts divers from all over the world to the island.

SHARK JUNCTION

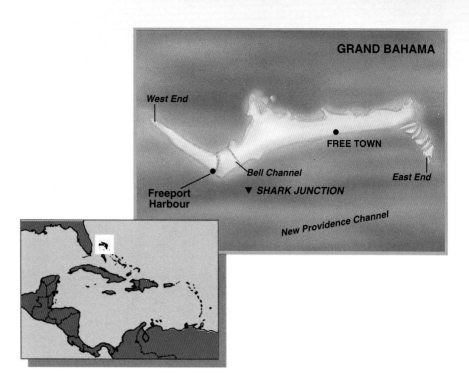

GRAND BAHAMA

West End

FREE TOWN

Bell Channel

Freeport Harbour

East End

▼ SHARK JUNCTION

New Providence Channel

0 m

16 m

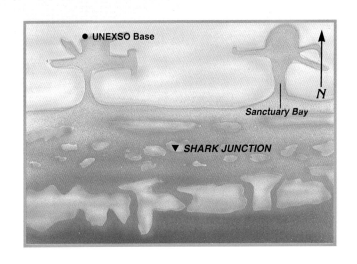

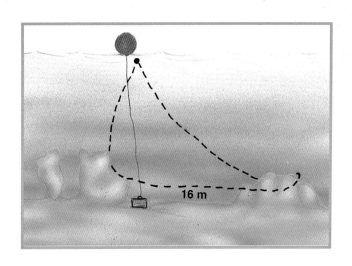

16 m

A - The encounter with sharks at Shark Junction is always preceded by a detailed briefing in the UNEXCO seminar rooms, to run through the different stages of the dive.

B - The shark carousel starts almost as soon as the sea bottom is reached; the divers are constantly supervised by lifeguards.

LOCATION

For divers there is no doubt that an encounter with a shark is the most unforgettable of experiences. The principle problem, however, is that these animals are extremely timid and under normal circumstances it is impossible to get close enough to observe them closely, film or photograph them. Here at Shark Junction on Grand Bahama Island visitors can dive in the company of no less than 20 Caribbean reef sharks *(Carcharhinus perezi)*. These close encounters take place in a circular sandy clearing on the sea bed, where the fish are fed by the divemasters. It is close to the medium reef, just over 1 mile from the Bell Channel and is marked by a permanent marker buoy used for both descents and surfacing. The area is at a depth of 15 metres. In addition to the sharks, which are the main attraction, you will see many other fish too. Enormous moray eels live hidden in the corals which surround the sand. They were attracted here in the past and it has become their fixed abode. You will often see big Southern stingrays here and more than 10 huge groupers are regular guests. It is worth moving

C - This picture shows how the sea bottom is transformed into an ideal arena, where sharks and divers come face to face and perhaps observe each other with the same degree of curiosity and fear.

D - The Caribbean reef sharks (Carcharhinus perezi) often bump into each other in their haste to tear a fish from the hands of the instructor.

A

B

C

D

into the open sea, not only because the outlines of the sharks make spectacular subjects for photographers, but also because large banks of jacks often cross through Shark Junction.

THE DIVE

The adventure begins with a detailed briefing at the UNEXSO base. The divemaster/feeder who will be in charge of feeding the sharks runs through the various phases of the dive with the aid of a blackboard. Although over the years the sharks have become used to these encounters, divers have to stick rigorously to the established procedure to guarantee their own safety and that of the other members of the group. The journey to Shark Junction only lasts 30 minutes. The 20 jacks used as bait are already at the dock, stowed in a special container. The feeder wears the "chainmail suit" in stainless steel which resembles those worn by the robber

E - The final instants of a shark's approach are always thrilling; the need to take precautions like chain mail are proof of how potentially dangerous the whole exercise can be.

F - Other fishes often mix in with the sharks, like these yellowtail snappers (Ocyurus chrysurus) which gobble up any food left by the bigger predators.

G - Some females, over two metres long, will let divers embrace and stroke them as if they had established friendly relations with anyone who brings them food.

H - At the end of the show the sharks spread, but never go too far from "the centre of their territory".

barons of the Middle Ages and which allows him to have greater control over the sharks. Sharks never bite without reason, but situations can arise in which two animals go for the same bait and their razor-sharp teeth can graze or wound the feeder's arm or hand in passing. In addition to the feeder, Ben Rose, there are two security guards and the cameraman. The descent down the buoy cable starts as soon as the dive boat is moored. The security men accompany the group to the sandy bottom, where there is an out-of-use decompression chamber, in front of which the divers kneel down in a

E

F

semicircle. Even while we are swimming towards the sand we can see some sharks circling. Some of them come to within a few metres of the waiting group and swim amongst the divers quite calmly. They are all females, their length varying from 1.5 to 2.5 metres. As we watch the place starts to fill up with other marine inhabitants as well as the sharks. Dark mottled groupers arrive from all directions, two Southern stingrays settle on the sand right in front of me and the water is alive with yellowtails. As if obeying a command all the fishes suddenly start to swim in the same direction. The reason is clear when Ben appears between two banks of coral with the food container. He has taken his fins off and, weighed down by the chainmail suit, he moves along the sand like a deep-sea diver, followed by a horde of sharks - he is guiding at least 16 gigantic Caribbean reef sharks towards the sandy clearing. Just two metres from the enchanted, but at the same time visibly-nervous divers, he extracts the first fish from the container. The sharks become animated, the circles around the feeder growing tighter, although the animals do not show the slightest tension and their movements are calm and controlled. Ben takes out a fish and waves it underneath the nose of the shark best-placed for the watching spectators. The whole action only lasts a few seconds from start to finish and you have to watch carefully to see the speed with which the shark raises its nose, thrusts its jaw forward and closes its eyes with their nictitating membrane. All this happens just two metres away from the spectators and the feeder is careful to ensure that they are in the best position to watch and photograph the action. Those without either a camera or video need not worry, as the UNEXSO cameraman is already in action. The whole dive is filmed so that every participant can buy a souvenir copy. The show has been running for about 20 minutes and I have the impression that many more sharks have joined us. As the group is continually moving it is impossible to determine the exact number. At this point the sharks start to close

in on the feeder as if they know that the food reserves are slowly running out. Ben is almost completely hidden by these huge bodies with their bright grey colours. I am struck by the way he manages to keep the situation under control. Some females over 2 metres long actually allow themselves to be embraced by him and rest on the sand to be stroked. Then, with the last bait in his hand, Ben sets off back, drawing the whole group of sharks out of the arena. These encounters with sharks have a much more far-reaching significance than many people might think. The fact that 100 million

G

H

sharks are exterminated every year is because they have earned a reputation as predators and the enemies of humans. So no-one worries about the destiny of sharks, destined to become extinct in a short time. Thanks to the show organised on Grand Bahama, and those in many other places, divers can stop being afraid of these animals. Anyone who has had the luck to see sharks close up at least once in their lives and to observe their behaviour, will fight for them in the future and, above all, will work to convince other people that sharks are not ferocious beasts and ought to be saved from extermination.

THEO'S WRECK

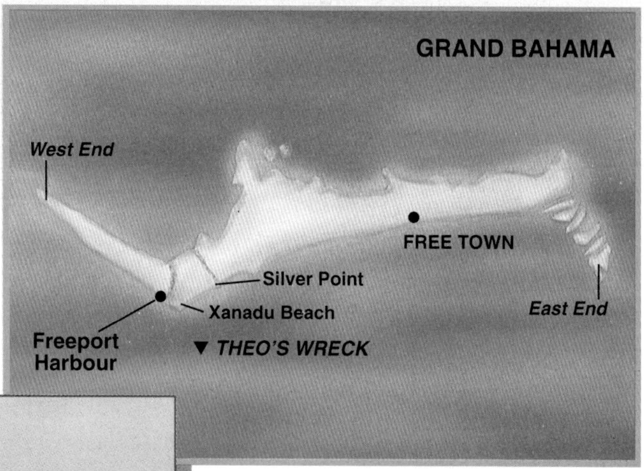

GRAND BAHAMA

West End

FREE TOWN

Silver Point

Xanadu Beach

East End

▼ THEO'S WRECK

Freeport Harbour

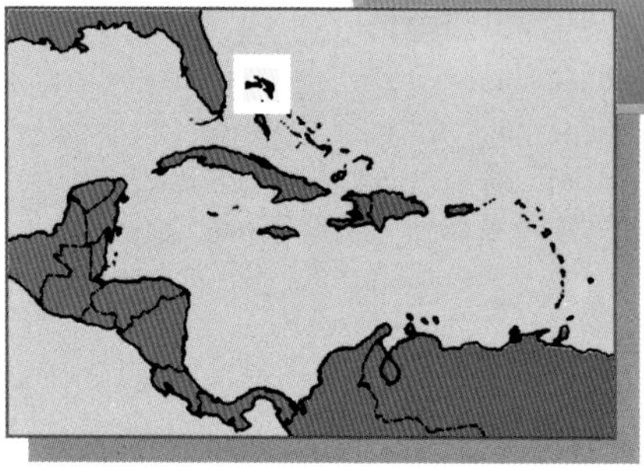

0 m

27 m

33 m

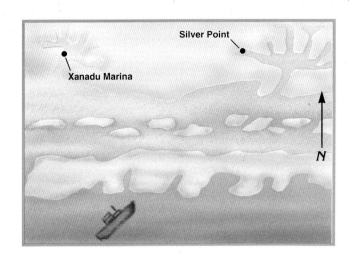

Xanadu Marina

Silver Point

N

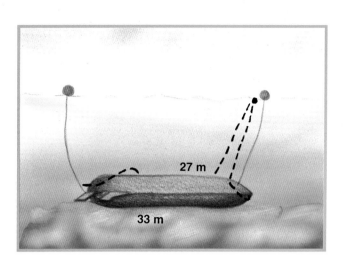

27 m

33 m

LOCATION

This dive site is to the west of Bell Channel, between Silver Point and Xanadu Beach, about 1.5 miles from the coast.
The wreck is about 70 metres long and rests on the ocean bottom on its port side at about 33 metres between the deep reef and the drop-off. The bows point towards land and the stern towards the open sea. Originally the rudder and propeller lay hanging over the edge of the ledge, until hurricane Andrew moved the wreck a few metres towards land.
It rests on a flat, sandy floor, with a few isolated coral banks.
Two permanent marker buoys,

A - *The ship's prow, with the anchor chain still in place, lies at a depth of around 30 metres and gives the impression of being slightly raised off the ground.*

B - *All the machinery on the bridge is still intact, but has been transformed by the encrustations into lively blotches of colour, which only artificial light can wake up.*

C - *The water is so transparent that virtually the whole outline of the wreck can be seen, even from a distance. The diver hanging in the water gives an idea of the scale.*

D - Theo's Wreck *has rapidly become one of the most popular dive sites in the Bahamas.*

one at the prow and one at the stern, mark the ship's position. The waters around *Theo's Wreck* are characterised by currents which vary according to the wind, the waves and the tides, but thanks to the buoys it is possible to dive and return to the surface without any problems.
The wreck has become home to numerous fish and has been covered with rich vegetation in the years since 1982.
The bow anchor chain, in particular, is covered with splendid gorgonian sea fans and the shaded part of the hull is completely covered with orange false gorgonians.

THE SHIP'S HISTORY

Built in 1954 amongst the mountains of Norway, the ship was given the name *M/S Logna*. Before being acquired in 1969 by the Bahama Cement Company, it was a cargo ship carrying goods between Norway and Spain.
In the Bahamas it plied the routes connecting Grand Bahama to Eleuthera and New Providence (Nassau) where it unloaded cement sand taken on at Ford Pierce in Florida. A million dollars was allocated for the restructuring of the ship, so that it could be be registered with Lloyd's in 1981, but as the investment could not be amortised the ship was decommissioned at the Bahama Cement Company dock. When the management decided to scuttle the ship in deep international waters, an engineer called Theopolis Galanoupoulos, an underwater sports enthusiast, suggested sinking it in shallower waters and turning it into an attraction for scuba divers. Thanks to backing from UNEXSO, the necessary authorisations were obtained and the specialists got to work on the procedure for scuttling the ship. On Saturday, 16th October 1982, everything was ready. The *M/S Logna* was towed to the spot and the valves in the ballast tanks were opened.
However, no-one had foreseen that the pipes would be so blocked by barnacles that the scuttling would last four hours.
The prolonging of the operation meant that the ship risked being lost as a strengthening wind got up, threatening to push the ship dangerously close to the drop-off.

Tension reached undescribable levels, but fortunately the *Logna*, known ever since as *Theo's Wreck*, sank in time. A few minutes more and it would have disappeared over the edge of the ledge for ever.

THE DIVE

Our boat is moored to the bows buoy. A glance over the parapet tells us there is a light current and the blue of the water is a guarantee of excellent visibility. The briefing is, once again, an important part of the dive and is done in detail and with care by the instructors. We start the dive along a cable which leads from the boat platform to the mooring buoy and right to the wreck. Visibility is quite exceptional. We can see the outline of the 70-metre boat clearly from the surface of the water and looking over the parapet I see a huge shoal of jacks and numerous barracuda. We enter at the bows where the anchor chain hangs down, covered with splendid gorgonians. The light of the strobe being used to make the film of this dive shows up the corals in all the splendour of their true colours. The depth is 33 metres close to the bows of the wreck. The exploration starts on the bow deck and we move on to the first cargo hold. An enormous shoal of grunts almost blocks the way and, totally ignoring the presence of the divers, disappears inside the ship. We use our fins to reach the superstructure at the centre of the huge holds easily. It is a good idea to take a torch with you because numerous animals hide in the nooks and crannies. Two enormous green moray eels are permanent lodgers here in the wreck, except for the summer months. The shoal of grunts has collected in front of us, almost as if they would like to be our guides, and they move as we pass by, revealing the superstructures. There is a lot of life down here. Many fishes are hidden amongst the struts, the braces and the ventilation pipes, and the shoal of jacks is still swimming around the deck and the chimney, which is horizontal instead of vertical because of the list. It is incredible

how in a few years underwater the ship has been covered in vegetation. The winches on the quarterdeck are beautiful. We intend to get as far as the propellers and the rudder and we leave the quarterdeck and head for the starboard parapet, where we feel the presence of the current from which we were sheltered on the other side of the ship and inside. It creates no problems for us though. The underside of the rudder is completely covered with flower corals in wonderful shades of orange, so are the enormous curved propeller blades. We see a long line of big lobsters at the point where the hull disappears into the sand,

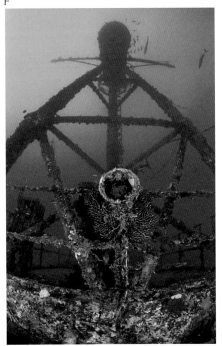

just a few metres away from the stark outline of the drop off. This is why you will often meet ocean fish, like sharks and rays and turtles near the wreck. A few days before I arrived on Grand Bahama divers had spent fifteen minutes with a school of spotted dolphins! Swimming towards the bows we are sheltered from the current by the deck and are able to admire *Theo's Wreck* in perfect tranquillity.

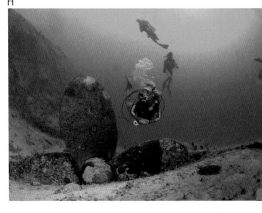

E - The inside of the huge holds has provided refuge for many fish.

F - The bridge scaffolding was quickly covered with organisms such as the huge deep-water gorgonians, sponges and corals.

G - The winches on the bridge are still perfectly recognisable even though they are covered with myriad encrustant organisms.

H - The huge propeller blades on the bottom mark the deepest part of the dive. The drop-off starts just a little way off and plunges to the abysses.

THE DOLPHINS EXPERIENCE

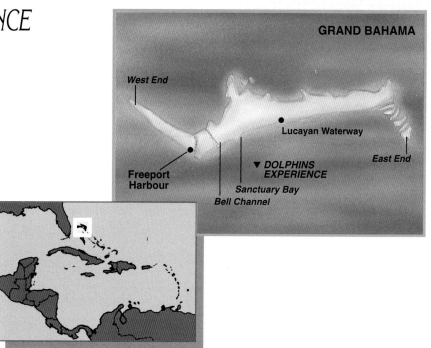

GRAND BAHAMA

West End

Lucayan Waterway

East End

▼ DOLPHINS
EXPERIENCE

Freeport
Harbour

Sanctuary Bay

Bell Channel

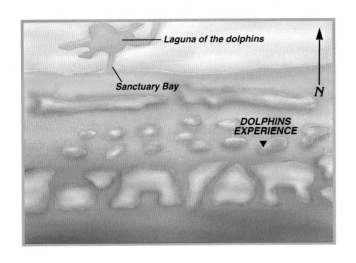

Laguna of the dolphins

Sanctuary Bay

N

DOLPHINS EXPERIENCE ▼

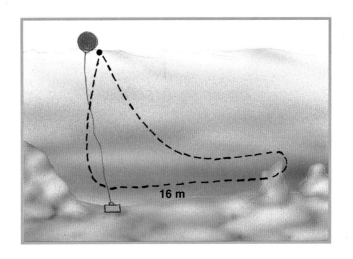

16 m

0 m

16 m

LOCATION

Very few experiences in this submerged world can beat the beauty, the grace and the energy of dolphins - rare encounters which take place in the wild of the ocean. On Grand Bahama underwater enthusiasts can dive whenever they want with dolphins that will even follow divers out into the open sea. The idea was Mike Schulz's. An ex-dolphin trainer, he decided to give up this job, which kept the animals imprisoned in tanks, to give them a chance to live in a more congenial environment. Before facing the open sea and heading for the coral reef the animals released from dolphinaria underwent months of training.

They live now in a lagoon called Sanctuary Bay to the east of Lucayan Marina, where they can swim in quiet, deep, protected waters kept clean by the tides. The group usually consists of six bottlenose dolphins *(Tursiops truncatus)*. The meeting point with the dolphins is on the medium reef

A - This photograph shows the UNEXSO base, starting point for dives with the dolphins.

B - During the trip to Sanctuary Bay the dolphins do their best to take part in the compulsory briefing before the dive.

at a depth of 15 metres, on an almost flat sandy clearing where there are big coral banks.

Its relatively shallow depth and the reflector effect of the sand make this stretch of barrier reef one of the best there is for photography and underwater film enthusiasts will be happy here.

These intelligent animals know the place well of course and come here even without the help of the support boat. The boat usually sets off from the UNEXSO base and the briefing is carried out during the trip to Sanctuary Bay. It is extremely important for all members of the group to know how they should behave in the presence of these marine mammals and to know the signals the dolphins respond to. Leaving Sanctuary Bay the dolphins follow our boat and the back-up boat towards the open sea. Not all the dolphins join in, but they are left to do as they wish - they are never forced in any way, as happens in dolphinaria. There is one rule to be followed here: no work, no food and visitors are reminded of this too. Even the length of time the dolphins

C - The dive with the dolphins starts from the moment the divers start kitting up in the boat.

D - The dolphins never fail to emerge to see their visitors and know how to interpret the signals they receive from them perfectly.

E - The dolphins will let all divers touch them as long as it is done gently and calmly.

F - The dolphins are completely free in these calm, sheltered waters and it is their own decision whether or not to approach the divers.

E

F

G - For all divers, it is an unforgettable experience to find themselves in close contact with these marine mammals.

H - The feeding session marks the end of each dive and contributes to reinforcing the bond between the instructor and the dolphins, although the animals are free to leave any time they like.

G

H

spend underwater is not fixed. If their attention is drawn by animals swimming close by, their interest in these bubble-producing beings soon disappears. Sometimes the group meets other dolphins of the same species - you can imagine what happens: once it was three days before the last dolphins came back to Sanctuary Bay.

THE DIVE

Keep a camera fitted with a light telephoto lens handy during the journey to the dolphin reef, the dolphins which follow the boat perform incredible acrobatics in and out of the bow waves. It is easy to judge at what point they will leap out of the water and the resulting photographs are splendid. On reaching our destination we all dive to a depth of 15 metres to a sandy bed, where we arrange ourselves in a circle and immediately four dolphins put in an appearance. They swim round us at speed, rushing towards the surface and then plunging back into the depths - they might almost be putting on a

demonstration of strength and skill for us. Their hydrodynamic bodies flashing through the blue water are a fantastic sight, they really can have fun here. But when the instructor goes deeper taking the bag of food with him the group calms down, as if the dolphins realise that the moment has come to do something for the guests. The programme changes each time, divers can either hitch a tow with a dolphin or feed them. The important thing is to know the signals which have been illustrated during the briefing, otherwise you run the risk of being totally ignored by the dolphins. Every movement they make is done with a tremendous amount of calm, which means you can take splendid photographs and magnificent films - one of the most interesting moments of the whole experience is when they go up to the surface to breathe. But not many of the dolphins' own games involve the divers and to live this unique experience in the company of these marine mammals you have to swim in their underwater world and observe them from close to.

25

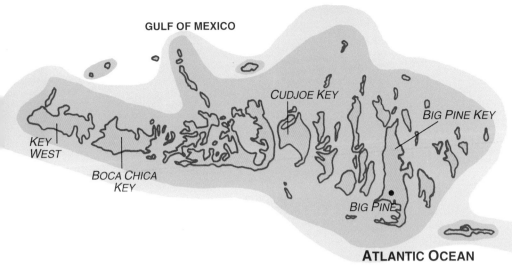

FLORIDA KEYS - KEY LARGO

GULF OF MEXICO

CUDJOE KEY

BIG PINE KEY

KEY WEST

BOCA CHICA KEY

BIG PINE

ATLANTIC OCEAN

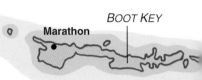

BOOT KEY

Marathon

A

B

The Spanish owe the discovery of Florida to the boredom from which Juan Ponce de Leon, governor of San Juan (today's Puerto Rico), suffered. The tranquil and monotonous life on the colony was not to his taste and he decided to abandon his position and dedicate his energies to adventuring.
After pulling all the strings he knew, in 1512 he obtained an agreement with the Spanish crown which authorised him to explore and colonise new lands. He had a rough idea of his point of departure from the legends of the local indians, which told of wide beaches to the north-west of the Bahamas.
In 1513 he set sail from the Bahamas in the hope of reaching this new land. No-one knows how long he stayed at sea, the only thing certain is that he did manage to reach those beaches, making landfall in what is today Cape Canaveral, in the Easter period. Easter in Spain is known as the festival of flowers *(flores)* and so he decided to call the land he had just discovered *La Florida*. De Leon earned himself a place in the history books thanks to this discovery. Rightly or wrongly?
Many critics maintain that the true discoverers were Christopher Columbus or other navigators. Whatever the case, de Leon headed south along the coast and the Keys. Some awful things must have happened during the voyage as his crew named the long, thin, chain of keys *Los Martires*, which means terror or fright. Might this pessimism have been transformed into a curse? For many ships travelling in this

area, including the famous Spanish silver fleet called the *Tierra Firma*, were forced onto the reef by hurricanes, and wrecked.
The Spaniards employed diving experts to salvage the treasure which had disappeared into the deep water. They were pearl fishermen from the island of Margarita in Venezuela, who used to dive to depths of up to thirty metres using heavy stones as ballast. Thanks to their help the Spaniards recovered most of the lost treasures.

THE GEOGRAPHICAL POSITION

The Florida Keys form an archipelago of more than 200 islands which is simply an extension of the characteristic Florida bow.
The Keys lie from north-east to south-west for over 212 kilometres. The sub-tropical vegetation and the warm climate are the result of its geographical position, lying in a chain along the Florida Bank, which channels in the warm water of the Gulf Stream. 34 of the 200 islands are linked by 42 bridges which form the famous highway US 1.
The 115 miles of road are marked by mile-markers which are essential for finding your way about the Keys. The centre of Key Largo is at mile-marker No.100.

DIVING IN THE KEYS

Comparison of the Bahamas sea bed formation and that of the Keys reveals that the coral reef proper is a long way from the coast.
The Florida Bank has an average width which varies between 7 and

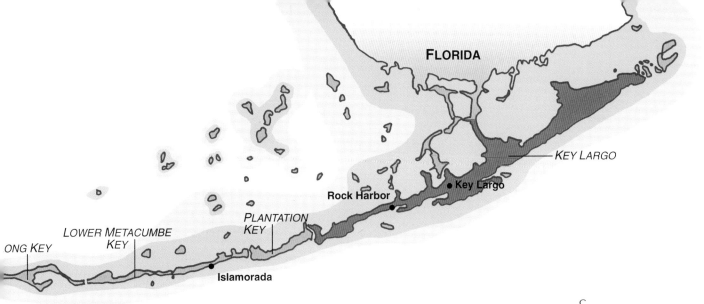

FLORIDA

KEY LARGO

Rock Harbor

Key Largo

PLANTATION
KEY

LOWER METACUMBE
KEY

ONG KEY

Islamorada

11 kilometres and is sub-divided into several zones.

The coastal zone is characterised by the presence of mangroves and zosteras; this shallow sea-bed is of enormous ecological importance, as it is the breeding ground for many marine species. The small fish spend the early part of their lives in these shallows. The mid-channel reef is made up from single coral banks, often surrounded by zosteras.

At this point the sea-bed is slightly deeper, although on average it is never more than 3-5 metres.

The off-shore zone comprises coral banks too, but they grow almost to the surface. In this section of the reef there are a good many buoys and light-towers to mark the shallows. This is the part of the Florida Bank where the most interesting dive sites begin, thanks to the transparency of the water. What is more, the sea bed slopes gently to the deep reef, where the corals create deep canyons, grottoes and long "fingers" along the sands. Out in the open sea, where the coral barrier gives way to a wide sandy bed, depths vary between 17 and 20 metres.

In view of the considerable distance of the reef it is impossible to dive along the coast and so all underwater activities require dive-boats. They can be hired privately, or excursions can be organised at one of the numerous dive centres. Like everywhere else, divers have to show a dive certificate. All the boats in use on the Keys are designed especially for this activity and have to be coastguard-approved. Everything is extremely professionally operated; on-board safety has

C

D

A - The sun rays penetrate through the blue surface enlighting the rich underwater world of Key Largo, Florida.

B - The torch of a diver let us admire the rich colours of the underwater fauna: gorgonians, sponges and corals create a unique view.

C - A grouper is curiously peering out from the delicate branches of a sea plume.

D - A pair of elegant grey angelfish swims close to the sandy bottom, not disturbed from the presence of the photographer.

absolute priority and full first-aid kit is always to hand. Detailed information is supplied about every site and visitors can opt for group dives unaccompanied by an instructor. The flora and fauna of the Florida Keys are typically Caribbean and can be compared to what you would find in the northern Bahamas. Divers will find all types of coral and a multitude of species of fish here; this is because the area around Key Largo is a marine sanctuary.

Set up in 1960, the first underwater park in the United States bears

the name of John D. Pennecamp, a journalist with the Miami Herald who was active in the battle around here to protect the coral reef and nature generally. In 1990 the park was enlarged when a further 2,600 square nautical miles was declared a protected area. The environment is an absolute priority here and the regulations which govern the large area (39 kilometres long and 15 kilometres wide) are very severe. The area stretches 5.5 kilometres into the sea and the water reaches depths of 90 metres.

THE WRECK OF THE DUANE

KEY LARGO

MARINA DEL MAR

Hawk Channel

Mollasses Reef   French Reef

▼WRECK OF THE DUANE

0 m

15 m

27 m

33 m

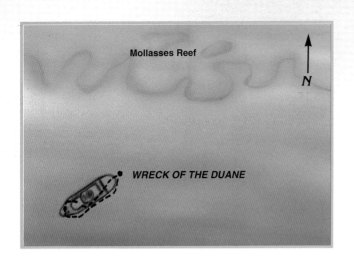

Mollasses Reef

N

WRECK OF THE DUANE

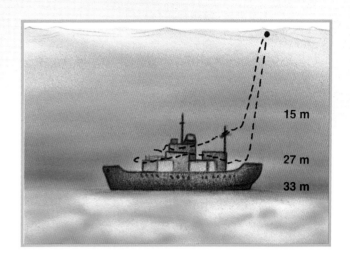

15 m

27 m

33 m

LOCATION

The wreck of the *Duane* lies at a depth of 33 metres on a large sandy bed scattered with small coral formations, 1.8 kilometres off the southern edge of Mollasses Reef. A single, large, yellow marker buoy signals its position and there are two moorings, below the surface of the water, for dive boats. The *Duane* was not shipwrecked: it was scuttled intentionally on 28th November 1987, to make an attraction for divers.

them over to the British authorities. The crew of the flagship were to distinguish themselves again, this time in the Mediterranean, when their ship rescued the 250 survivors of the tragic sinking of the troop-carrier *Dorchester*. On 15th August 1944 the ship took part in the Allied invasion of southern France. At the end of the war she was once again reconverted, this time as an aircraft carrier and commissioned in the Atlantic. The *Duane* played guardian angel once more when the Finnish merchant vessel *Bornholm* went down in the middle of the ocean on 4th May 1957 and the 27 members of the crew were rescued by the *Duane*. In December 1967

she was assigned to Coast Guard Squadron III and used in military action along the coastline of South Vietnam against enemy positions. At the end of this turbulent existence the *Duane* was finally pensioned off into her well-deserved retirement. Now that she rests on the ocean bottom, the memory of her heroic feats lives on amongst the divers who visit her.

THE DIVE

Although the sea is quite rough, the big yellow marker buoy over the wreck can still be seen from a long way off. Our instructor, Im, holds the briefing while we were still in the relatively calm waters of the Florida Bank, in order not to tire the members of the group unnecessarily. After attaching *Ocean Diver II* to the mooring buoy we complete our preparation for the dive. A taut cable connected to the platform helps the group reach the buoy where they enter the deep waters. Like almost all the wrecks in the Caribbean, there are enormous barracuda circling the buoy line. The outline of the *Duane* appears slowly out of the dark blue which surrounds us. We reach the quarterdeck and our reaction is one of wonder: the ship is truly enormous. I realise immediately that an in-depth exploration will require several dives. Although the wreck

A

B

C

THE STORY OF THE *DUANE*

Named after the American Secretary of the Treasury, William J. Duane, the coastguard vessel was commissioned in 1936. Initially she plied the route linking her port of registry, Oakland in California, with the Alaskan coast. Ship and crew were put to the test in 1939 when the vessel was transferred to wartime duties. On their first north-Atlantic patrol they saved the crew of a British steamship which had been torpedoed. When the United States became actively involved in the war the *Duane* was armed and in 1943 she attacked a German submarine. The *Duane* used depth charges, forcing the sub to surface, and sank it with cannonfire. The *Duane* picked up the 20 survivors and handed

has only been lying on its side on the sea bottom for a few years, there is already a lot of vegetation covering it. The first superstructures we see are covered with big gorgonians, their dark red colours lit up by our torch beams. We can make out a high structure, the eagle's nest, on top of these first superstructures, around which a group of jacks and several barracuda are swimming. The sight of their silhouettes seen against the light is a magnificent one. Moving along the parapet of the wreck, sheltered from the current, we come to the chimney stack and head for the equipment at the centre of the ship. The view from the flying bridge, above the upper deck, is spectacular. The bulwarks plunge vertically downwards on both sides; they too are completely covered with soft corals where huge parrotfish are intent on searching for food, while a shoal of blue-black surgeon fish pay diligent attention to what is going on in front of the bridge. Right beneath me, where some steel panels have given way, two enormous eyes are staring upwards - they belong to a brown grouper over one metre long. You could stay here for hours, but unfortunately a glance at the divecomputer strapped to the wrist and the tank pressure gauge tells us that the time has come to head for the surface. But before going back to the buoy we go for another look at the bridge. Certain measures were taken to make the *Duane* safe for diving and of course anything which might damage the environment was removed. All the metal cables and struts, in which divers might have become entangled, have been removed, as have the doors, including the internal ones. We are just reaching the ship's interior from the bridge through what was once one of these doors. Of course there is nothing left of the ship's instrumentation. It doesn't matter though, the vegetation and the animals are, without doubt, more exciting. An enormous shoal of snappers grudgingly leaves us room to get through, preceding us inside. A diffused light shines through the portholes, creating a mystic penumbra, where the torch beams

pick out the magnificent colours of the bulkheads and ceiling. As I said before, you have to do several dives to do justice to any exploration of the wreck. The foredeck is just as interesting. It is worth going down to the propeller too, but this needs special preparation as it is at a depth of 33 metres and not 27 like the quarterdeck, or different depths like the superstructures. You can see by the vegetation which has taken root on the *Duane* that the presence of currents is frequent around the wreck. This does not prevent diving, although it does require skills a little higher than basic. The important thing on sites like this is to enter the water and resurface close to the buoy. The wreck can be explored on the leeward side, where you are sheltered from the current.

D

E

A - Thanks to the transparency of the waters, the wreck of the Duane *is soon visible, even though it is too big to see in a single dive; this photo had been taken just after the sinking of the* Duane.

B - The huge propeller of the Duane *lies at a depth of 33 metres and a specific preparation is required to reach it.*

C - The bridge superstructures of the Duane *are entirely covered in dense encrustations of colourful organisms.*

D - Even if the Duane *lies on the sea bottom since many years, most of the metal structures are perfectly preserved.*

E - The inside of the bridge of the Duane *has become a huge aquarium where tens of smallmouth grunts (Haemulon chrysargyreum) swim undisturbed.*

DRY ROCK
THE CHRIST OF ABYSS

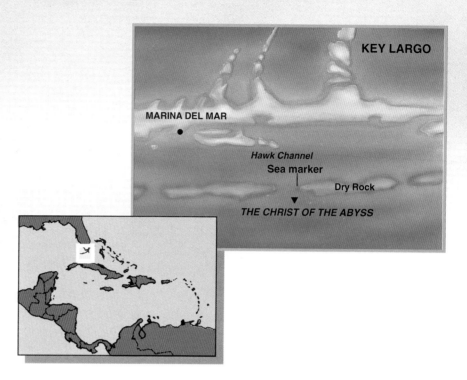

KEY LARGO

MARINA DEL MAR

Hawk Channel
Sea marker
Dry Rock

▼

THE CHRIST OF THE ABYSS

0 m

4,5 m

7,5 m

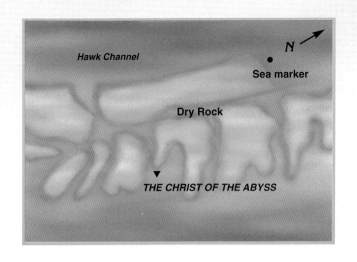

Hawk Channel

Dry Rock

THE CHRIST OF THE ABYSS

N

Sea marker

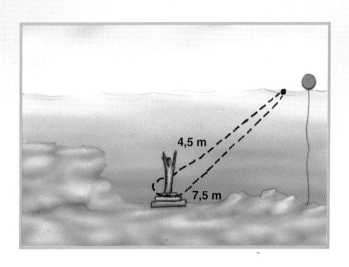

4,5 m

7,5 m

LOCATION

Dry Rock is one of the best known of the superb dive sites in the Key Largo marine park, for it is home to the statue of the Christ of the Abyss, the sanctuary's symbol. Dry Rock is not in the open sea like Elbow or Mollasses and lies to the north-east of Marina del Mar. The latter is a popular dive site and has been fitted with 12 permanent buoys for the dive boats.

The Christ of the Abyss is also an ideal place for keen snorkellers, as the coral reef almost reaches the surface of the water.

prawns and lobsters too.

Large numbers of big barracuda live here permanently, the most famous of which was, indeed still is, Smoky. Smoky, almost 1.5 metres of him, had become the photographers' favourite, because he was driven by his curiosity about the lens to come within a few centimetres of the camera. The last time I was there my luck was out and I did not see him, but all the divemasters were sure that it was only a temporary absence and that Smoky would find his way back to Dry Rock very soon.

A - This picture will be strangely familiar to many Italian scuba divers who know the statue of Christ of the Deep which has been protecting divers at San Fruttuoso, off Genoa, Italy, since 1954.

B - The transparency of the water and the encrustations are very different, but the wonder of this face remains the same here on the sea bottom in Florida.

C - Big barracuda are permanent presence on the Dry Rock sea bottom and they are happy to approach divers and allow them to take photographs from close to.

D - Divers at Dry Rock will find themselves surrounded by compact crowds of yellowtail snappers (Ocyurus chrysurus).

A

B

C

D

The statue rests at a depth of 7.5 metres on a cement base buried in the sand; the coral barrier extends to the right and the left of it, forming a kind of canyon. But the statue is not the only attraction; the place teems with fish which seem perfectly untroubled by the numerous visitors. In addition to the commoner species of fish which live on coral reefs, divers will sometimes meet big shoals of yellowtail snappers swimming in formation above the reef amongst the elkhorn coral and around the statue.

The corals around the statue form a maze of canyons and tight corridors and it is worth taking a closer look at them as these coral formations are the natural habitat not only of invertebrates but of big

My advice to underwater photographers is to take along two cameras or two lenses. You need a 15-20 mm lens to capture the statue of Christ close up in all its majesty and a wide-angle for the shoals of fish. For individual fish or other creatures you need a 35mm lens or a macro.

E - Snappers, grunts and goatfishes often form mixed shoals which take shelter amongst the massive corals. They rise from the sea bed, their growth favoured by the virtual lack of currents.

F - A large adult male stoplight parrotfish (Sparisoma viride) *appears to be proudly showing off its lively range of colours.*

G - An indigo hamlet (Hypoplectrus indigo) *swims in front of a real forest of sea plumes.*

H - A Florida stone crab (Menippe mercenaria) *comes threateningly to the door of its den at the bottom of the reef, ready to rush back to safety if approached too suddenly.*

THE DIVE

I have already seen a Christ of the Abyss figure like the one I am looking at now, its arms stretching upwards, but it was in the Mediterranean. There is an identical statue on the sea bottom at San Fruttuoso, near Genoa in Italy. The statue is the work of the sculptor Guido Galletti and represents the patron saint of divers, fishermen and all sea-going folk. In 1954 it was lowered into place on a prepared base, at a depth of 15 metres.
Like the original, this bronze copy is three metres tall and weighs 1,800 kilos. Cast from the same mould, it was presented to the American Underwater Society by Egidio Cressy, the Italian diving-equipment manufacturer.

Here though, it is not the multicoloured fish of the Mediterranean which are swimming around the statue, but yellow tail snappers and bright blue parrotfish searching around the base for food. Depending on the position of the sun the statue provides a series of different backdrops for exciting photography.
Today, during our morning dive, the sun is still far to the east and the figure of Christ is a powerful image seen against the light.
After taking the required photographs of the park's symbol we head into the canyon to explore

the surrounding rocks, which form a kind of vertical wall.
The most striking things are the many, huge, brain corals and the numerous shoals of snappers. Dry Rock has no strong currents and although this makes diving easier it does have its drawbacks too, as the water is not as transparent, which means that visibility is a few metres less than on the outside of the reef.
Despite this, the Christ of the Abyss should be a compulsory outing for anyone diving at Key Largo.

MOLLASSES REEF

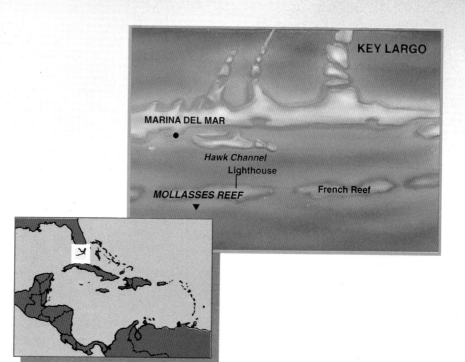

KEY LARGO

MARINA DEL MAR

Hawk Channel
Lighthouse

MOLLASSES REEF
▼

French Reef

0 m

3 m

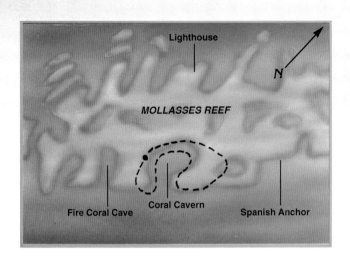

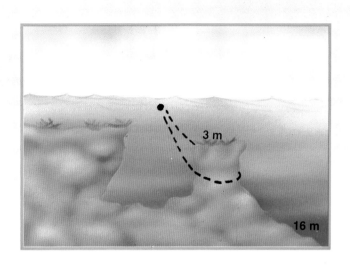

LOCATION

Ask divers who have visited Key Largo about their favourite dive site and the answer is unanimous: Mollasses Reef. I agree, this stretch of outer coral reef, at the southern perimeter of the marine sanctuary, is its most interesting part.

The famous wreck *Duane* also lies close by where it was scuttled specially for divers. Alongside it there are many other ships which came to grief when they foundered on the fatally dangerous coral barrier reef. Nowadays Mollasses Reef houses a big light-tower.

The Gulf Stream which laps the reef brings clean, fresh water to the area, so the water is transparent and attracts large pelagic fish from the open sea here. The reef is very interesting topographically, although divers must not expect drop-offs at great depths.

The barrier is rich in canyons and sandy clearings.

A

B

A - A huge anchor, called the Spanish anchor, bears witness to a past shipwreck on the dangerous Mollasses Reef, which is today marked by a lighttower.

B - Wide gorgonian fans grow high up to take better advantage of the plankton-rich currents.

C

The plateau starts close to the surface of the water and then goes straight down. Maximum depth is around 17 metres.

In some points the Miniwall plunges vertically and it is rare to see such masses of fish as the ones which congregate beneath it.

There are numerous hollows and swim throughs to be explored. Mollasses Reef is impressive and interesting all the way along, quite independently of the point at which you start your dive: from Fire Coral Cave to Miniwall and right to Wellwood Side.

On the sea bottom close to Hole in the Wall there is a huge anchor known as the Spanish Anchor, which makes an interesting photographic subject when posed with a diver in the background to give an idea of the dimensions involved.

C - A small group of Atlantic spadefish (Chaetodipterus faber) *swims close to a diver, reflecting the bright silver rays of the sun.*

D - A white-spotted filefish (Cantherines macrocerus) *is here pictured in its unusual orange livery.*

D

THE DIVE

The 10 kilometres which separate Mollasses Reef present no problem for the dive operators' powerful boats, which means you get more underwater time too, generally around an hour. Afterwards the boats move on to another site close by, the tanks are changed and you get another one-hour session underwater. Thanks to these fast boats divers will get back to base for lunch. It is a splendid later summer day, hot and perfectly still. Mollasses Reef appears before us in all its splendour.

Visibility is perfect and the water is so flooded with light that I have to adjust the aperture and set the fastest exposure time possible in order to get a dark enough background for my shots. I swim slowly along the reef. There are brown elkhorn corals growing as far as the eye can see along the edge of the wall and on the plateau, they look like gigantic fingers. These corals are common in both the Caribbean and the western Atlantic, the shallow reefs of the Florida Keys which go from Key Largo to Key West constitute their natural habitat. They are very fragile however, and divers must move along the reef carefully, paying attention to how they move their fins. Whatever type of coral formation I am photographing, there are always small groups of fish in its shade: French grunts, blue-striped grunts and white grunts. I even manage to find a trumpetfish, hiding stiff and unmoving between the coral branches. This is an old trick these fish are employing: they camouflage themselves amongst the coral branches and their prey, ignorant of the danger, goes right past their mouths. Two big French angelfish have been following me for a few minutes, but whenever I try to get in close to them for a photograph they disappear into the coral. It is almost as if they are teasing me: they come back immediately, but keep out of the way of the camera. All the members of this family are here on the reef: from the grey angelfish to the queen angelfish with its gaudy colours.

It is like being in an aquarium: wherever you look there are fish of all colours and all kinds, from moray eels to groupers. But there is plenty of movement out in the open sea too. As well as the yellowtails, at least eight Atlantic spadefish *(Chateodipterus faber)* are swimming above the corals. These fish resemble the batfish of tropical seas, even though there is no family connection at all. They can grow up to half a metre in size. A word of advice for diving enthusiasts: when exploring Mollasses Reef you will find that time and films finish fast.

E - This shoal of colourful yellow grunts swimming close to the reef, is made up of several different species, in particular can be recognized Haemulon chrysargyreum and Haemulon flavolineatum.

F - This trumpetfish (Aulostomus maculatus) seems to observe the photographer and at the same time it tries to camouflage among the branches of a gorgonian.

G - A French angelfish (Pomacanthus paru) shows to the camera its characteristic and brilliant colouring, the yellow opercular spine can be easily recognised.

H - A queen angelfish (Holacanthus ciliaris) with its

splendid yellow and blue livery swims close to a huge barrel sponge.

I - A few schoolmasters (Lutjanus apodus) with their characteristic yellow fins swims amongst gorgonians and elkhorn corals, their usual habitat.

THE ISLAND OF CUBA

C uba - land of history and of legend, of adventure and of illusion. Seven thousand kilometres of beaches, magnificent bays and some of the best diving in the whole of the Caribbean. Thanks to its position perched on the edge of the Mexican trench its ocean floor is richer in life than that of almost any other island. As in all parts of the Caribbean the sea

L'Avana

CUBA

Trinidad

CARIBBEAN SEA

Camagüey

ISLA DE LA JUVENTUD

CAYO LARGO

CABEZERIA DE CAYO BLANCO

LOS JARDINES DE LA REINA

Santiago de Cuba

A

B

bed is divided into two spheres of influence: in shallower waters the gorgonians dominate, deeper down it is the sponges. Absolute domination, i.e. proof of the independent evolutionary course of this sea, isolated from other oceans for millions of years - from the moment that the isthmus of Panama sealed off its last contact with the Pacific. Sponges: there are all shapes and sizes, from the minute, invisible ones which live by excavating tunnels inside the coral, to the elephant's ears which grow up to 3 metres in diameter. Thousands of cells living together in colonies, assuming different shapes and characteristics according to their environment and the depth at which they live. They draw in the surrounding water

A - The big island of Cuba is surrounded by thousands of islands with coral sands and turquoise seas, still for the most part unexplored.

B - Divers will come across gorgonians of differing shapes and species, according to the environmental conditions.

C - The gorgonians dominant wide tracts of the sea bed with their ramified branches.

C

D - Unbelievable though it may seem, most of the organisms in this photograph are gorgonians. Despite the difference in shapes, they all belong to the same family.

E - Against the blue of the sea bottom the bright colours of the sponges are always one of the major attractions in the Caribbean.

through thousands of little flowers which open outwards, then filter and exhale it, through the big central aperture, the osculum: two hundred kilos of water every 24 hours, for an average-sized sponge. Nowadays there are plenty of places off the Cuban shoreline where diving is a possibility, but the most interesting sites are those along the edge of the continental shelf, which in many points runs close to the coast: the renowned Isla de la Juventud, which has been a magnet for globetrotting scuba divers for decades, Cayo

G

D

H

E

F

Largo and Los Jardines de la Reina, two Cuban destinations recently discovered by divers. Diving is great all year round in these waters, with the exception of September and October: from May to November the weather is hot, the rest of the time it is more temperate, with lowest temperatures - 23/24 degrees - in January and February. However, there is more to Cuba than scuba diving: this is a land of history and of legends. The European version has everything starting on 27th October 1492 when Columbus discovered the island. In the centuries which followed it became a pirate cove, so much so that Robert Louis Stevenson set his novel *Treasure Island* on the Isla de la Juventud (Isla de Pinos at the time). His imagination did not have far to go from the facts: there were plenty of pirates. Pie de Palo, for instance (pegleg) - a privateer paid by the French and English governments to undermine the Spanish hegemony in South America - who ammassed fabulous treasures by attacking the loaded ships returning to Spain, treasures which they say are still hidden here, underwater perhaps.

F - A school of blue tang (Acanthurus coeruleus) moves over the reef looking for seaweed-rich areas on which to feed.

G - The fairy basslet (Gramma loreto) is one of the best known and most colourful species of fish in the Caribbean and is also easy to recognise because of its two-tone livery.

H - The grey angelfish (Pomacanthus arcuatus) is the largest angelfish in the Caribbean and can measure up to 50 centimetres in length.

ISLA DE LA JUVENTUD
CABO FRANCÉS

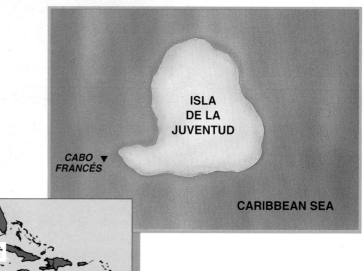

ISLA
DE LA
JUVENTUD

CABO
FRANCÉS ▼

CARIBBEAN SEA

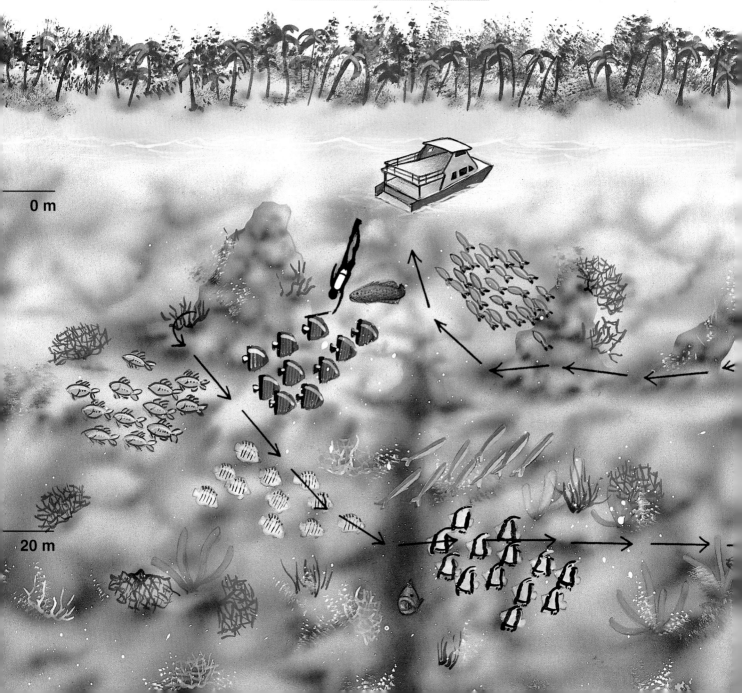

0 m

20 m

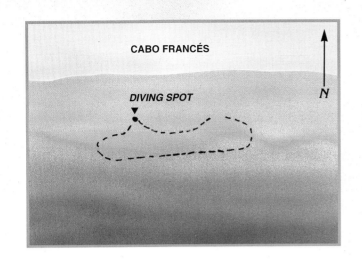

CABO FRANCÉS

DIVING SPOT

N

20 m

LOCALIZATION

The dive sites at Cabo Francés are a 45 minute trip from the Marina by one of the fleet of fast support boats belonging to the island's only dive operator. There are two scheduled dives a day: the first along the outer reef wall, the second one on the platform behind the reef, with a pause for lunch and a spot of relaxation between dives at the "Rancheron". This is a restaurant built on the pile-supported platform running along the stunning white beach. A large number of shoals of yellow snappers gather in the water around the structure's pile. There is a once-weekly scheduled night dive at Cabo Francés.

A - A shoal of French grunts (Haemulon flavolineatum) surrounds a squirrelfish, a fellow tenant of this particular piece of shady sea bed.

B - The grey angelfish (Pomacanthus arcuatus), although is fairly common, never ceases to fascinate divers and sometimes approaches them spontaneously.

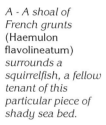

THE DIVE

Scuba diving in Cuba is synonymous with Cabo Francés: for decades the Isla de la Juventud has been a "must" for divers of all nationalities, lured by the transparent waters, the great depths and the giant sponges.
The world underwater photography championships were held on this stunning wall, which plunges right off the continental shelf and in a few hundred metres drops more than 1000 metres.
You can dive along this same wall for weeks on end without ever running the risk of boredom.
A series of buoys has been positioned along the edge to mark the dive sites. The buoys numbered 1 to 34 are on the wall and the others indicate shallower dives on the reef behind the wall.
The edge starts at 20 metres and disappears into the deep blue, hitting the ocean floor only after several hundreds of metres.
The lords and masters of this wall are the sponges, of all shapes but just one size only: giant.
Don't just look at them from a distance: sponges are not merely inert beings of outsize dimensions, but growing animals, which reproduce and fight amongst themselves.
Diving close to No. 4 buoy in particular you will find several engaged in silent but deadly battle for space and light.

There are caves along the wall, the one near No. 7 buoy is especially interesting. There is one particularly large one which goes down to a depth of 50 metres. The top of the cleft is open and you can see the Caribbean tarpon with their huge silver scales swimming slowly against the illuminated backdrop provided by the surface of the water. The poetically-named "tunnel of love" is a deep vertical cleft in the wall which divers can swim down, between the gigantic sponges that grow on the inside walls of the tunnel. Behind the wall is the coral plateau which never goes any deeper than 15 metres.
There are numerous hard coral formations on its sandy bed and

and purple prawns, whose job is to clean the animals of parasites, hide. Around here you will often come across groupers with their mouths open as they good-temperedly undergo the prawns' painstaking and energetic ministrations.
If you want to see the beautiful purple fans of the gorgonians, you will find whole forests of them on the walls of the gully at No. 56 buoy, which descends from a depth of 10 metres to 15 metres, to the sandy floor: the characteristic of this point is the unusual amount of splendid flamingo tongues, molluscs found only in the Caribbean, which you will see on the branches of the coelenterates.

G

F

H

even the most well-travelled scuba divers will find plenty of interest. At No. 38 buoy there is a huge coral arch where lots of tarpons congregate. Squads of fish swim unceasingly under a rocky arch three or four metres high.
There are groupers everywhere and they are easy to approach too (especially at No. 40 buoy, as divers often take food to them. Even a group of surgeonfish does not disdain a snack between meals. "El Cabezo Solitario" (No. 46 buoy) is, as its name suggests, a lone reef with plenty of cleaning stations run by crustaceans. Look into the nooks and crannies for the characteristic sea anemones with their curly tentacles: this is where transparent

C - A school of schoolmasters (Lutjanus apodus) swims slowly above the rich coral beds which surround the Isla de la Juventud.

D - Sometimes schools of big tarpons (Megalops atlanticus) are non-migratory and can always be found in the same places on the reef.

E - The big tube sponges (Agelas sp.) are a common spectacle in all dives in the Caribbean reef system.

F - The yellowline arrow crab (Stenorhynchus seticornis), is easily recognisable by its long, disproportionate, legs.

G - In the areas of the reef exposed to constant weak currents it is not uncommon to see tufts such as these: the branchial crowns of feather dusters worms (Bispira brunnea) which are quickly withdrawn at the slightest vibration.

H - A huge gorgonian lifts its wide fan towards the surface.

CAYO LARGO
CABEZERIA DE CAYO BLANCO

CABEZERIA DE
CAYO BLANCO

CAYO LARGO

N

0 m

10 m

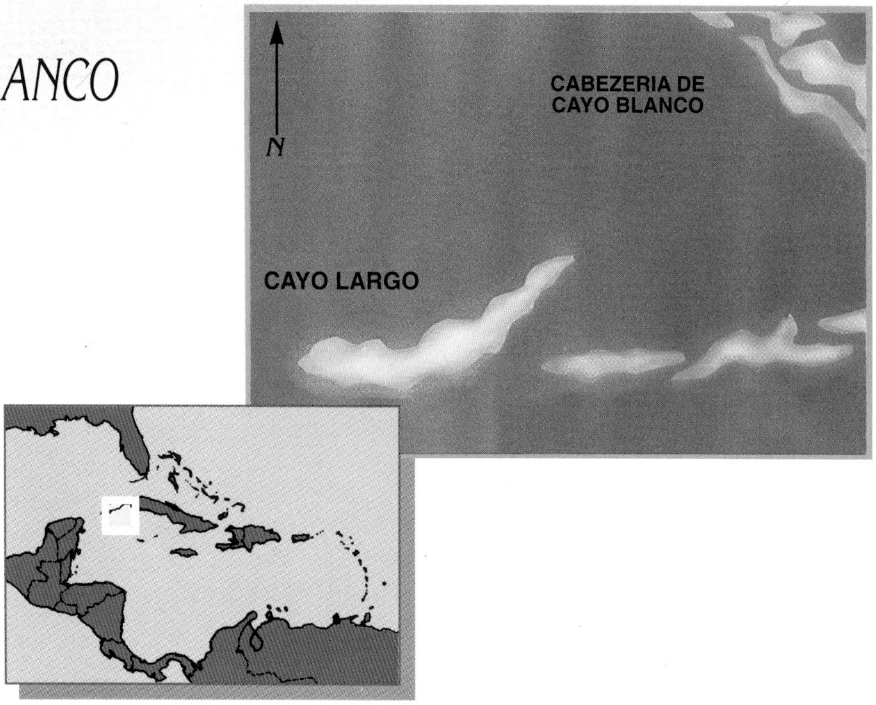

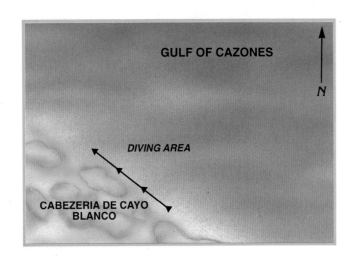

GULF OF CAZONES

N

DIVING AREA

CABEZERIA DE CAYO BLANCO

10 m

LOCALIZATION

Cayo Largo and the Los Canarreos archipelago of which it forms part are all that lies above water of the huge, low-lying Jardines de la Reina Bank, the last strip of Cuban territory to surrender to the deep waters of the Gulf of Mexico. Just by studying the marine charts you can see that the diving potential of this island is considerable: in addition to the southern coast, which reaches a depth of 1000 metres just over half a mile from the shore, north of the archipelago a deep channel runs between the Jardines Bank and Cuba. Its sheer walls drop straight from 0 to 200 metres and run for tens and tens of miles before exiting

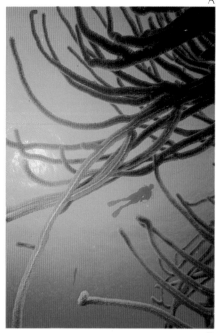

A

A - The vertical wall is broken by the branches of the sea-rod gorgonians, whose arms are covered with thousands of polyps that filter the rich water for their nourishment.

B - A Southern stingray (Dasyatis americana) swims with slow wingbeats over one of the wide sandy clearings which link the numerous reefs of the Cabezeria.

C - A gigantic yellow-orange tube sponge (Aplysina fistularis) appears to be colouring the sea plume behind it (Pseudopterogorgia bipinnata).

D - These two sponges, rising from a common base, look like signposts against the blue of the surrounding sea beds.

E - A large vase sponge can conceal fishes and other organisms inside.

B

C

D

E

into the Gulf of Cazones.
The Cabezeria de Cayo Blanco, a long stretch of reefs and sand spits which disappears at high tide, lies along this wall. The 200 metres isobath runs right along the edge and where the sea bed plunges swiftly to great depths there is, of course, more chance of abundant wealth of marine life, including the big predators in the early months of the year.

THE DIVE

It is difficult to pinpoint one specific dive site along the Cabezeria, which is a relatively new area still being explored. The wall buzzes with underwater life - you will find corals, sponges and gorgonians and you will be surrounded by masses of fish: giant dentex, tropical groupers and nurse sharks. This is big predator country: sharks (including the whale shark), eagle rays, and jacks. The whole of the Cabezeria edge is interesting and suited, for the main part, to more experienced divers. This is not because it is necessary to reach dizzying depths to catch a sight of the big ocean-going predators, as they come almost to the surface, but because the current is often very swift and strong and many dives are done using the drift system. But there is something for all tastes: even for beginners, who can stick to the shallower levels where there will be no lack of opportunities

F, G - Whatever their shape, the Caribbean sponges seem determined to reach their maximum size here. They are an important part of the sea bottom because they are transformed into substrates on which small gorgonians become established.

H - A school of Atlantic spadefish (Chaetodipterus faber) illustrate how their characteristic dark bands can differ from one individual to another.

I - A pair of spotted eagle rays (Aetobatus narinari) swims with their usual elegance.

for encounters with the great lords of the sea.

For everyone, there will be the unique sensations aroused by diving on a virtually unknown sea bed: it is the sheer amount of fish - giant groupers, sea-bream which are so huge they co-habit with one or more remoras, eaglerays, stingrays - which shows that until now this sea has barely been touched by human beings.

Cayo Largo is only just starting to be discovered, only a tiny fraction of the Los Canarreos sea bed has ever seen a diver.

The best period for diving in the Gulf of Cazones is from June to December, when the prevalent wind is east-southeast.

LOS JARDINES DE LA REINA
THE OCTOPUS'S LAIR

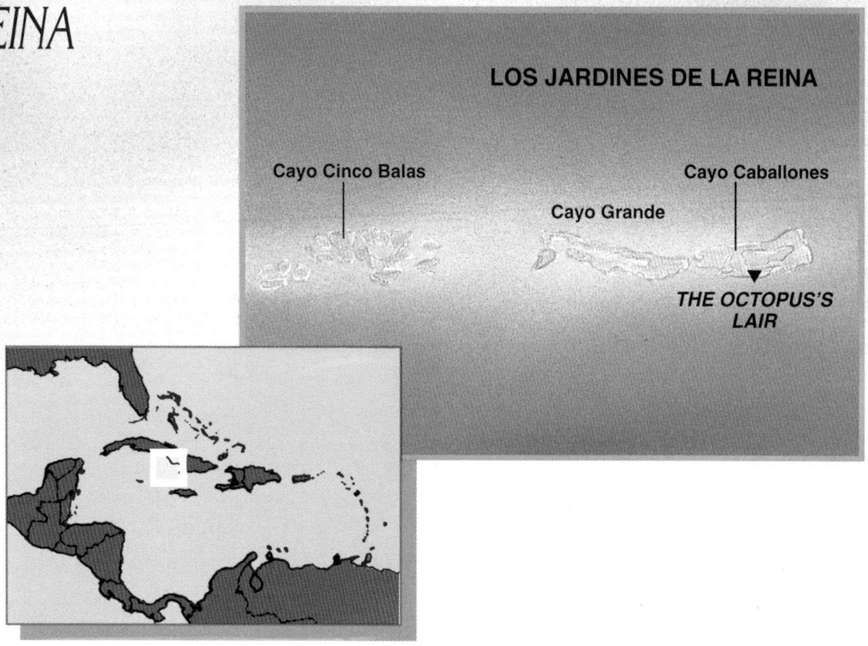

LOS JARDINES DE LA REINA

Cayo Cinco Balas

Cayo Caballones

Cayo Grande

THE OCTOPUS'S LAIR

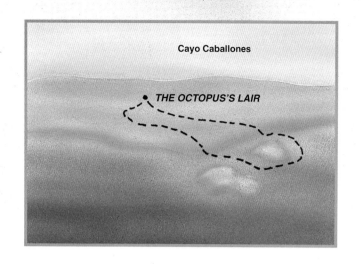

Cayo Caballones

THE OCTOPUS'S LAIR

A

LOCALIZATION

The Jardines de la Reina archipelago consists of more than two hundred cayos stretching in an arc over two hundred kilometres long and lying parallel to the south coast of the island of Cuba. The archipelago, which boasts one of the longest coral reefs in the world, is separated from the main island by the Golfo del Ana Maria and can be reached by cruise boats in just a few hours' sailing from Marina di Jucaro, not far from the small town of Ciego de Avila.

At the moment the Jardines de la Reina archipelago is uninhabited and the only way to visit it and dive on its reefs is on a scuba-divers' cruise: decades of total isolation have contributed to making it one of the most unspoilt of all the dive sites in the entire Caribbean.

A - The tall sea plumes are strange gorgonians which can grow in several different habitats, to heights of over two metres.

B - Numerous plankton-feeding organisms, such as gorgonians and sponges, like this pink vase sponge (Callyspongia plicifera) grow along the steepest parts of the reef wall.

C - Big barracuda (Sphyraena sp.) can often be found close to the reef, drawn by the wealth of the marine life on the sea bottom.

D - Divers will be struck by the size of the silvery tarpons (Megalops atlanticus), which can be over two metres long.

B

C

D

THE DIVE

One of the best dives is at a site known as The Octopus's Lair, so called because it consists of a huge crater about 12 metres in diameter, fringed with heaps of rocks which are neatly laid out along the edges, just as if it really were the lair of a giant octopus. But far from concealing a monstrous octopus lying in wait, the crater is simply the hideout of a spectacular green moray *(Gymnothorax funebris)* - and myriad small reef fish, especially grunts *(Haemulon sp.)*, gregories *(Stegastes sp.)* and chromis. After exploring the crater, which is about 15 metres down and is usually first stop on the dive programme, you can move on first to the banks of coral and gorgonians which surround it and take time out to admire the huge resident shoals of grunts *(Haemulon flavolineatum, Haemulon sciurus* and *Anisotremus virginicus)*, the butterflyfish *(Chaetodon capistratus)* and the ever-present trumpet fish *(Aulostomus chinensis)*, before

E

E - The green moray (Gymnothorax funebris) *is a nocturnal creature, this species stays hidden in its den during the day and will often allow divers to approach it.*

F - Tiger groupers (Mycteroperca tigris) *can often be found suspended immobile in the water. Although shy, they are quite curious about divers and let themselves be approached.*

F

G

H

going further down where a landslide of reefs covered with corals including the huge black bush species and, more especially, sponges of the genera *Aplysina, Callyspongia* and *Xestospongia* which are home to a fascinating selection of animals: morays *(Gymnothorax moringa* and *Gymnothorax miliaris)* the emperor fish *(Holacanthus ciliaris)* and *Pomancanthus paru*, sea-anemones *(Bartholomea* and *Condylactis* genera) with their delightful dining companions the cleaner prawns *(Periclemenes pedersoni)*. A merry population of warlike giant crabs *(Mithrax spinosissimus)* as well as lots of other lesser, but by no means less interesting, species.

This is a dive you will enjoy doing a second time, after the sun has gone down, when you will often catch sight of the elegant flamingo's tongues *(Cyphoma gibbosum)* and the surreal arrow crabs *(Stenorhynchus seticornis)* on the gorgonian sea fans.

G - One of the amazing underwater panoramas at Octopus's Lair. Like other parts of the Jardines

de la Reina, submarine life is plentiful, thanks to the relative isolation this area has enjoyed up until now.

H - All the reef walls are encrusted with marine organisms which transform the sea bed into a maze of life.

MEXICO
COZUMEL ISLAND

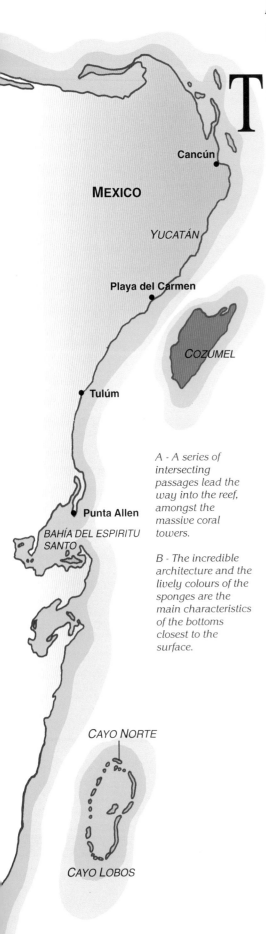

The Mexican island of Cozumel lies 12 kilometres off the north-east coast of the Yucatan peninsola. It is not a large island, just 46 kilometres long and 14 kilometres wide. Its highest point is 14 metres a.s.l. Cozumel is the largest of the three islands - the others are Mujeres and Contoy - which front the north-eastern coast of Mexico. The underwater world of Cozumel is part of the world's second largest reef, the Belize Reef, which stretches 320 kilometres from the southern tip of the island Mujeres to the Gulf of Honduras. The pre-Colombian history of Cozumel evolved parallel to the rise and fall of the Mayan civilisation. It was quite by chance that the Spaniard Don Juan Grijalva discovered the island while trying to reach Cuba. In the years which followed the Spaniards used the island as a base from which to launch their attacks on the Mexican mainland. In the late 16th century the island was turned into a base for fearsome pirates,including the infamous Jean Lafitte and Henry Morgan. When the period of the pirates, with their alcohol and their skirmishing, finally came to an end after more than 200 years, they had caused considerable devastation to the lives of the small, peace-loving groups of Mayans and Spaniards and in 1843 the island was totally abandoned. In 1848, refugees from the troubles which were ravaging the mainland landed on Cozumel, repopulating the island with fishermen and farmers. Strange though it may seem, it was chewing-gum, invented in America around the year 1900, turned this island into an industrial centre. During the Second World War the Americans built an airstrip and a submarine base on the island and the Marine Corps divers used the island to train for upcoming events in Europe and the Pacific. It was these men who at the end of the war went back to the island to enjoy themselves and spread the word about the island and its extraordinary dives.

A - A series of intersecting passages lead the way into the reef, amongst the massive coral towers.

B - The incredible architecture and the lively colours of the sponges are the main characteristics of the bottoms closest to the surface.

DIVING ON COZUMEL

Practically all dives on Cozumel are on the western coast which is in the lee of the wind. Although the reef surrounds virtually the entire island, it is impossible to dive off the east coast because of the massive breakers. But with the exception of when the North, North-West winds blow in the late autumn, the water on the western side is generally flat. You can also dive from the shore on Cozumel. At the points along the coast where the reef narrows, the drop-off is reached after a 50-metre swim. The whole of the Cozumel coast is accessible to all inhabitants and tourists, and this includes access to the sea in front of the hotels.

On presentation of a dive certificate known as the C-Card equipment can be hired practically anywhere and you can roam the coastline in a hired car. A list of all the shore access points is available in every one of the 20 dive shops. Up to ten years ago all dives were made from small boats. In general it used to take a whole day to do two dives on the southern and northern reefs. Nowadays there are fast, modern and well-equipped boats which leave from the bases and the hotels. You can do two dives along the coast between 9 a.m. and 1 p.m., what is known as a two-tank boat-trip. The bases are also available for afternoon and night trips. All craft are equipped with radio and oxygen equipment for emergencies.
The northward-flowing Guyana current strikes the southern tip of Cozumel, producing secondary currents of varying intensity. Currents are a constant presence here and generally flow south-north, but they can sometimes change direction without warning. This is why all dives starting from boats have to be done using the drift-diving technique, which will probably be new to most people. The technique involved is explained before every dive and at the start divers are always accompanied by extremely expert local divemasters. You will see straightaway that this kind of dive is simple, practical and safe. At the end of the agreed time, the divers are picked up by the boats which have been following the bubbles. Dives are carried out under CADO (Cozumel Association of Dive Operators) equipment and safety regulations:
- 40 bar (500psi) minimum air pressure in tanks;
- 40 metres depth limit;
- no deco-dives;
- 3-minute safety stop at 5 metres;
- it is forbidden to remove anything.
Respect for nature when diving is fundamental here on Cozumel and you need to be well acquainted with a stabilizer jacket or buoyancy compensator to take part in the dives. The underwater universe around Cozumel does not differ from other regions of the north-eastern Caribbean. The drop-off is very close to the coast, only 50 metres away at some points. The reef can be divided into three categories: shallow reef,

medium reef, drop-off reef. The entire area, especially close to the medium and drop-off reefs, is broken up by canyons at right angles to the coast - these are the sand shuts, which were dug out by enormous masses of water during the Ice Age when the entire territory was at sea level. Today everything is covered with corals and sponges which have created a fantastic underwater world. Thanks to the constant presence of currents, the waters around Cozumel are always transparent and visibility is often over 50 metres. Water temperature is constant all the year round, oscillating around 25 degrees Celsius in winter and over 29 degrees in the summer. There is a rich variety of fish; even in the absence of enormous ocean-going fish, along the drop-off and the

medium reef divers must expect to meet eagle rays, barracuda, jacks, grey and blacktip sharks. Schools of stingrays rest on the sandy floor and enormous nurse sharks hide in the nooks and crannies all along the reef. But it is the angelfish which are the real bosses of the reef and can be found in every corner of it. There are snappers too, especially on the intermediate reef. You might also encounter a native species, which exists only here, the splendid toadfish (Sanopus splendidus), which hides in the reef during the day but comes out and swims on the top of the reef at night. But be warned, do not to touch them, they bite with great speed. The snapping of their jaws constitutes the soundtrack during nigh-time dives.

C

C - One of the most unusual encounters in these waters: a splendid toadfish (Sanopus splendidus), with the characteristic striped head and long barbels underneath its mouth. Despite its funny shape, this fish is dangerous and it might bite if touched

D

D - A close up of this squirrelfish, showing its big eyes, a characteristic of its adaptation to this fish's nocturnal life style.

E - Big, solitary barracuda (Sphyraena sp.) swim along the sea-bed of the reef, ready to take advantage of any careless move by its prey.

E

SANTA ROSAS WALL

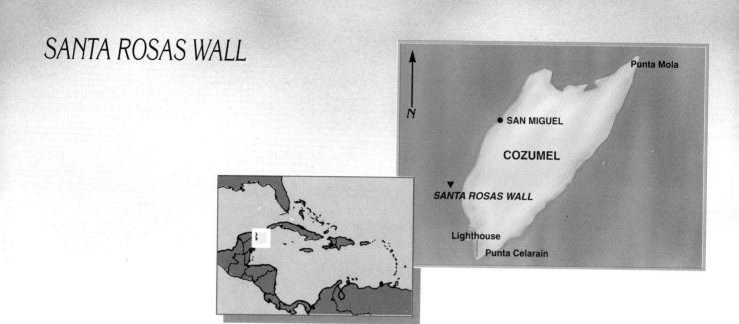

Punta Mola

● SAN MIGUEL

COZUMEL

▼ SANTA ROSAS WALL

Lighthouse

Punta Celarain

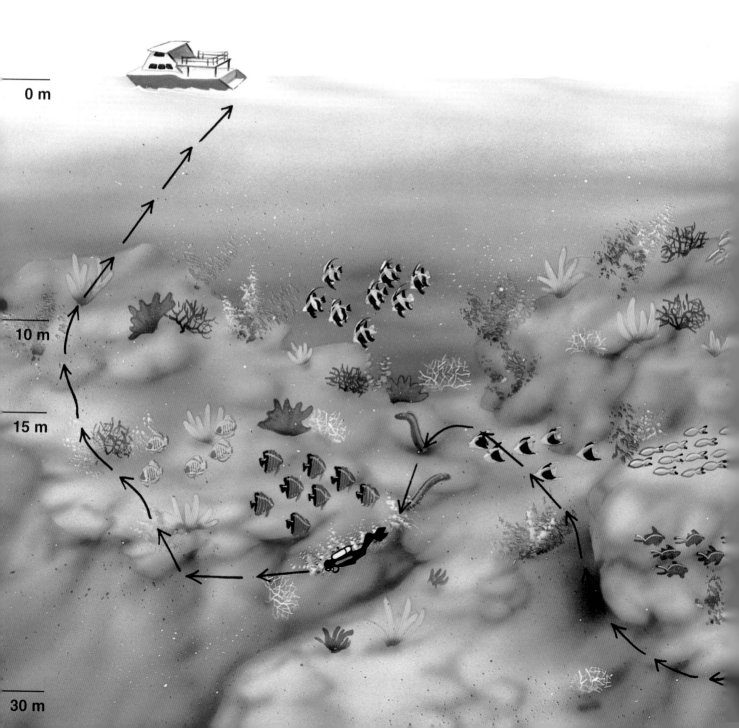

0 m

10 m

15 m

30 m

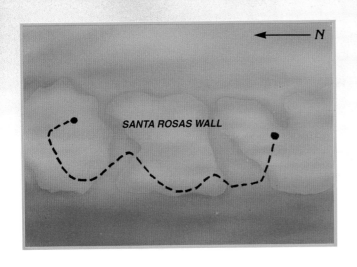

SANTA ROSAS WALL

N

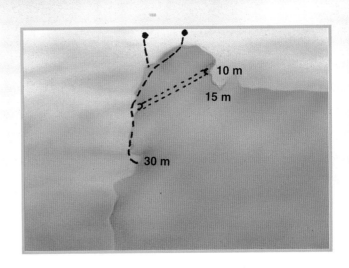

10 m

15 m

30 m

A

LOCALIZATION

The Santa Rosas Reef is the most northerly of the three dive sites described here. This section of the reef is very long and even with the help of a favourable current it would be impossible to swim it all on one tank. Here at Santa Rosas the current normally flows south-north and although it can be quite strong its main characteristic is its unpredictability. Generally, however, divers have no difficulty in finding shelter from it in one of the many troughs or passages which lead straight to the reef. With progress broken up in this way, there is more time to take an attentive look around at your surroundings, take photographs or film footage.
The so-called down currents can be a nuisance. These currents flow towards the coral platform and push you down the sheer wall of the reef towards the ocean bottom. It would be a mistake to inflate your stabilizer jacket in these conditions because it would simply supply the current with a larger surface area on which to work. The only thing to do is to keep calm and fin hard towards the reef, where the current will pass you by, allowing you to slip into one of the many canyons and continue the dive. The southern part of the reef is quite flat and only slopes slightly. Here in the northerly section, on the Santa Rosas Wall, the wall plummets from the reef platform, which is at about 10-12 metres, to breathtaking depths. If you get the right tunnel you can swim through the reef and look straight down into the deeps at the exit. The wall is covered with deep-water gorgonians and whip corals and, once again, the dominant sponges. There are enormous orange elephant ear varieties and yellow tubes over a metre long. There are fantastic tunicates to be found amongst the black coral formations or on the branches of dead gorgonians. At depths of over 20 metres it is the landscape which catches ones attention, while at shallower depths it is the fish.
It is not unusual in this area to meet enormous black sea-groupers (Mycteroperca bonaci) and green morays (Gymnothorax funebris) stretch their bodies out of their holes. Sometimes there are whole schools of spiny lobsters underneath the canyon rims.

THE DIVE

As is usual here, our boat drops us behind the reef. We head west over the slightly-sloping, pale sand, the first dark shadows of the reef visible in the distance. The wall is broken by sand shuts leading straight out onto the slope.
The bottom of this canyon is covered with sand as white as snow and the walls of the reef above are inhabited with soft corals and sponges; the brilliant colours of the rope sponges make a splendid

B

C

D

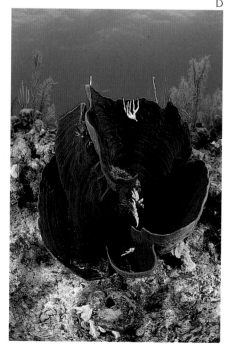

A - The big yellow tube sponges (Aplysina fistularis) are a recurring note in the steep walls which plunge downwards into the dark blue water.

B - The sponges, a constant companion on every dive, always make the brightest blotches of colour.

C - A close-up of a large green moray (Gymnothorax funebris). This is the largest eel in the Caribbean, measuring up to two metres long.

D - One of the enormous, unmistakable, elephant ear sponges scattered all over the steep Santa Rosas Wall.

E - The branches of this deep-water gorgonian have developed and interwoven with the branches of a red rope sponge.

F - A yellowline crab (Stenorhynchus seticornis) *easily recognizable by its long legs, is lying on a orange sponge.*

contrast with the deep blue of the water. We cannot feel the current yet, inside this passage, but looking at the air bubbles from another group of divers we realise the speed with which water is flowing in front of the sheer outer wall.

This is the point at which we too are caught up by the current, which slowly but inexorably carries us along. Abandoning yourself to your emotions and allowing yourself to be carried along the reef wall is a tremendous experience.

From a distance I spot two enormous sponges under an outcrop on the reef. The contrast with the blue of the water will make a good photograh.

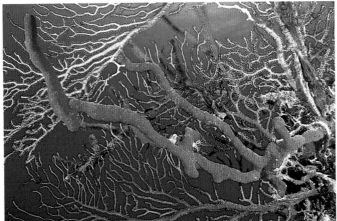

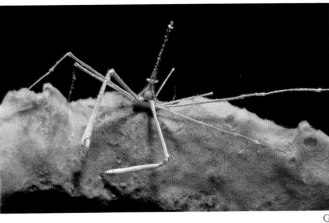

A few finstrokes and I am close to the reef where the current is very weak, no longer creating any problems for photographers. The water is so clear that we can see well below the depth we have fixed for our dive. Although the temptation to let ourselves go down into the blue expanse is great, it is always better to restrain oneself in this kind of drop-off. Three huge black groupers draw us through a canyon to the reef - this looks like their territory, if the way they run circles around we photographers is anything to go by. By using every passage and tunnel in the reef they manage to be everywhere, all the time, and not just in front of the lens. This is where our boat will pick us up after the 45 minutes' planned dive and the compulsory 5-minute stop at 5 metres.

G - The splendid toadfish (Sapodus splendidus) *is one of the main attractions at Cozumel, the only place this fish has so far been found.*

H - Large black groupers (Mycteroperca bonaci) *are quite common below 20 metres, where they hang immobile in the water, well clear of the bottom.*

I - The first part of the reef ends in a sandy platform. Divers can move backwards and forwards along the wall and take time to admire the shapes and colours of the encrustant organisms.

PALANCAR CAVES

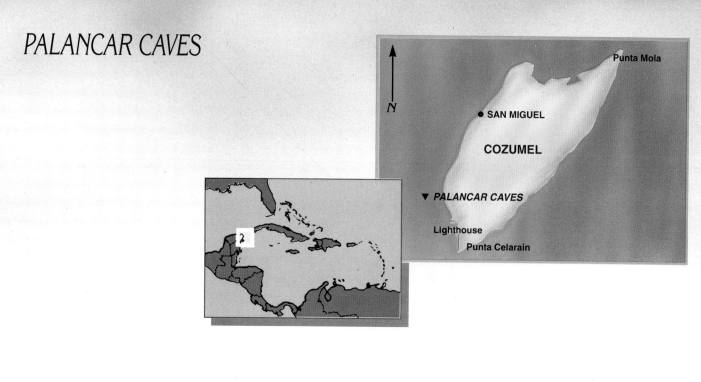

Punta Mola

● SAN MIGUEL

COZUMEL

▼ *PALANCAR CAVES*

Lighthouse

Punta Celarain

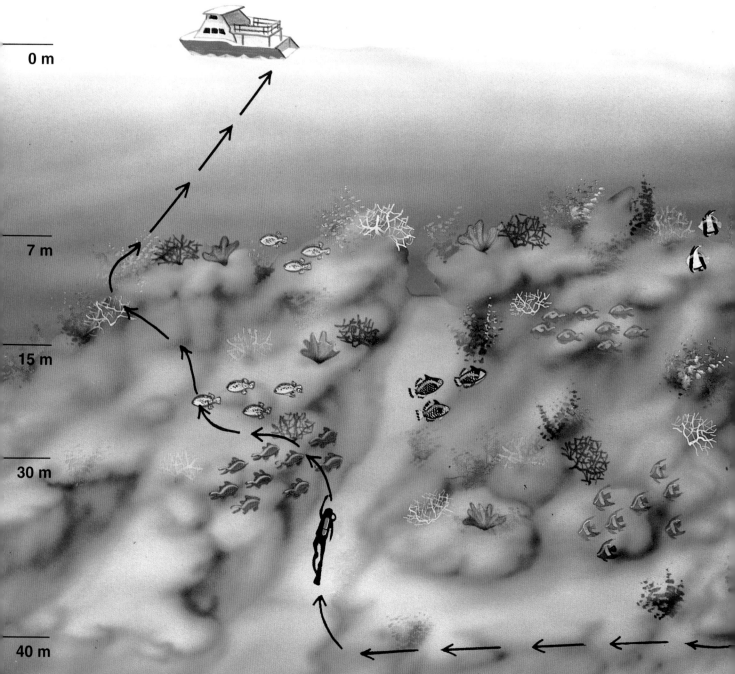

0 m

7 m

15 m

30 m

40 m

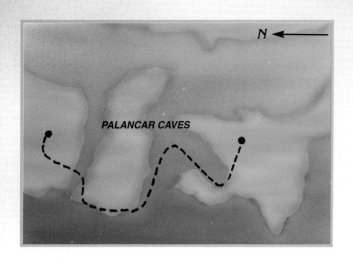

PALANCAR CAVES

N

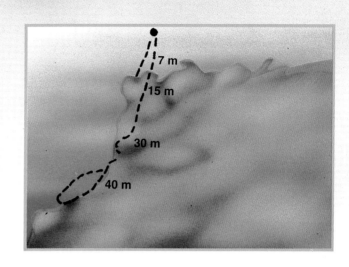

7 m

15 m

30 m

40 m

LOCALIZATION

The Palancar Cave system stretches for around 5 kilometres and is one of the favourite dive sites on Palancar Reef at Cozumel.
At this point the reef does not always plunge straight down to the sea bed and there are long flat sections known as the Palancar Shallows. The Palancar Horseshoe is another, more northerly, section of the reef; Palancar Caves are separated from the shallows through a sandy trench which varies in depth from 7 to 10 metres.
The wide structure of the Palancar Caves is as full of holes as a Swiss cheese - it is a labyrinth of holes, tunnels and coral towers criss-crossed by canyons and sand shuts.

A

B

C

The roofs of the tunnels are mainly covered with brilliant orange sponges. There are much fewer soft corals here compared with other places, no doubt due to the passage of hurricane Gilbert which hit the island in 1988 and caused a good deal of damage, especially here at the Palancar Reef.
The extraordinary landscape and the fact that you can swim in and out of the blocks of reef at will quite make up for this disadvantage.
The outer reef wall drops sheer to a depth of about 30 metres on a sandy slope which leads to the drop-off. The real drop-off is further than the permitted depth, which in most of the dive sites is between 30 and

40 metres. In this part of the reef the current is light to medium, visibility is generally between 30 and 50 metres. There are some particularly strange types of fish for divers to see here, including filefish, boxfish, red-finned parrotfish, puffer fish and spotted drums.

THE DIVE

Right after the drop, looking into the distance, we see that the water is transparent. Visibility is over 50 metres. Perfect conditions for diving in the Palancar Caves which, I ought to point out, are not particularly rich in fish. The dominating factor here is the scenery created by the underwater landscape.
The current flowing south-north is virtually imperceptible. To get an idea of the bizzarre reef formation we purposely swim a few metres above the reef platform. The Palancar Caves live up to their name. Innumerable canyons and troughs tempt the explorer and it is extremely difficult to decide where to start. We slide along the bottom of a canyon hidden by a huge outcrop. Underneath it there are weird sponges and further back, next to a crack, quite unmoving, are three big spiny lobsters.
In view of the incredible visibility, we choose to get an overall impression of our surroundings rather than go into details.
The wall drops away right at the canyon exit where the walls of the reef, decorated with enormous

D

gorgonians, rise upwards. With the partial filtration of the colours of the spectrum they look almost black to human eyes. It is only when lit up by the strobe or a torch that they reveal their true red. We are at the foot of the reef now, at a depth of 30 metres. This is where the very steep sandy bottom starts, stretching right to the drop-off. A glance at the dive computer confirms that we are running out of our allotted time. Our attention is drawn to a tunnel ending in a point, which we should like to explore. The sun's rays filter in through a narrow slit in its roof, reflecting on the sandy bottom and enveloping the landscape in an enchanting light blue. In such situations, where divers like to spend a long time taking photographs and watching the marine life, one learns the advantages of drift diving. But it is important for the team to reach the surface at the set time and to travel in the same direction as the current. The exit from the Blue Grotto, as I have decided to call it, leads into the sandy expanse behind the reef. Here we have plenty of time to check out the sandy floor for stingrays or the other fish which inhabit this world.

E

E - A shoal of bluestriped grunts (Haemulon sciurus) moves slowly along, keeping close to the bottom.

F - A spotted trunkfish (Lactophrys bicaudalis) appears to be eyeing up the photographer out of curiosity.

G - One of the most lively liveries, the early, female one, which accompany the growth and sex-change of this parrotfish (Sparisoma viridis).

H - The underwater area at Cozumel is the ideal environment for the Caribbean spiny lobster (Palunirus argus).

F

G

A - The Palancar Caves are a real maze of hollows, tunnels and canyons with sandy bottoms, inside coral towers.

B - The amazing tunnelled landscape of the Palancar Reef provides plenty of settings where underwater photographers can combine natural and artificial light.

C - A large stove-pipe sponge (Aplysina archeri) seems to drawn new life-giving nourishment from the waters from below.

D - A large black grouper (Mycteroperca bonaci) appears before the divers without warning from one of its many possible lairs in these walls.

H

COLUMBIA WALL

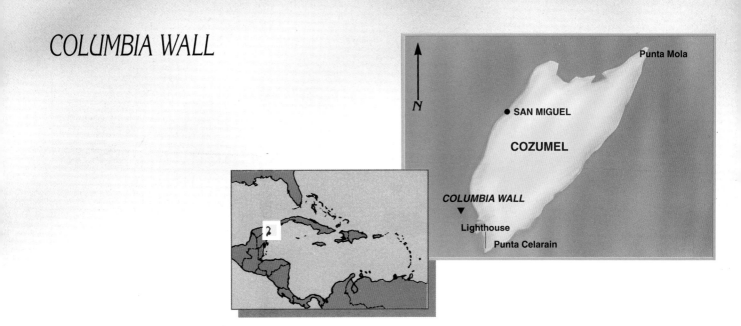

Punta Mola

SAN MIGUEL

COZUMEL

COLUMBIA WALL

Lighthouse

Punta Celarain

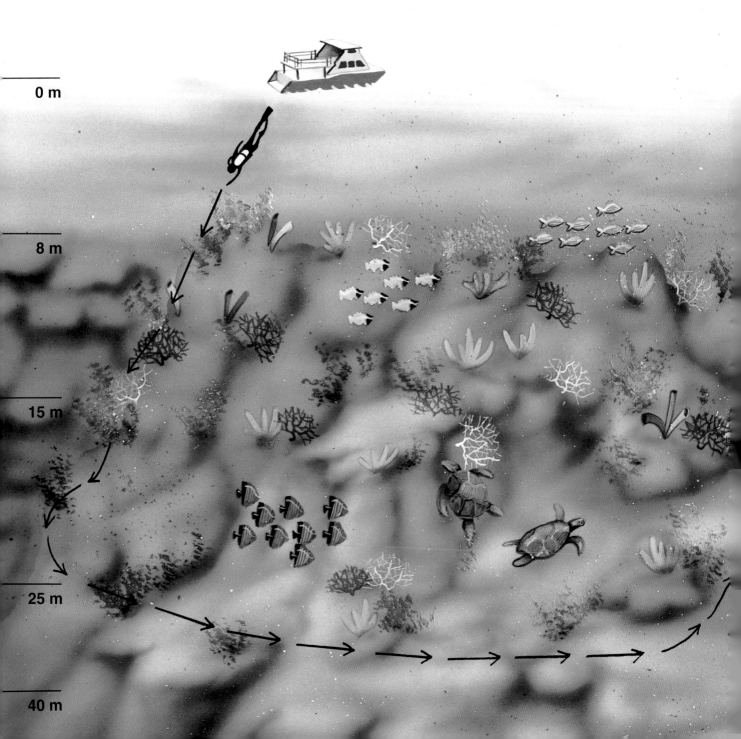

0 m

8 m

15 m

25 m

40 m

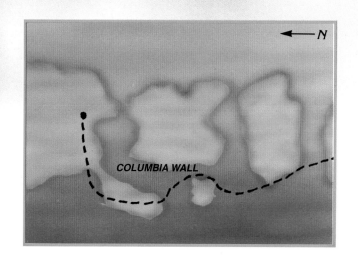

COLUMBIA WALL

N

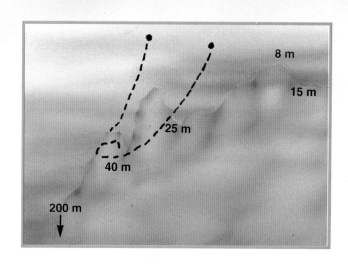

8 m

15 m

25 m

40 m

200 m

A

B

LOCALIZATION

The Columbia Wall is between the southern tip of the Palancar Reef and Punta Sur Reef. This area is a really spectacular drop-off, with massive coral towers which grow right up to the surface from depths of up to 18 metres. The reef is very wide here, starting from a depth between 6 and 8 metres and continuing in a single unbroken slope right to the sheer wall. Canyons and pathways run through the length and breadth of the coral base block, until they reach the drop-off which plunges into the void. This is one of the reasons why a maximum depth of 30 metres has been set for dives along the wall.

C

A - A series of arches appears to indicate the ideal underwater pathway through the Columbia Wall reef.

B, C - Carried along by a medium-strength current and by keeping the buoyancy controller well-adjusted, divers can take time to admire life on the reef without any problem.

D - The biggest caverns in the Columbia Wall maze are dominated by dense schools of silversides, their silvery bodies reflecting and multiplying the light filtering in from above.

D

This dive site does not just have an amazing underwater landscape however, there are plenty of fish too. You will meet huge formations of yellow-tailed snappers, jacks and Bermuda chub. It is not unusual to see turtles, groupers and eagle rays either, and during certain periods blacktip sharks appear on Columbia Reef, staying for several weeks, as the divemasters will show you. The surface of the reef, the canyons and the outcrops are all covered with rich vegetation and gorgonians cling to the sheer outer wall. Any kind of sponge will grow here and the most striking are the tube sponges, in all colours and sizes.

The luxuriant vegetation and the great number of fish is, of course, the result of the current which is practically always present, varying in intensity from medium to strong. All these factors combine to make the Columbia Wall a site suited to expert divers.

The water is generally very clear in this area, but in some cases a strong current transports a lot of particles. Although these do not affect visibility, they can be a nuisance for photographers. If the light is used too close to the camera or is too strong the suspended particles will appear on the final print as white spots.

THE DIVE

Today we want to explore as much of Columbia Wall as we can and we have Enrice with us. He is one of the "Aqua Safari" divemasters, and he knows this reef like the palm of his hand - a guarantee that the dive will be an exciting one. We shall be diving for an hour and our plan is drawn up to give us the best possible ratio between depth and time, using our dive computers. We enter the water close to the shallowest part of the reef and after a few metres we reach the first coral blocks. In some places these coral formations go more than a metre under the surface; we shall be able to spend a long time here on our ascent. We go quickly towards the drop-off. Enrice points out an outcrop further down on the reef, where there is an entire shoal of silver-grey snappers; eyes wide open they stare into the camera, quite unfrightened by the flash. At this point the reef slopes gradually down and the depth is already 15 metres in this central part. We already had some idea of the lay of the land thanks to a sketch Enrice had done earlier so we know that the drop-off is not far from here now. As we swim over the edge of the reef, the wall below us plunging vertically into the deeps, the fantastic sensation of drop-off diving becomes a reality for us. We let ourselves sink down to 30 metres and swim slowly along the wall, supported by a medium-strength current. We could do with a pair of fish's eyes to make sure we miss none of the marvels down

E

F

G

H

here; in front of us there are gorgonians and soft corals growing straight out into the void. Upwards, the reef wall with its wierd outcrops has the look of a huge curtain through which we can look into the open sea, checking for the appearance of any large marine inhabitants. Our depth time passes in the twinkling of an eye and we begin to ascend slowly towards the tunnels and hollows of the coral masses. Enrice leads us into a twisting path across a first canyon which leads us inwards and then a second one which takes us out. He also knows a series of crossways which take us through the reef, but not in a straight line. They are all wide enough to be crossed without any problems by a fully-kitted-up diver without touching either the walls or the bottom.
When we arrive back at the boat we are in the grip of euphoria. Columbia Wall has shown us its best - we have another page to add to our diary of memorable experiences.

*E - A spotted eagle ray (*Aetobatus narinari*), with its unmistakable shape and colouring, comes out of one of the tunnels in the reef beating its great winged fins.*

F - This forest of gorgonians waves slowly in the current, on the edge of the drop-off.

G - A large turtle swims slowly, using feet which have evolved into wide paddle-like fins.

*I - A shoal of horse-eye jacks (*Caranx latus*) patrols the waters in front of the reef. They sometimes approach divers of their own accord, attracted by the air bubbles and the glitter of the apparatus.*

G rand Cayman is 481 miles south of Miami, between Cuba and Central America. This island has always been an almost excessively tranquil island. During his fourth voyage towards the New World in 1543 Columbus "discovered" the island quite by chance. He actually set foot on Little Cayman, to be precise, which was called *Las Tortugas*, after all the turtles there. These animals

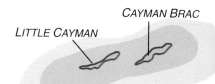

CAYMAN BRAC

LITTLE CAYMAN

GRAND CAYMAN

Georgetown

CAYMAN ISLANDS

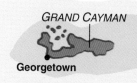

A - Tall sea plumes (Pseudopterogorgia sp.) rise from the bottom and spread themselves in the current. Despite their shape they are part of the same family as the gorgonians.

B A group of bluestriped grunts (Haemulon sciurus) - easily recognised by the blue stripes all along the animal's body and the black tail.

A

B

were also the reason why the Caymans became a favourite with the Spanish sailors, who used to stock up on fresh meat here. Such excesses were not without consequences and forty years later the turtles were so reduced that the interest in the island died away. Later maritime maps called the islands by the name *Lagatargos* and, in 1530, *Las Cayman*, from an Indian word meaning "little crocodile". Sir Francis Drake stopped at the Caymans after sacking Santo Domingo and described the islands as uninhabited by humans and populated with huge serpents called *caymanas*. With their predominant position in the Caribbean under threat the Spanish launched an offensive to clear French and English ships from the waters. The English responded by legalising piracy in the form of privateers whom they supported in their attacks on Spanish ships. Following the conquest of Jamaica, the first English colonists reached Grand Cayman. Generalised peace in the Caribbean, declared in 1713, brought an end to legalised piracy and the last pirates, including the infamous Blackbeard, took refuge on Grand Cayman - so it is not surprising that even today there are endless rumours about hidden treasure. In 1788 something happened which was to have repercussions on the island's future. Known as the "wreck of the ten sailing ships", it is reported in all maritime history books. On that terrible day, strong winds

drove the flagship of an English merchant fleet onto the eastern tip of the reef. Despite warning signals, all ten ships went down. Thanks to a heroic effort by the island's inhabitants, a catastrophe was avoided and none of the passengers or crew lost their lives. Following this the magnanimous British government awarded its colony "freedom from taxation in perpetuity", a generous move which was a starting point for the spectacular development of the island. In a few years the Caymans became one of the major offshore financial centres, attracting an infinite number of investors. There were soon more banks and companies registered in Grand Cayman than there were people living there. This financial growth played a decisive part in the development of tourism: hotels, boarding houses, appartments, condominiums, its own airline and the best infrastructure for scuba diving in the world.

DIVING IN THE CAYMANS

Diving goes on all round the island. West Bay where the reef fronts the coastline along Seven Mile Beach, is the most popular area and the one where most of the main hotels are concentrated. This side of the island has the calmest waters and diving goes on all year round. There are, however, some spectacular dive sites along the north coast too, on the North Wall West off North Sound.

C

D

C - A diver is closely observing a splendid composition of large tube sponges of varying sizes.

D - Stingrays, with their powerful wingbeats, can raise clouds of sand.

These places are a long way from the mainland and so the success of the dive depends on weather conditions. Strong winds and waves can limit dives or even prevent them from taking place at all. East End, which as its name suggests is the eastern end of the island, has spectacular landscapes and is as yet not very developed for diving. These areas are a long way from the hotels and from the dive centres and you need large craft to reach them. The 22-mile long South Shore lies on the west side of the island, within reach of all dive boats. Along the South Sound you can dive off the rocky coastline from George Town to Queen's Monument. Sunset House is an extraordinary place to visit and you can hire air tanks from the dive centre too. The reef which fronts it is something quite unique and will thrill all underwater photographers. You can get your films developed at the

Sunset House Photocenter. There are tourist submarines operating on this reef too, run by Atlantis Submarine Adventures and with a bit of luck you may come across them underwater. Grand Cayman has 111 dive sites, most of which are equipped with permanent moorings. Rules in the Cayman Marine Park are extremely strict and it is absolutely forbidden to fish, shoot and pick up anything off the ocean floor. Where there are no mooring buoys the anchor must be dropped on the sand and the divemasters on the boats are responsible for ensuring that dives are carried out with total respect for the environment. They follow the American methods here and the day starts with a two-tank trip. This means that in a 3-4 hour trip there will be a deep dive and an ascent via a medium reef in quite shallow water. In the afternoon the boats go out again for a single-tank dive. Do take the

opportunity to do some night-time diving, which is always on the programme. Many of the dive centres have larger dive boats which can be used for all-day excursions, during which the furthest sites can be reached. They always include three longer, deeper, dives. For divers who prefer a floating hotel there are live-aboard dive boats all around the island. Dives are regulated here by the Cayman Islands Watersports Operators Association and their rules do not only cover the main dive techniques, which on the whole are not much different from international norms, but also the standards for divemasters, skippers and safety equipment. This means that the dive centres are staffed exclusively by certified divemasters and skippers and that all dive boats carry oxygen, VHS radio and first-aid equipment. Grand Cayman is surrounded by a reef which lies very close to the coast, with the exception of the huge North Sound lagoon. Except for the sandy Seven Mile Beach, the coast consists of flat rocks which carry on into the water. The ocean floor on Cayman, like other places, is divided into three categories: shallow reef, medium reef and deep reef. On the drop-off, known as the wall here, the reef descends vertically for several thousand metres. At right angles to the reef edge there are deep gulleys and hollows filled with corals which make spectacular dive sites, especially on the wall.

Grand Cayman is home to the entire range of Caribbean fish and some species are so numerous here that there is talk of "marine miracles" - Stingray City for example and Tarpoon Alley. The water here is fantastic, 50-metre visibility is guaranteed. Temperature is practically constant all year, around 27 degrees Celsius in summer and 24 degrees in winter. Currents around the island present no difficulty to divers and many of the dive sites are totally free from currents.

STINGRAY CITY

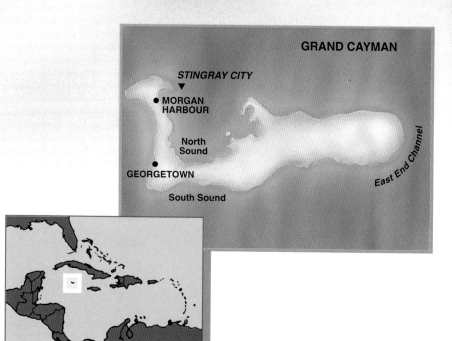

GRAND CAYMAN

STINGRAY CITY
▼

● MORGAN
  HARBOUR

North
Sound

● GEORGETOWN

South Sound

East End Channel

0 m

5 m

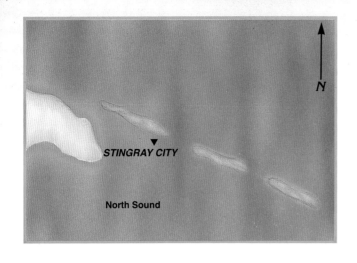

STINGRAY CITY

North Sound

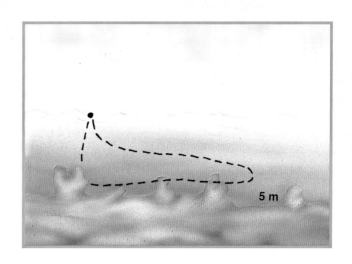

5 m

LOCALIZATION

Stingray City is in the lagoon behind the reef, not far from the entrance to the North Sound. This enormous sandy expanse is 5 metres deep and protected from the wind and the waves. It is one of the most famous of all dive sites and belongs to the special chapter on marine miracles, like Code Hole in Australia. For decades fishermen have been dropping anchor here and hauling up their treasure. They were the first to notice and record the high proportion of stingrays which appreciated the remains of the fishermen's catches. Curious to investigate the fishermen's accounts, the first scuba divers visited the site in 1987. They could hardly believe their eyes when they were surrounded by a vast number of rays *(Dasyatis americana)* who revealed neither fear nor aggressivity. Naturally the circle of visitors increased rapidly and Stingray City became the number one attraction on Grand Cayman. As the rays were fed by the divers too, the site turned into an underwater zoo and soon a procedure was instigated. Gloves and knives are strictly forbidden and the only food given to the animals is the sardines and the octopus brought by the divemasters. The technique for sharing out the food correctly is clearly illustrated before it is divided between the divers. This may seem like taking it all a little too far but it is by no means easy to get food into the mouth of a massive ray. The mouth is on the underside of the body and therefore the animal cannot see the food, but simply smells it, so the diver has to guide the animal's nose with a closed fist and release the food at the right moment. Many of the adult stingrays have become very pushy and enjoy knocking the divers onto the sand. There is no need to worry about the poisonous sting at the end of their tails, in view of the fact that in all these years and with thousands of visitors, no-one has ever been harmed. Of course, marine biologists have done a series of different surveys to check on whether this enormous mass

A - In this picture can be seen one of the many dive-boats which ferry divers to Stingray City.

B - Thanks to the transparency of the water and the shallowness, the Southern stingrays (Dasyatis americana) *are visible from the surface.*

C - The stingrays show no fear at all and swim gently around the divers on the lookout for food.

D - The bottom at Stingray City is not just home to the stingrays, but also to bar jacks (Caranx ruber), *black surgeonfish* (Acanthurus sp.) *and yellowtail snappers* (Ocyurus chrysurus).

of visitors and the constant feeding of the animals could have any negative consequences. Fortunately this has not been the case. Year by year the number of the animals increases and recently the number both of male specimens and of births has increased.

The exact number of the population of Stingray City is hard to calculate, but it is estimated in the hundreds.

THE DIVE

To avoid long journeys many dive centres keep a boat moored at the North Sound specially for the Stingray Dive and in this case the trip across the flat lagoon only takes about 30 minutes. Stingray City is right behind the reef in the breakers and towards the east there is the only channel which links the North Sound to the open sea. Here in the lagoon the water is perfectly calm and transparent. The sea bed is flat and the dark stains visible on the bottom are individual blocks of coral scattered all over the uniformly white sand. I have been daydreaming about the rays for the entire trip and now I am here there is no need to search for them. As soon as we put our feet into the water a whole group closes in on us just like an aircraft squadron. They are all sizes and colours, from the dark adults to the light-coloured baby stingrays. In a short time they have surrounded us, like big birds, and it does not take them long to identify Kevin, our divemaster, who is carrying the sack with the food in it. He demonstrates the feeding procedure to the divers and we can see how experienced he is. Kevin literally takes the biggest of the rays by the nose and pushes the food into the mouth - it might be a scene from *Dances with rays* - giving the photographers a chance to capture a spectacular sight. Then he distributes the food to the divers, who look for all the world like wild-animal tamers. I swim around the edges of the action to take photographs of the individual animals. Stingrays are still coming in from all directions, mainly in groups of three or more. As I have no food they soon lose

interest in me and look elsewhere for better luck.

The blocks of coral on the sandy sea bed are worth investigating too. They are inhabited by groupers and big moray eels which are naturally also fed with the food distributed to the rays and which live here permanently. We are not the only visitors. There are groups of divers kneeling all over the sand, sharing out food to famished sets of stingrays. Despite the hordes of visitors, diving at Stingray City is a tranquil, well-organised affair. Each visitor has the opportunity to appreciate the experience and will talk about this marine miracle for a long time to come. Divers of all levels can visit Stingray City and so can snorkellers.

E - Swimming in such shallow water with animals as large as the divers themselves is an unforgettable experience.

F - Up to several hundred stingrays can be found together on the bottom of this lagoon.

BABYLON

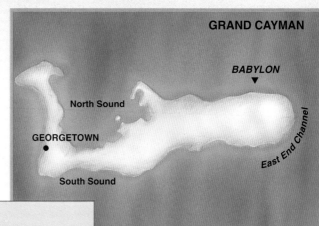

GRAND CAYMAN

North Sound

GEORGETOWN

South Sound

BABYLON ▼

East End Channel

0 m

18 m

30 m

40 m

↓ 200 m

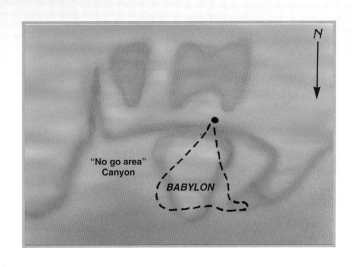

"No go area"
Canyon

BABYLON

N

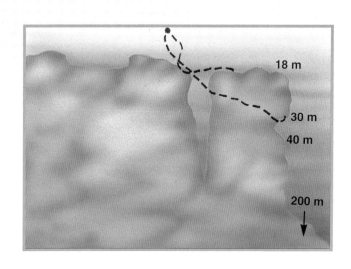

18 m

30 m

40 m

200 m

LOCALIZATION

Babylon is on the west side of the North Wall, a long way from both West Bay and South Sound where most of the dive sites are. Babylon is one of the places where not much diving goes on, but an increasing number of centres are being visited by the large dive boats moored at North Sound and they bring visitors to this part of the island too.
In addition, live-aboard boats are becoming increasingly popular and, naturally, nowhere is ever big enough for these floating hotels. Babylon is a colossal platform colonised by corals, which emerges

A

B

C

D

A - A narrow canyon separates the huge coral platform called Babylon from the reef.

B - A large, almost fluorescent, vase sponge stands out against the deep-sea blue with an amazing 3-D effect.

C - The blocks of rock rising from the sand are transformed into extraordinary coloured gardens; there is always something for the diver to look at amongst the thousands of details and the unusual shapes.

D - A school of snappers (Lutjanus apodus) makes a high, living, wall, hiding what is happening on the other side.

from the depths in front of a sheer wall. Only a narrow canyon separates it from the reef which is totally colonised by soft corals and has been declared a no-go area in order not to disturb their proliferation. But just a glance left and right into the canyon and one realises that the panorama is something quite amazing and that these natural wonders should indeed be left uncontaminated.
The coral shelf, like the tip of Babylon, is 15 metres deep, from there the walls drop sheer for thousands of metres.
The huge coral base however is only a part of the spectacular topography of this dive site.
As the map shows, to the west there is a platform which grows in the water like a huge table.
Depending on the dive plan, which is always adapted to the participants' abilities, you can actually go underneath this.
To the east of Babylon there is another huge canyon which leads right inside the coral shelf like a knifethrust. Travelling through this canyon at the end of the dive will allow you to swim right back to the

sandy surface where the boat anchored. The coral vegetation both on Babylon and on the drop-off is fantastic. Enormous corals slanting downwards and growing in almost symmetrical ranks make the structure look like a mushroom. From 20 metres there are huge bushes of black corals and gorgonians, some bigger than 2 metres. On the western side of Babylon, at around 18 metres, there are masses of sea anemones. On the same plateau there are all kinds of fish and other marine life: angelfish, snappers, parrotfish and, underneath the ledges whole lines of lobsters are on the march.
Something is happening in the blue water along the drop-off: schools of black jacks (Caranx lugubris) advance from the depths in perfect formation and eagle rays propel themselves forward with elegant wingbeats along the sheer wall. Underwater photographers need to take two cameras with them: a wideangle lens to capture the extraordinary panorama and a lens with greater focal depth to pick up the tiniest details.

THE DIVE

The boats drop anchor, according to the regulations, in one of the sandy expanses about 40 metres behind the edge of the reef.
Our dive, during which we shall swim north towards the drop-off, starts right here.
To compensate our bottom time we move off midway between the sea-bed and the surface.
Horizontal visibility is about 30 metres and we can already see the edge of the reef and the pear-shape of the top of Babylon outlined against the intense blue of the water.
We cross the canyon, the barrier which separates the edge of the reef from the coral bank like an arched black line.
The plateau lies to our left, at a depth of 40 metres.
The dive plan is for a rapid visit to this monstrous protruberance after which we shall investigate Babylon and then backtrack through the canyon to the boat.
The view is quite astounding, covered with enormous bladed corals the rocks look like a manmade monument. This is my first dive on this part of the island and I have the impression that the vegetation is healthier than in other parts. Pelagic fish, especially jacks swim by us continually, while a whitetip reef shark swims along the edge of the reef. Sharks are not habitual visitors here on Grand Cayman, which makes this a particularly interesting encounter. Unfortunately the predator is too far off to be captured fully on film. But immediately afterwards I am more fortunate, as a gigantic turtle heads impassively straight for me. The canyon we take on the return journey to the boat is an ideal foil for photographs against the light. The group of divers should swim above the photographer so that the edges of the gulley are on the left and right of the photograph. The decompression stop is taken underneath the boat by the deco bar, a ballasted pole, at a depth of 5 metres. The pole has two automatic respirators with regulators attached, supplying enough air even for divers whose reserve is running low.

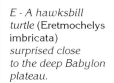

E - A hawksbill turtle (Eretmochelys imbricata) surprised close to the deep Babylon plateau.

F - A big snapper with an unusual, all-yellow, livery looks at the photographer from the secure refuge offered from the reef.

G - A formation of horse-eye jacks (Caranx latus), identifiable by their yellow caudal fin, swims in the blue abyss.

H - An adult male stoplight parrotfish (Sparisoma viridis), one of the most widespread of the parrotfish, swims amongst the corals and the sea fans at a depth of about twenty metres.

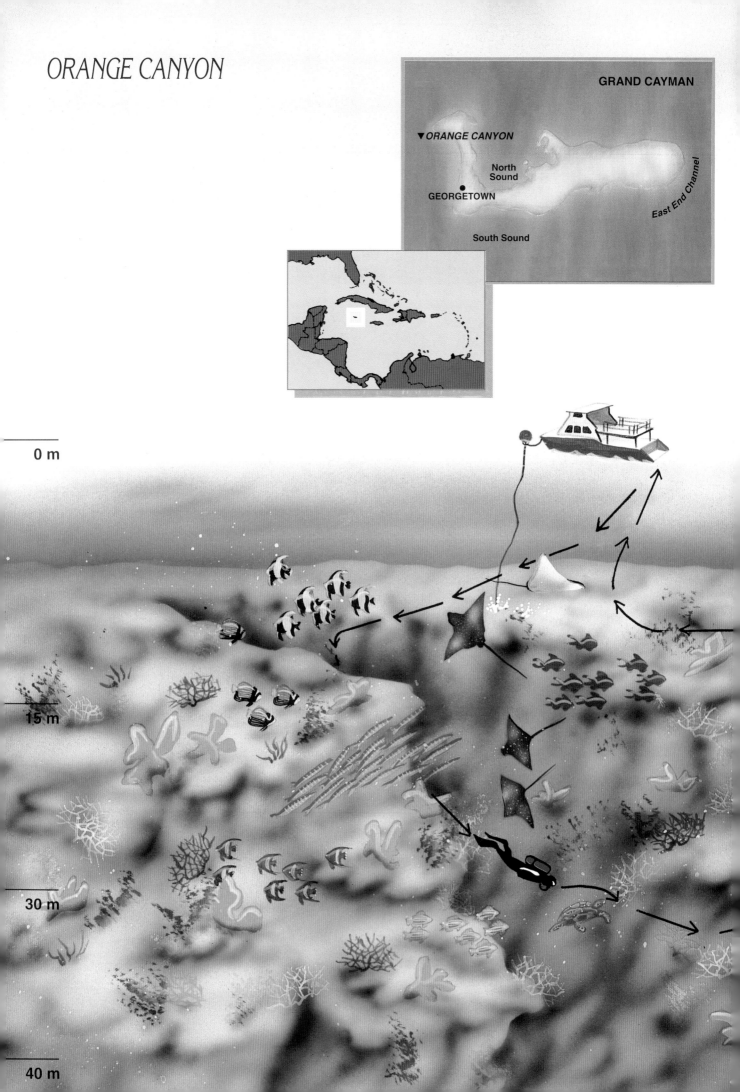

ORANGE CANYON

GRAND CAYMAN

▼ORANGE CANYON

North Sound

GEORGETOWN

East End Channel

South Sound

0 m

15 m

30 m

40 m

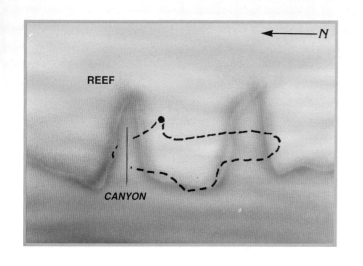

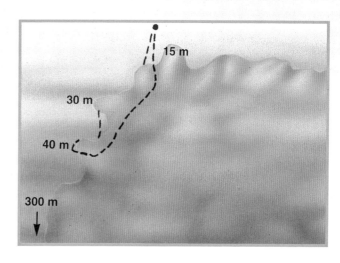

A - The wealth of life on the rocks is even more obvious when compared to the empty sand oases in the midst of the coral.

B - The orange sponges are the dominant motif in the underwater scenery at Orange Canyon. In the middle of the photograph a diver is observing a grey angelfish.

LOCALIZATION

Orange Canyon is on the west coast, on the west coast drop-off, to be more precise. This part of the reef is a series of massive balconies and terraces overhanging the chasm, which plunges vertically down for thousands of metres. Here at Orange Canyon the current varies from light to medium. The big gorgonians which grow here are proof of its presence, as they feed on the plankton it carries with it. The outstanding feature of this dive site, from which it got its name, is the mass of orange sponges. They grow here to quite impressive sizes and are scattered all over the reef. Orange Canyon is a paradise for wideangle enthusiasts. However, the landscape is not just characterised by the massive amount of sponges. There is another attraction although it is not always guaranteed, in the form of a group of triggerfish. These rather tubby fish, which swim using only their back and ventral fins, follow

A

B

C

D

the divers at a safe distance. On the reef plateau, at a depth of 15 metres, there is always a shoal of snappers (Lutjanus apodus). There are angelfish in pairs living permanently in Orange Canyon. They have completely overcome their fear of visitors and follow them like faithful puppies. They can actually be a nuisance for photographers as they swim backwards and forwards in front of the lens all the time. It is worth looking out for bigger forms of life on the drop-off, where the sea-bottom drops away into the depths. You can encounter barracuda, turtles, eagle-rays and schools of jacks. Like all the other dive sites on the west coast, Orange Canyon has a permanent mooring buoy - which is important as it prevents boats having to drop anchor - and here on Grand Cayman divers will be able to see the results. Although the island is one of the most popular diving resorts in the world, no serious damage has been done to the reef. Obviously, environmentally-friendly and conscientious diving has also played its part in this.

C - This wide gorgonian sea fan looks as if it was protecting the big tube sponges.

D - This group of Haemulids seems immobilised just above the sea bottom.

THE DIVE

Thanks to its position opposite North West Point, there is often a current at Orange Canyon. It is never very strong and divers will have no problem in returning to their buoy.
You will see more fish on days when the current is flowing and the water is clearer, which will make photographers happy.
Today is one of those days as we realise immediately on entering the water, where visibility is exceptionally good.
The reef surface, at a depth of 15 metres, and the jagged line of the drop-off stand out clearly and brilliantly against the intense blue of the water.
We find a pair of French angelfish in yellow and black waiting for us and they make an excellent subject for underwater camerawork.
I see a group of silver snappers grazing on the reef surface.
But the real object of this dive is not just to immortalise the small forms of life, but the sponges which make up the landscape too.
The afternoon sun is in the perfect position and its light is not only shining directly onto the drop-off but is also penetrating into both canyons. This is where most of the gigantic orange sponges grow; they are best photographed at a 45-angle to the surface.
This provides enormous depth and if another diver is swimming in the background then the result will be perfect. Of course, we discussed the photography while we were approaching the site in the dive boat, so that we do not waste time we could spend exploring other areas of Orange Canyon.
I try out several different perspectives and quickly find a well-placed group of sponges.
I can even get the boat in the top half of the frame and my partner moves over the reef as we agreed. Despite the antics of two angelfish which keep swimming backwards and forwards in front of the camera I manage to get the pictures I want without losing too much time and we can continue our exploration. The exit from the canyon leads

E - A shoal of horse-eye jacks (Caranx latus) easily identifiable by their yellow caudal fin, goes off in search of calmer and richer hunting waters.

F - The French angelfish (Pomacanthus paru) has such a colouring and such an harmonious shape that make it a favourite for underwater photographers.

G - A couple of barracuda (Sphyraena sp.) shows to the photographer their brilliant silvery body.

straight onto the sheer wall of the reef. The landscape is truly grandiose, like an enchanted forest. The jutting rocks are totally covered with soft corals whose colours stand out against the blue sea. It is hard to resist the temptation to go deeper.
As we have already taken so much time with the photographs we dare not go any further than our 25-metre limit and, guided by the dive computer, we go back to the no decompression limit.
A second canyon, much less disjointed and with less inhabitants,

takes us back inside the reef and from there to the platform.
Here, at 15 metres, our computer translates the reduced oxygen saturation into a decompression stop of 14 minutes, no less, which means that we have time to explore the shallower parts of Orange Canyon.

THREE SISTERS

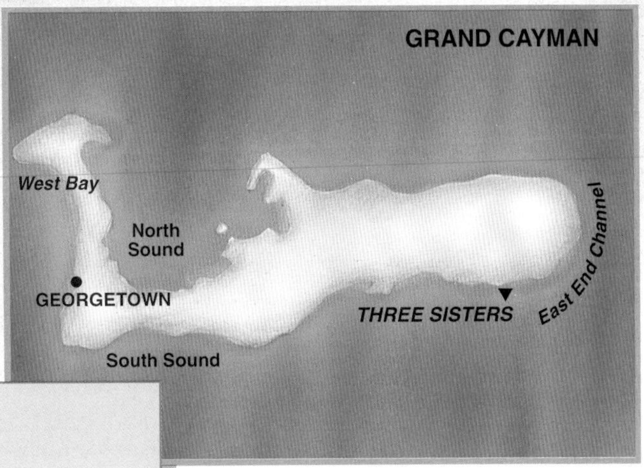

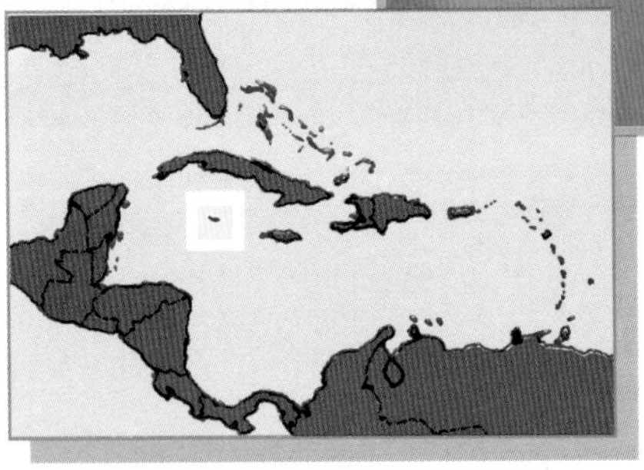

GRAND CAYMAN

West Bay

North
Sound

GEORGETOWN

South Sound

THREE SISTERS

East End Channel

0 m

15 m

22 m

40 m

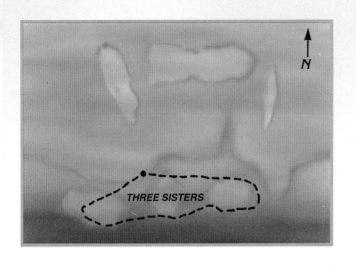

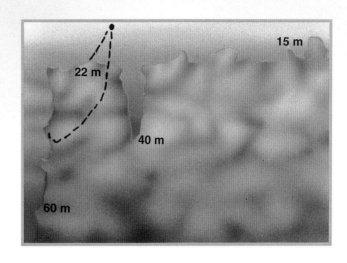

LOCALIZATION

Like Babylon, the Three Sisters dive site is a distant one and it requires a long journey to reach it. It is almost at the tip of the south coast, not far from the corner which leads to East End Channel.
An important feature of this part of the island is that the drop-offs are deeper than on the West Wall. Here at the Three Sisters the reef only comes up to 22 metres below the surface. The Three Sisters are enormous rocky plinths fronting the reef wall. They are totally cut off and you can swim through the canyons which traverse them without any problems. These gullies are rich in vegetation and you

canyon. This is naturally more spectacular and reaches a considerable depth through the reef. However, there are repercussions on time and air consumption, which are not usually sufficient to explore the entire region. The Sisters are rich in vegetation and brilliant with the many deep-sea gorgonians and several kinds of sponges. There are orange elephant ear sponges practically everywhere and huge tube sponges rise in the open sea like cannons. The fish and lower animals you find here are as varied as at other sites here. In addition, it is not uncommon to encounter large fish near the East End Channel, including eagle rays, sharks and other predators.
This is a paradise for divers, with its bizarre underwater landscape, rich vegetation and the crystal-clear water which is virtually constant in this part of the island.
Because of their depth and the need to keep strictly to the dive plan, the Three Sisters dive is only recommended for expert divers.

THE DIVE

The briefing is a very important part of the dive and its value is often underestimated.
The presentation by the divemaster does not only deal with subjects such as time and depth, but the configuration of the sea-bed and the places to be explored.
The briefing is normally worked around an underwater map of the reef, on which the place where the dive boat will be moored and the quickest way to reach the best sites are marked. However, the briefing is also important for the group's safety and confidence: it deals with currents, entrances, exits, emergency procedures and other subjects. Our on-board briefing was so perfect that we have no problems in keeping to the dive plan specially drawn up for our requirements. We want to explore the whole area to get the most complete picture possible of the Three Sisters.
The anchor has been dropped on one of the sandy expanses about 40 metres behind the reef and we

should take care in travelling through them not to damage the corals. To explore all three of the Sisters satisfactorily, plan your dive very carefully, as the masses are spread out over a distance of about 80 metres. Calculations must include the distance from the dive boat to the edge of the reef.
To save air and time it is recommended you travel along the drop-off in the open sea, rather than on the reef, at a depth of about 5 metres. In addition to the advantages mentioned above, it will give divers a good picture of the lie of the sea-bed and orientation will be easier. Another way of doing it is by direct access through the

A - The rocky outcrops of the Three Sisters are intersected by deep canyons, whose walls are covered with sponges, gorgonians and black corals.

B - The deep gorges of the Three Sisters make it possible to go right into the canyons from the open sea swiftly, and to see walls packed with rich marine life.

C - A close up of a dense colony of sea-rod gorgonians (Plexaurella sp.) standing out against the transparent waters, through which the outline of the dive-boat can be seen.

D - A group of large orange sponges, looking more like pillars than the tubes which give them their common name.

E - A large group of young Creole wrasse (Clepticus parrae), identified by their characteristic purple livery, swims close to the surface of the reef.

F - A green turtle (Chelonia mydas) resting on the bottom with two large remoras.

G - Some reef sharks (Carcharhinus perezi) making a brief stop near the reef where it is interrupted by a sandy beach, probably they are observing the photographer with curiosity.

start our dive here. Even from afar, we can see the huge rock rising from the depths. It is a virtually square mass, separated from the reef wall by a deep canyon.
We descend onto the plateau at a depth of 22 metres and start our exploration.
I am struck right away by the shoals of creole wrasse *(Clepticus parrae).* They are purple, which means they at an early stage of their colour development, which will eventually include a yellow tail. I find a notable specimen of a sea-perch under the jutting sheet corals. It is a tiger grouper *(Mycteroperca tigris)* and it observes the camera curiously. Finning across the canyon with its soft corals, we see another group of divers in front of us, but they have chosen the shorter, deeper route through the canyon to the drop-off.
Now we can see the second of the Three Sisters. It is slimmer and ends in a point, creating the impression of a gigantic finger. There are a lot of gorgonias here too and framed against the sunlight above us they make fantastic silhouettes. Below me the sea-bed drops away into the depths and I let the sensations of floating in the void take hold of me. We could stay here for hours if the passage of time did not bring us back to reality. However, the journey to the third rock is longer than foreseen. It is a bigger rock, but no less fascinating.
Having stayed a long time at depth we can only spend a short time exploring the top of the rock, at 22 metres. None of the divers from the other group seems to have come this far, as we can see

two big green turtles *(Chelonia midas)* resting quietly amongst a group of soft corals. It is not usual to meet up with marine turtles on Grand Cayman, even though in the past they were practically wiped out, first by sailors and then by the "Cayman Turtle Farm".
This name covered an operation which involved removing the turtle eggs from their natural environment, then incubating them and then raising the animals until they were big enough to be slaughtered. Now that marine turtles have been classified as animals in danger of extinction and thanks to the export ban

instituted by many countries, this farm has lost a lot of its international standing.
However, it is still a rather dubious tourist attraction, selling turtle steaks and souvenirs and we recommend all divers and all friends of animals to avoid buying such products, thus removing support for this enterprise.
As for the two here: although marine turtles have lungs and need to return to the surface to breathe, they look as though they arrived here a long time before us.
A glance at our instruments tells us that we have to head back to the boat.

BELIZE

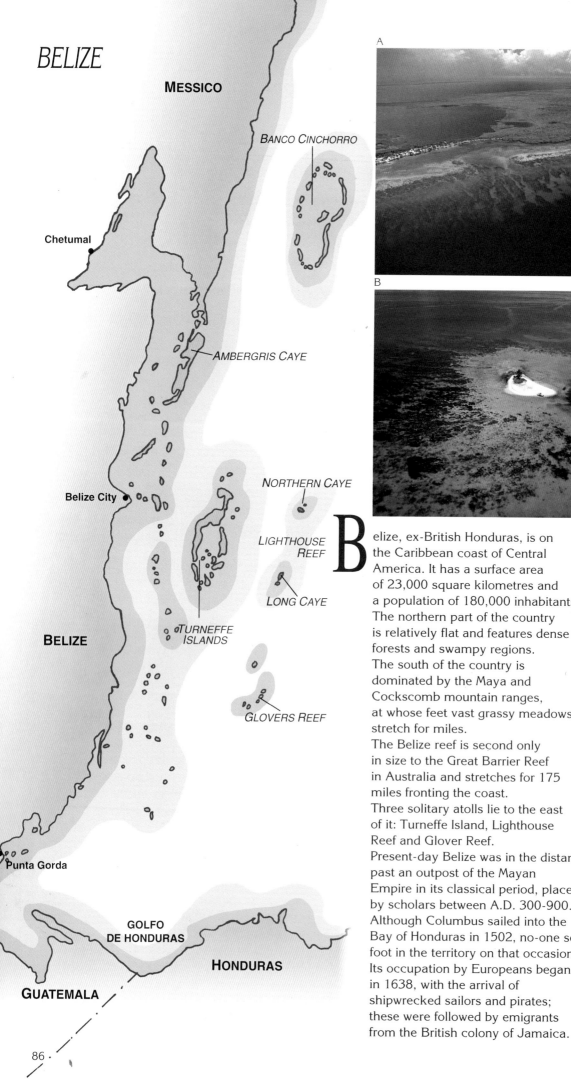

MESSICO

BANCO CINCHORRO

Chetumal

AMBERGRIS CAYE

Belize City

NORTHERN CAYE

LIGHTHOUSE
REEF

LONG CAYE

TURNEFFE
ISLANDS

GLOVERS REEF

BELIZE

GOLFO
DE HONDURAS

HONDURAS

GUATEMALA

Punta Gorda

Belize, ex-British Honduras, is on
the Caribbean coast of Central
America. It has a surface area
of 23,000 square kilometres and
a population of 180,000 inhabitants.
The northern part of the country
is relatively flat and features dense
forests and swampy regions.
The south of the country is
dominated by the Maya and
Cockscomb mountain ranges,
at whose feet vast grassy meadows
stretch for miles.
The Belize reef is second only
in size to the Great Barrier Reef
in Australia and stretches for 175
miles fronting the coast.
Three solitary atolls lie to the east
of it: Turneffe Island, Lighthouse
Reef and Glover Reef.
Present-day Belize was in the distant
past an outpost of the Mayan
Empire in its classical period, placed
by scholars between A.D. 300-900.
Although Columbus sailed into the
Bay of Honduras in 1502, no-one set
foot in the territory on that occasion.
Its occupation by Europeans began
in 1638, with the arrival of
shipwrecked sailors and pirates;
these were followed by emigrants
from the British colony of Jamaica.

*A - In Belize, the
calm, sandy,
waters between
the reef and the
mainland are
scattered with little
islands covered in
mangroves, whose
closely woven roots
hide the densely-
inhabited shoals
where these trees
originate.*

*B - A solitary coral
islet in the throes
of formation just
visible amongst the
surrounding reefs,
like a white stain
produced by
natural forces.*

Interest in the country was stimulated mainly by the extraordinary abundance of mahogany and other hardwood trees and a thriving industry grew up in the 18th century. The Baymen, this was the name given to the inhabitants of the Mosquito Coast, were increasingly threatened by the Spaniards, who had already colonised land to the north and the south of them. After the last bloody battle on St. Georges Cay, won once more

C - The grey angelfish (Pomacanthus arcuatus) is one of the most attractive species found in the Caribbean. Fifty centimetres long, it is the largest angelfish in these waters.

C

D

D - A diver and an angelfish are getting close to a group of huge sponges.

by the astute Baymen, the enmity was resolved by diplomatic means. The territory was annexed to the British colony Jamaica, with the name of British Honduras. After the government was set up in 1961 the country changed its name and since 1981 Belize has been an independent state and member of the Commonwealth. The Belize coast might have been created specially for diving. A massive reef lying between 8 and 15 miles off the mainland provides 175 miles of an underwater world which is in part still untouched.

The reef is a majestic barrier which runs parallel to the coast itself. Between the reef and the mainland, the calm, sandy waters are scattered with mangrove-covered islets, called Cays. Towards the east a deep marine trench separates the three coral atolls of Turneffe, Glover Reef and Lighthouse Reef and it is here that the best dive country lies.
The flora and fauna of the waters of Belize are virtually identical to those in the Caribbean reef system. However, there are some unique differences in types, behaviour and presence of living things.
There are places in these waters where every year thousands of groupers return to mate, stingrays meet up for their honeymoon and dolphins visit regularly just to make contact with humans.
The reef's favourable off-shore position in an ocean rich in currents is reflected in the rich and varied population of corals and fish.
Divers along the outside edge of the atoll will be stunned by its plummeting walls, known as drop-offs, which plunge vertically for more than 1000 metres.
Water temperatures are practically constant the whole year round, varying between 23-25 degrees Celsius in winter and 25-28 degrees in summer, which means that a 5mm wetsuit will provide sufficient protection from the cold.
Practically all the beach resorts on the islands along the reef and on the atolls have diving centres, which take tourists to the dive sites on half- or full-day excursions.
In addition, there are the live-aboards, comfortable boats providing unlimited opportunities for dives, both day and night.
Dive standards are American in terms of equipment, safety and planning.
It is essential to respect the environment underwater as well as out of it.
Most boats apply the "no glove rule" and perfectly regulated buoyancy to prevent contact with the reef are an essential for taking part in the excursions. Furthermore, it is forbidden to take away anything you find on the sea-bed.

THE BLUE HOLE

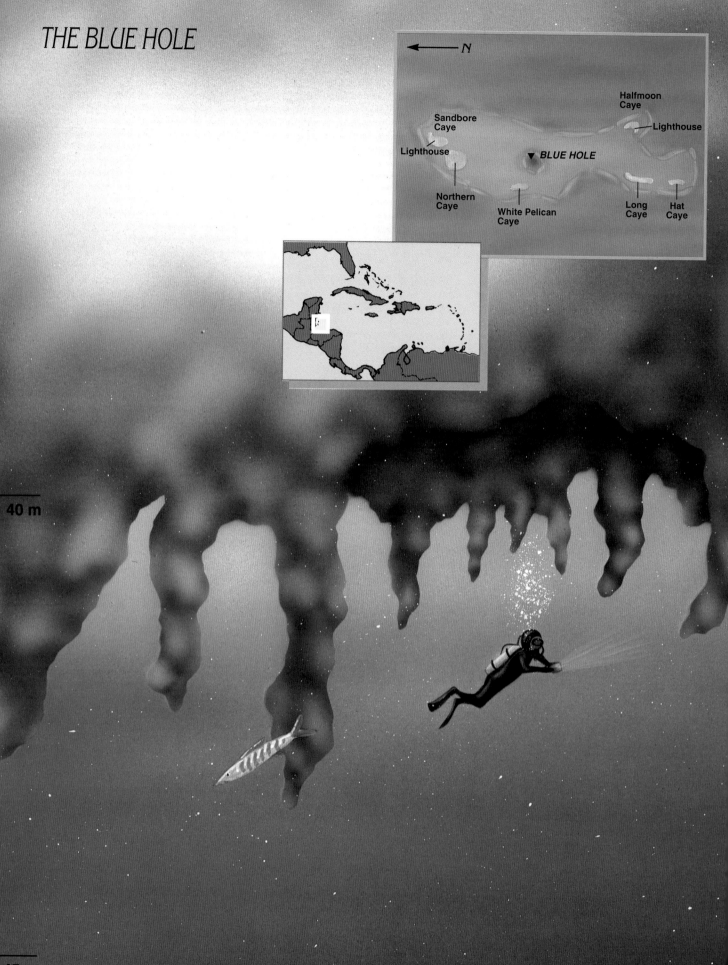

N

Sandbore
Caye

Halfmoon
Caye

Lighthouse

Lighthouse

▼ BLUE HOLE

Northern
Caye

White Pelican
Caye

Long
Caye

Hat
Caye

40 m

45 m
↓

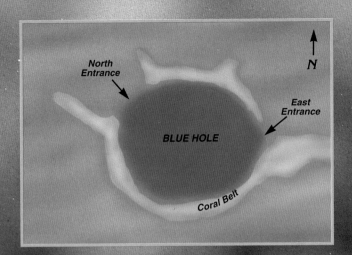

North
Entrance

BLUE HOLE

East
Entrance

Coral Belt

N

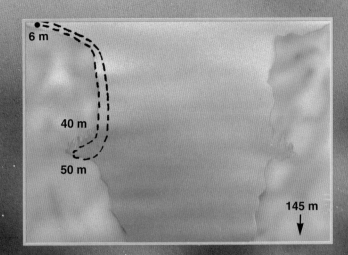

6 m

40 m

50 m

145 m

A

B

C

D

LOCALIZATION

Blue holes are by no means a rarity here in the Caribbean; they can be found on Andros Island for example, or on Great Bahamas.

But the biggest of them all is in the middle of Lighthouse Reef. These karst hollows were formed during the Ice Age, during which huge volumes of water eroded the sandstone and the sea level was a good deal lower, sometimes by as much as several hundreds of metres. The presence of stalactites reveals that these hollows were originally out in the open, and divers will find them in the Blue Hole of Belize. It was only later, when the water level rose to cover the entire region, that the roof caved in, leaving the characteristically-shaped hollow, likened to a "sink hole".

In 1972 the eminent oceanographer Jacques Cousteau revealed the blue holes' secret. In the course of a thrilling expedition he manoeuvred the *Calypso* inside the Blue Hole and explored it all, right down to the bottom, with a miniature bathyscope.

The rumour that Cousteau used dynamite to force his way into the blue hole has absolutely no basis in truth. The Hole has two natural entrances which allow the smallest of craft to pass through. The Blue Hole has a diameter of approximately 400 metres and is 145 metres deep. The walls are vertical and at a depth of 40 metres divers will find gigantic stalactites, some up to 3 metres in length, attached to the underside of the rim, hanging from the roof like enormous pine cones.

From the point of view of marine life the Blue Hole offers nothing special, but this is not the source of the extraordinary experience diving in the Blue Hole provides. The enduring, indeed the irradicable, impression all divers take away with them is of having made a leap into the past.

The fact that the dive goes down to a depth of more than 40 metres, on a sea floor over 145 metres deep, calls for several very strict technical requirements.

The dive is preceded by a detailed briefing during which the route,

A - An enormous, perfectly circular, dark-blue blotch in the middle of the bright blue of the sea, looks like the result of ancient magic, the same kind which draws divers here.

B - Below the black line which marks the edge of the Blue Hole, the big stalactites stand out against the blue like freshly-cast statues.

C - The big stalactites hanging from the vault of this ancient cavern regained from the sea are like milestones in a dive which takes us back into the past.

D - The sun's light as it penetrates from above seems to come to a halt in the labyrinth of the many-shaped submerged columns in the Blue Hole.

E - The big pillar stalactites give the impression of being inexorably and constantly drawn towards the dark bottom 100 metres below.

F - The play of lights, both natural and artificial, might almost be substitutes for the echoes and sounds of a cave on land.

G, H - In the darkness of the cave the torch's rays throw a ghostly light on the rocks, where darkness reigns unchallenged.

the times and maximum depth are established. Divers are normally accompanied by a divemaster. The light which manages to penetrate through the circular aperture really is minimal and depending on the time of day and weather conditions visibility could vary from poor to nil. It is essential to take a torch with you, which will not only enable you to see the gigantic stalactites better, but will pinpoint the divers too, ensuring a certain degree of safety. Photographers are recommended to use 200 ASA/ISO film to make the most of the light which filters through. Do not use too powerful a strobe as the ascending air bubbles cause particles in

F

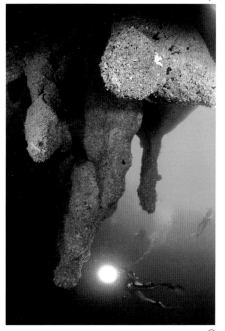

E

suspension to break up at face level and they appear on the film in the form of white spots. Video-camera users will, of course, have to use artificial light in order to avoid seeing nothing but the silhouettes of this amazing landscape of stalactites.

G

H

THE DIVE

The stalactites on the north-western side of the Blue Hole are our first destination. This point is not far from the north entrance and it is on the sandy floor of this slightly sloping channel that our dive will later end.

It is an ideal place for a quiet decompression stop after a deep dive. The beginning of the dive is generally marked by a small buoy, whose cable leads to the slope from where the descent into the deep blue waters begins.

Great care is needed to maintain perfect buoyancy as we shall be hovering on a sea bottom which is about 150 metres deep. Compared to the walls of the open reef these look bare and are covered with a kind of hard, bluey-green algae.

Although the sun is shining brilliantly above us, at a depth of 30 metres the light is already very poor - and we turn the underwater flashlights on.

Forty metres down! We can see the black line of the rim beneath which the stalagtite landscape begins. Every diver in the group adjusts their buoyancy with extreme precision and we slowly make our way into the darkness.

The beam from our torches throws a ghostly light onto the gigantic, cone-shaped figures which hang from the vault.

Some are twisted like corkscrews, others are perfectly straight - it truly is a fantastic sight. The background noise coming from the depths is already perceptible and it makes this an unforgettable experience. But unfortunately the time down here passes in a flash and we slowly swim back to the edge of the reef to begin our ascent.

We come out of the Hole at the gently sloping sand channel which is a natural passage in the reef. On the surface, under the sun, the view which fills our eyes is once more of life, for as far as we can see. We can stay a long time here, at a depth varying from 6 to 4 metres, but no time will ever erase the profound impression that the enormous Blue Hole of Belize has made on each of us.

THE LONG CAYE AQUARIUM

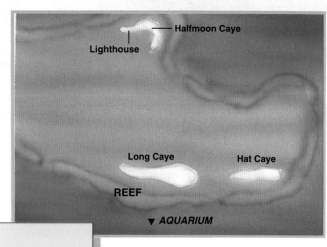

Halfmoon Caye

Lighthouse

Long Caye

Hat Caye

REEF

▼ *AQUARIUM*

0 m

10 m

30 m

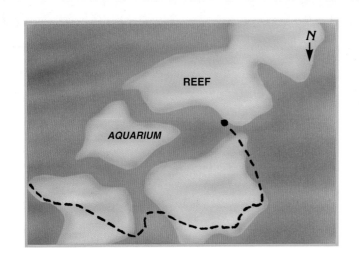

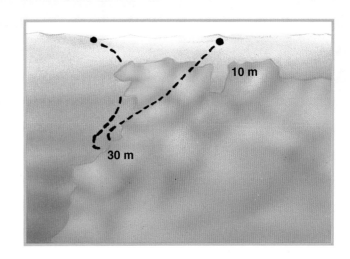

A - The island of Long Caye is totally covered in dense vegetation which comes right down to the edges of the white coral beaches.

B - Great blocks of rock rise out of the sandy bottom, covered with sponges, sea fans and sea plumes.

C - The big encrusting corals form ideal platforms for the establishment of these bright red ramified rope sponges (Aplysina sp.).

D - The topography of the bottom alternates sandy tracts with rocks and coral, where life is particularly exuberant.

E - A pair of large grey angelfish (Pomacanthus arcuatus) swims close to the summit of the reef. These fish are not very shy and will often approach divers spontaneously.

A

B

C

D

LOCALIZATION

The place known as the Aquarium gets its name from the astounding variety of fish to be found there and the brilliant colours of its vegetation. There is no need to dive deep here as the reef surface which positively teems with vivacious life is only 10 metres down. The Aquarium is only one of the numerous top-flight dive sites on the reef lying to the west of Long Caye. The island itself, flat and elongated in shape, is totally covered by low-growing vegetation. Many salty streams constitute the ideal hideout for mosquitos and it is absolutely essential to provide oneself with adequate protection from these

E

insects when visiting Long Caye. There are no resorts on this island. The base at Ambergrise Caye to the north of the island regularly houses groups of tourists for a few days at a time in bungalows and tents. It is an ideal base for scuba divers as the best dives are close to the island.

The water around Long Caye is generally transparent and the constant light current ensures that it is rich in plankton and food. This is one of the reasons why you meet every possible kind of fish there.

The topography of the sea floor is particularly favourable for divers as the reef's surface is not too deep and the drop-off starts at 10 metres. However, from this point the wall plunges vertically, only broken by a few small shelves and by outcrops of mushroom coral. It is sensible to keep an eye on the open sea as you move along the steep wall. Huge shoals of jacks and sometimes sharks or eagle rays patrol the wall.

The reef is continually broken up by sand shuts. These canyons are either partially covered with coral or form actual tunnels.

The commonest fish are the yellow and black French angelfish and the splendid yellow and blue queen angelfish.

Photographers and video enthusiasts will find an interesting subject in the shoals of blue damselfish which graze on the coral in loose formation, their amazing blue-violet livery glinting as light strikes it.

The canyons are inhabited by green morays and the longspine squirrelfish *(Holocentrus rufus)*, hover beneath the reef's outcrops. Shoals of bluestriped grunts *(Haemulon sciurus)* move backwards and forwards over its surface, or hover immobile in perfect formation below the soft corals.

THE DIVE

We leave the buoy and swim west towards the drop-off.

We follow the classic dive pattern, inspecting the widest part first and then ascending slowly according to the computer, making the most of every minute of 0-time.

The sea floor literally comes to an end, plummeting down before our eyes with a vertical wall inhabited by soft corals, sponges and outcrops of mushroom coral.

We launch ourselves into the void like expert base jumpers and the sensation is indescribable.

We descend the first 30 metres with no difficulty, keeping a strict watch on our time and air reserve. The current pushes us towards the south and so we start the dive from the opposite direction.

Enormous bushes of black coral grow freely in the water, their real life colour actually a reddy-brown.

F

F - It is common to encounter the big silvery tarpons (Megalops atlanticus) *in the most sheltered parts of the reef.*

G - The waters over the drop-off are the reign of the big schools of horse-eye jacks (Caranx latus)*, mixed here with yellowstriped rainbow runners* (Elagatis bipinnulatus).

G

H - A close-up of a large French angelfish (Pomacanthus paru)*. Its yellow eyes are an almost unmistakable feature.*

H

Our way is often blocked by huge stove-pipe sponges, some of them are longer than 2 metres and wave in the current as if part of the trumpets of a giant fanfare. We keep a look out towards the open sea as there is a strong possibility of encountering large fish on this reef.

Sure enough, here is one now: an enormous eagle ray slides majestically by before our eyes, propelled by its imperceptible wingbeats. We ascend rapidly and discover that there are a lot

more fish around at a depth of about 15 metres than in deeper waters. In front of us, in the reef wall, is the mouth of a chasm which ends in a tunnel.

Taking very great care not to stir up the sand and not to touch the vegetation, we swim through it and onto a wide stretch of pale sand behind the reef. We are keeping perfect time with our dive plan and head for the reef surface in order to have the full hour's dive.

HALFMOON WALL
THE CHEMINÉE

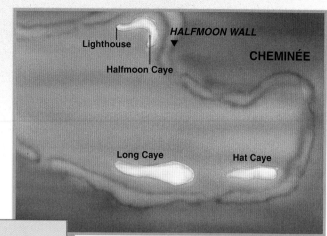

0 m

15 m

30 m

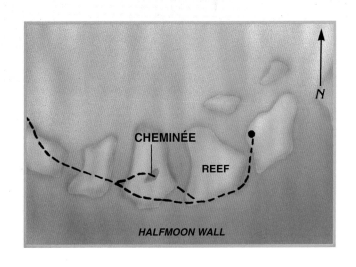

CHEMINÉE

REEF

HALFMOON WALL

N

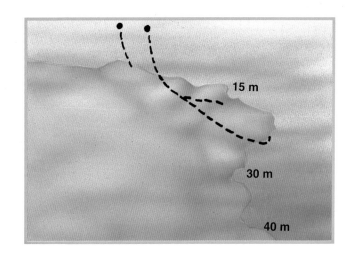

15 m

30 m

40 m

LOCALIZATION

The south-eastern part of the Lighthouse Reef atoll does not only have some outstanding dives, it also has an idyllic little island covered with palm trees and with its own lighthouse.
Halfmoon Caye, which gets its name from its shape, is home to a bird reserve. Thousands of red-footed boobies and frigate-birds nest amongst trees and bushes on the southern part of the island

B

A

C

D

A - The variety of species and the shapes of the Caribbean sea fans is unequalled in any other sea.

B - Halfmoon Island: given its shape, the name of this idyllic islet, dominated by a lighthouse, could not have been different.

C - The numerous forms of benthic life create such colourful, intricate, landscapes that we have to keep our distance in order not to damage them.

D - The play of the currents has encouraged the establishment of a large number of sea plumes (Pseudopterogorgia sp.) which have transformed the rock into a gigantic plumed flower.

and in addition to these species, 98 different types of bird have been recorded on the island. Halfmoon Caye is inhabited by a lighthouse keeper who is also warden of the bird reserve and keeps his eye on the tourists. This sociable gentleman, many tourists pass the time of day with him, keeps a guest register in which nearly every tourist is entered. He built the platform which rises above the tops of the trees and from which you can take excellent pictures of sitting boobies and flying frigate-birds. To get good pictures of the birds you need a telephoto lens with minimum 200mm focal width. The start of the dive, known as the Cheminée because of its chimney shape, lies off the island's southern coast, next to Halfmoon Wall. A shallow sandy floor separates the island from its belt of reef and at this point it is relatively narrow. This has the advantage that after exploring the drop-off, there is still

enough time to visit the back of the reef, which is in shallower waters. Hundreds of garden eels live in the sand here and from a distance they look like a huge asparagus bed, waving in the undertow. But as soon as we approach they shoot back below the sand. There are large rays here, which bury themselves in the sand to sleep. The reef surface is at about 15 metres and numerous sand shuts lead straight to the wall. The steeply sloping Halfmoon Wall is truly spectacular, and thanks to its east-west lie it gets the sun practically all day long.
The occasional presence of strong currents in this corner of Lighthouse

Reef is reflected in the rich vegetation. The soft corals which adorn the surface of the reef grow in forests and the edge of the drop-off is covered in sponges, black corals and gorgonians, transporting the diver into an enchanted world. The Cheminée represents another attraction. This natural tunnel in the reef can be crossed without any difficulty as long as the diver feels comfortable despite the narrowness, the desolation and the darkness which dominate the scene in some parts.
There is also the advantage of being able to ascend from a depth of 30 metres to 15 metres, where the exit is. Not only is this correct

E - The presence of numerous schools of horse-eye jacks (Caranx latus) is proof of the richness of the waters around this island.

F - A hawksbill turtle (Eretmochelys imbricata) swims along the sea bottom at Halfmoon Wall. Although this species is not uncommon in the Caribbean, encounters are not frequent.

G - The most shaded walls are the ones preferred by the ramified sponges, which create lively blotches of colour, intermixed with the filiform white gorgonians.

colours of coralline vegetation. The tubular sponges, which in the twilight of the depths look brown, light up into bright red, and the gorgonians, seemingly an anonymous greenish colour, show up in lively yellow-orange. Unfortunately out time goes by swiftly and we have to ascend. We pass through one of the numerous canyons in the reef, out onto the sandy expanse to watch the garden eels and the sleeping rays.

from a technical point of view, but we also have the opportunity to admire the effect of the rays of light filtering through the surface of the water. There are fish of all varieties here. It is worthwhile keeping an eye open towards the open sea as there are quite often whitetip ocean sharks and cute turtles which come to Halfmoon Caye to lay their eggs.
The sponges are a constant presence, especially at the rear of the reef where the vast sandy stretch of floor starts and where the giant barrel sponges grow. Some are so big that even a diver could hide inside one, but you are advised not to test this theory personally! Sponges are living things too and can be damaged as a result of any kind of physical contact.

THE DIVE

We start from the sandy tract behind the reef belt.
From here we head through one of the numerous canyons and reach the drop-off.
In some points the narrow chasm is right on top of us, totally covered with overhangs of soft and hard corals.
The water is like glass and in front of us we see the exit towards the steep wall, against a background of indescribably deep blue.
At the very moment that our companions disappear into the darkness we spot the arrival of a large shoal of jacks and the sunlight filtering through from the surface sparkles on their lean bodies. We let ourselves drop, maintaining constant buoyancy, to the planned depth of 40 metres and move off along the vertical wall towards the east.
In some points the drop-off is so prominent that looking upwards it creates a curtain against the pale surface. One of our team has fixed two powerful lights to the videocamera and their light shows the true marvel of the

H - The white sandy bottoms are the ideal habitat and place to admire the big Southern stingrays (Dasyatis americana) with their pointed wings and their long tail armed with large venomous spikes.

99

THE HONDURAS BAY ISLANDS

The Bay Islands are 40 miles off the northern coast of Honduras and are the result of a volcanic eruption and the proliferation of corals. Archeological research has proved that the islands were inhabited by the Payans, close relations to the Mayans, 600 years ago. But their tranquil existence was interrupted around 1502, when Christopher Columbus landed here on his fourth voyage and named the islands *Islas de Pinos*, because of their pine forests. The islands were annexed by the Spanish crown and like all the others were exploited indiscriminately and their inhabitants massacred.

For 400 years, the island were fought over by the Netherlands, Spain, France and England, until the latter ended the conflict in 1800 and annexed the Honduran islands. The Bay Islands consist of Cayos Cochinos, Utila Roatan, Barbareta and Guanaja, the most distant. Guanaja is one kilometre long and four kilometres wide in the north-eastern part.

The island is a single rocky mass, with no plains and no roads. The only way to travel from one place to another is over the water. The three little villages on the island, Bonacca, Savanne Bight and Mangrove Bight are either built on stilts or cling to the rock, exploiting the last inch of available surface. There is a landing strip on the island for small DC3-type craft from Ceiba on the mainland, or Roatan.

Guanaja has plenty of freshwater springs and rivers which provide high-quality drinking water all year round. It is surrounded by reefs which provide a wide range of dive sites for all levels of ability. The flora and fauna are typically Caribbean - the reefs are inhabited by soft corals, gorgonians, feather stars and sponges.

At the drop-off the sea bed plunges vertically for thousands of metres and on the north-west of the island there are underwater lava landscapes to be explored. The entire palette of Caribbean animal life is present here.

A - The rugged Guanaja coastline makes the island a prisoner of the sea; the water is therefore the only means of communication between two points.

B - A school of bluestriped grunts (Haemulon sciurus) swims amidst a "wood" of sea plumes (Pseudopterogorgia sp.), probably the fish are looking for crabs and prawns to eat.

A

B

BELIZE

BAY ISLANDS

GUANAJA

ROATÁN

Puerto Castilla

Trujillo

UTILA

GOLFO DE HONDURAS

Puerto Cortés

La Ceiba

GUATEMALA

HONDURAS

DIVING IN GUANAJA

The dive sites are reachable
by boat. The Posada del Sol hotel,
built in the style of an old Spanish
locanda, has three dive boats
which ferry divers to the 28 sites,
all named. Each site has permanent
buoys to prevent damage to the
habitat caused by constantly
dropping anchor.
Some of the sea floors, such
as the Black Rocks described
in this chapter, are drift-dive sites.
The dives are organised to

D

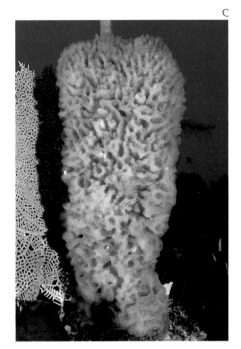

C

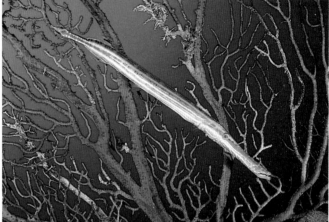

E

F

American standards and the base
provides all the necessary services,
from a dive shop to a film
developing laboratory.
Careful briefing sessions mean
that divers can become familiar
with the site and then, depending
on their experience, dive either
in independent groups or with
a divemaster.
Respect for the environment is
a top priority here, stab jackets
or BCs are compulsory and "no
gloves" is the rule everywhere.
It is severely forbidden to collect
mollusks, live or dead.

*C - The intricate
bas-relief sculptures
are characteristic
of the soft tissues
of this vase sponge
(Callyspongia
plicifera).*

*D - This picture
shows a series of
pillar corals
(Dendrogyra
cilindrus) which
have grown in
a tight cluster.
The numerous
fully-expanded
polyps on the
surface of these
hard animals give
it a soft-textured
appearance.*

*E - A streamlined
trumpetfish
(Aulostomus
maculatus)
camouflages itself
amongst the
branches of a large
gorgonian.*

*F - A young
yellowtail snapper
(Ocyurus
chrysurus) is
engaged in a
solitary patrol of
the waters
surrounding
the reef.*

*G - A group
of porkfish
(Anisotremus
virginicus), easily
recognised by the
two black bands
on their heads,
swims above coral
and sea plumes.*

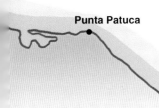

Punta Patuca

G

THE WRECK OF THE JADO TRADER

REEF

GUANAJA

Southwest Caye
▼ JADO TRADER

0 m

12 m

25 m

35 m

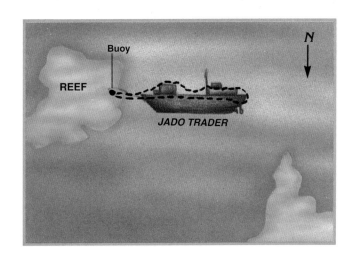

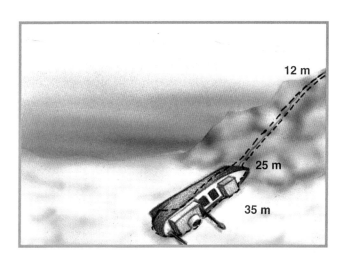

A - The big holds designed to take the cargo have been turned into lairs for the fish.

B - The old merchant vessel rests on its starboard side; abandoned by humans, it has become the ideal habitat for a large number of species.

LOCALIZATION

The *Jado Trader* was scuttled in 1977 as an attraction for divers, after it had been left abandoned by its owners for years.
A 70-metre merchant vessel, it lies on its starboard side almost 2 miles off the coast to the south-east of South West Caye at a depth of 33 metres. The prow is pointing towards a huge coral rump which rises from the sea-bed to 12 metres below the surface. The huge anchor chain leads from this coral rump to the wreck.
After exploring the ship you travel back along the same route and the

B

C

D

ascent is by the buoy cable up the coral. Those with enough time and air can stay on the reef plateau, which is completely covered with soft corals and where you can see huge shoals of fish. Its depth of 33 metres, the possibility of currents and the need to follow the dive plan exactly, mean that the *Jado Trader* is classified as a dive for experts.

THE DIVE

We start our dive following the anchor chain. Here can be light to medium currents and if this is the case it is wise to reach the wreck along the sea bottom. Depending on visibility, which in most cases is excellent, the silhouette of the wreck should already be standing out against the deep blue.
A group of 4 or 5 enormous groupers appears, forming a reception committee. They are regular guests at the wreck and are awaiting the food brought

C - Transparent waters with currents of varying strength make it possible to see most of the wreck clearly.

D - The black silhouettes of groupers who live in the wreck and the lights from the divers' torches stand out against the dark background of the Jado Trader.

by the divemaster. There is an extraordinary wealth of fish life both inside and around the wreck. Angelfish, blue surgeon fish and hogfish are all hunting for food in the hull and there are shoals of jacks all around the superstructure. The wreck is just like the ones you see in books. Still fully intact, it lies on its starboard side and stretches away into the void with its hawsers still attached to the mast and the cargo cranes and masts covered with all kinds of organisms.
We start our exploration through the cargo hatches. You are advised to take a torch with you on this

of over 30 metres and time passes quickly, but do not omit to take a last glance at the poop.
There are schools of silversides inside the rear deck too and divers can sometimes take a last look at the enormous perch which lives in the wreck, before it disappears into the hull. For a better view of the arched poop, which looks more like a pirate ship than a merchant vessel, it is best to keep a certain distance away from the wreck, the rudder and the propellor.
There is another chain leading from this part of the ship to another coral block close by.
About 10 metres away from the

E - The ship's bridge rises upwards like a wall, providing safe shadow for a big black grouper (Mycteroperca bonaci) which has made the vessel its own territory.

F - The uncountable encrustations covering the hull have transformed inanimate sheet metal into a gallery of colours which only the divers' torches can awake.

G - Cables and parts of superstructure still hang from the ship's cargo masts, creating strange, contorted bundles, brightened up by the organisms which have set up home even on these slim supports.

E

F

dive. Following the light we enter the hull where hundreds of thousands of silversides dart in the cone of light. A huge green moray eel, over one and a half metres long, lives here too, but it is absolutely innocuous and actually follows the divers around during their visit to the wreck. The mast rising from the superstructure and the chimney stack make good subjects for photographers, stills or film, especially when there is another diver in the background carrying a flashlight. Although it is possible to go inside, it is strongly discouraged for obvious safety reasons. The passages are extremely narrow and cables obstruct some of them. You must not forget that you are at a depth

G

wreck of the *Jado Trader* there is a big red gorgonian which makes a good subject for photography. The way back towards the prow takes us up, along the backbord reling, to a depth of 23 metres, which means we can save on air and, when the conditions are right, take a look at the coral plateau which is right beneath the dive boat, moored to the buoy.

JIM'S SILVER LODE

REEF

GUANAJA

Southwest Caye

▼ JIM'S SILVER LODE

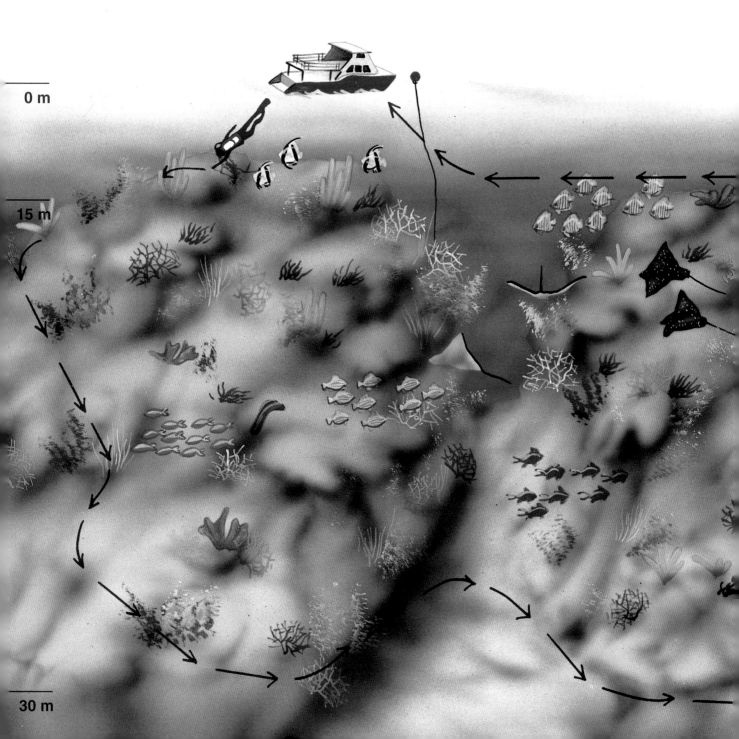

0 m

15 m

30 m

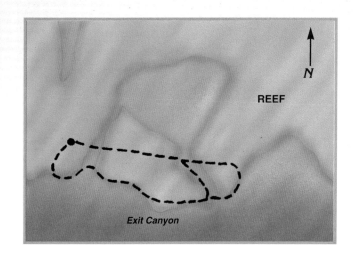

REEF

N

Exit Canyon

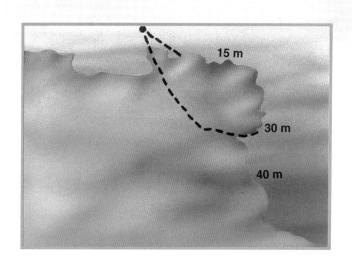

15 m

30 m

40 m

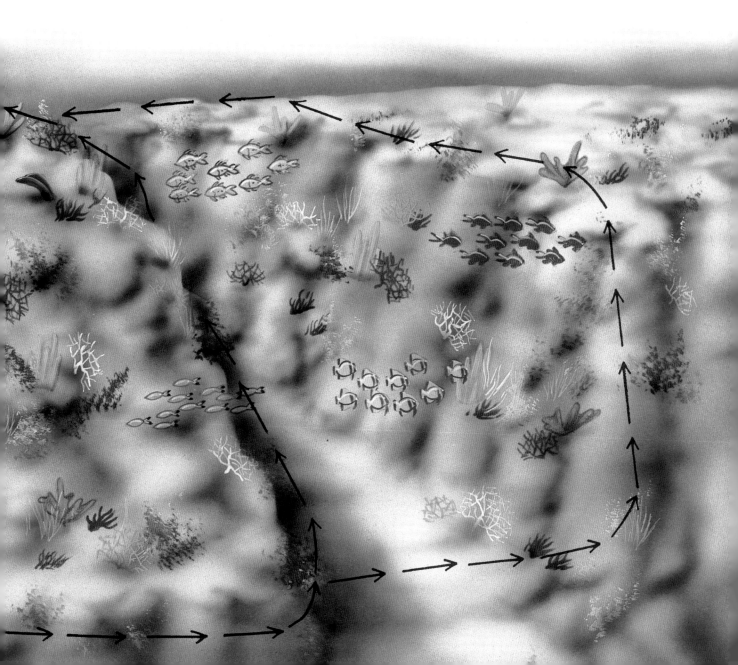

LOCALIZATION

Jim's Silver Lode is without doubt one of the most popular dive sites around Guanaja. It is south-east of South West Caye. Here too there is a permanent buoy to moor the craft. The site is named after the schools of silversides which divers find in the hollows of the drop-off. The reef's sheer wall is truly spectacular. From the edge of the reef, which is at a depth of about 15 metres, the wall falls vertically for another thousand metres. You often meet very big fish here, schools of jacks or stingrays. The divemasters have created a practically perfect circular expanse of sand right behind the reef proper as a fish feeding station. The reason

why you can feed fish here is because it is protected from the local fishermen and only the most expert divemasters do the feeding. The groupers you find here just get bigger and bigger and they are fearless when confronted with divers. Other inhabitants of the reef include two enormous morays and a big barracuda. There are groups of adult yellowtail snappers, royal triggerfish, butterflyfish and angelfish are everywhere. Strong currents are rare and it is always easy to get back to the buoy or to the dive boat. Jim's Silver Lode is a suitable site for divers of all levels of experience. Good buoyancy control is essential to swim along the drop-off and remember that at this point of the wall the reef plunges vertically into the void.

THE DIVE

There are 5 or 6 enormous groupers waiting for us immediately underneath the boat. Their interest is, of course, caught by the white food basket which one of the divemasters has brought with him. The fish know quite well what will be waiting for them at the end of our tour and so they accompany our group for the entire length of the dive. Leaving the huge sandy expanse behind us we head through a narrow canyon covered with soft and hard coral. To stop our fins damaging the coral we have to swim along its widest part. Photographers and cameramen have to work with a great care inside and out of the canyon because of the particles

A - The sandy sea-bottom winding inwards amongst the rocky walls of a long canyon attracts both mainstream divers and photography enthusiasts.

B - The canyon exit stands out against the deep blue of the drop-off, where divers can hang in a watery universe which plunges downwards for hundreds of metres.

C - The underwater panorama of the Caribbean includes sea fans, hard corals, sea plumes, sponges and colourful fish like the purple blackcap basslet (Gramma melacara).

D - A dense group of orange and yellow tube sponges (Aplysina fistularis), one of the most common types in the Caribbean.

E - This particular coral ledge stretching into the deep blue provides an ideal substrate for the slim red stick sponges and deep-water sea fans.

F - A black grouper (Mycteroperca bonaci) almost a metre long checks out the movements of the divers.

G - A rare gilded grouper called a coney (Epinephelus fulvus), which is quite common in the most sheltered parts of the reef, where it stays close to the bottom.

H - A green moray (Gymnothorax funebris) leaves its lair, a rare opportunity for any diver in open waters.

I - The sculptures of elkhorn corals (Acropora palmata) become a familiar sight after a few dives.

which become detached from the roof by the rising air bubbles.
The exit opens onto a deep, deep blue, right on the drop-off. Depending on the current you can go right or left here.
The sensation you experience swimming along the wall of the reef, knowing that the floor is over a thousand metres below is an undescribable one. The drop-off, which starts at a depth of around 13-15 metres, has a rich vegetation. Next to "forests" of soft corals we encounter all kinds of sponges. The photographers' attention is immediately caught by red rope sponges and azure vase sponges - the photographs taken against the blue background are bound to be fantastic. From 30 metres we come across an increasing number of what are known as deep-sea corals. They are sea whips corals for the most part and big reddy brown clumps of the well-known black corals. Despite the amazing landscape set out in front of us as if seen through a wide-angle lens, it is worth looking into the reef's hollows and crannies and underneath the outcrops. This, at depths of 30 metres and below, is where the rare blackcap basslet lives. If the briefing has been carefully listened to, or if the dive is lead by an expert divemaster, you can visit the "silversides crevice".
This is a grotto 20 metres down which is packed, quite literally, with these silvery fish, which shine like lightening in the sun's rays that penetrate through the surface.
It is a fascinating subject for photographers, but they have to use a very light flash gun, to avoid excessive reflection from the fish themselves in their shiny livery.
We go through a large sand shut - the name given to a crevice between two blocks of coral - to the sandy area. We meet up with the groupers again here, which have been joined by a large green moray eel.
Lunchtime for them at last.
The divemaster shares out the food skilfully and with determined impartiality. You can watch the show kneeling comfortably on the sand or do a final tour of the reef surface at about 10 metres, in the opposite direction to the drop-off.

BLACK ROCKS

REEF

BLACK ROCKS

GUANAJA

10 m

20 m

Sand tunnels

N

Sand

Cave

REEF

BLACK ROCKS

6 m

10 m

20 m

LOCALIZATION

The black lavic rocks are on the leeward side of the island, to the north-east of the little village of Mangrove Bight. The whole of the sea bed is of volcanic origin and divers are confronted with a bizarre lanscape, featuring caves, crevices and hollows, which is quite unique in the Bay Islands. This area is one of the most popular dive sites. Black Rock is a reef 2 kilometres long and, canyon after canyon and crevice after crevice, you can get a long way inside. The depth of the plateau is between 1 and 6 metres and the sea bed, and therefore the floor of the caves and the crevices, is never more than 20 metres. The water is generally crystal clear. In this kind of transparency the black rocks imbue the landscape with a unique kind of coldness which exerts its own particular fascination. There are the same species of fish as we saw at other dive sites on Guanaja, although there are not as many species here as in other

A - A strange landscape made up of caverns, canyons and grottoes opens up between the surface and the sea-bottom.

B -The volcanic nature of the rocks and the many shady areas prevent encrustant organisms from creating the rich colourful palettes seen on other Caribbean sea-beds, but the dives are no less attractive as a result of this.

places. Furthermore, the geological structure of the sea bed is less suitable for coral than limestone and there is less of it. However, divers will meet thousands of copper sweepers in the hollows and the caves of the reef. These triangular, copper-coloured fish are nocturnal and spend the entire day inside caves and crevices. Huge nurse sharks are quite common in the

Black Rocks too, as bottom-dwellers this area is particularly suitable for them. But it is the chasms and the grottos which make this a unique place - it is not so much the long passages, which require special care, but the fact that every 20-25 metres the roof opens up through a lateral landscape to the open sea. Depending on the weather conditions, the sun's rays penetrate

either through the surface or are refracted on the corners of the reef, making a spectacular sight. Sometimes you have the feeling of being inside a Gothic cathedral or else in a discotheque full of psychedelic lights.
Underwater photographers and video enthusiasts naturally find the challenge of capturing these light plays an exciting one. A good underwater torch is an absolute must for a visit to the Black Rocks.

THE DIVE

There are no permanent buoys at the Black Rocks and drift diving is the technique usually used. Depending on the currents, divers are dropped at a point on the reef and picked up at the other end. It is very comfortable to let oneself be carried along by the current and divers have the advantage of not having to worry about making their way back to the boat. As you let yourself be pushed gently along there is more opportunity to concentrate on the underwater world. As soon as you enter the water you will catch your first sight of the volcanic sea floor

E

F

G

E - A dense "forest" dominated by the big fans of the gorgonians grows on the reef.

F - During the day the darker corners of the caves are inhabited by dense shoals of glassy sweepers (Pempheris schomburgki) with their golden reflections.

G - A group of spadefish (Chaetodipterus faber), typical inhabitants of the Caribbean, swims intermixed with some snappers at the base of the caves.

H - The sandy beds inside the volcanic caves are the ideal place for the nurse sharks (Ginglymostoma cirratum) and many chose to establish their lairs here.

H

C - The black volcanic rocks and the deep blue of the sea create richly fascinating, cathedral-like settings, the joy of adventurous photographers always on the look out for original angles.

D - The Black Rocks caves are not at all frightening for those who want to explore them; in many places they have large openings towards the open sea.

and you cannot fail to note the cold sensation I mentioned earlier. On morning dives the sun is on the reef plateau, the sheer walls are in shadow and this accentuates the atmosphere and the contrast even more. The reef is full of canyons and cavities which offer divers an infinite choice of routes. We go into one of these dark passages. The cone of light from the torch shows practically bare walls, bearing colonies of bright yellow anemones, carpeted with red sponges, black corals and whip corals. On the "V"-shaped roof of the tunnel there is a shoal of copper sweepers, their shiny bodies reflecting the light. To capture them on film photographers have to use the underwater flashgun at half- or even quarter- strength, to avoid overexposing them. Bright and in bands like laser beams, the sun's rays penetrate through the opening in the ceiling. The exit is just a little way ahead already. It is a rugged crevice through which the sunlight enters the cave. Now that we are in the open sea, we move along the lava wall on which soft corals and sponges grow. We stop to admire a group of nurse sharks underneath the flat outcrops.

Thanks to a slight current, we are thrifty with our air reserve and we pay a short visit inside one of the volcanic caves. This passage which travels over 100 metres into the reef is called Sandtunnel. Sometimes it is so wide that a lorry would easily fit in. Numerous side passages and exits through the roof let the sun's rays in and they reflect on the sandy floor and wrap the whole labyrinth in a mysterious halflight. The Sandtunnel is the end of our visit to the Volcano Caves. We go through a huge hole out into a sandy expanse where our diveboat is anchored to take the teams back on board.

The far-flung French territories of
Martinique and Guadeloupe, which
lie between the Atlantic and the
Caribbean, are like non-identical
twin sisters - close but very different.
Originally inhabited by the peace-
loving Arawaks who came from the
Orinoco, the islands were later
invaded by the fearful Caribs, who
were warriors and cannibals. In 1493
Christopher Columbus landed on
Guadeloupe, while Martinique -
Madanina, the island of flowers -
was discovered in 1502. From 1635
both islands became French
colonies. In 1946 Martinique and
Guadeloupe became French
overseas departments. There are
two seasons in the French Antilles:
one is cooler and drier and goes
from December to April, the other,
from May to November, is more
humid and warmer and is sometimes
interspersed with gales and cyclones
(mainly in September and October).
The mountain chains on the islands
make the climate particularly
variable and it is marked by short,
tropical rain showers which
periodically soak the land and by the
Trade Winds, constant winds blowing

*A - This
extraordinary
aerial view shows
the two small
islands known as
Iles de la Petit Terre,
lying south-east of
the main Grande
Terre island,
Guadeloupe.*

*B - However
delightful, the
island coastline
is not always ideal
for easy access for
diving.*

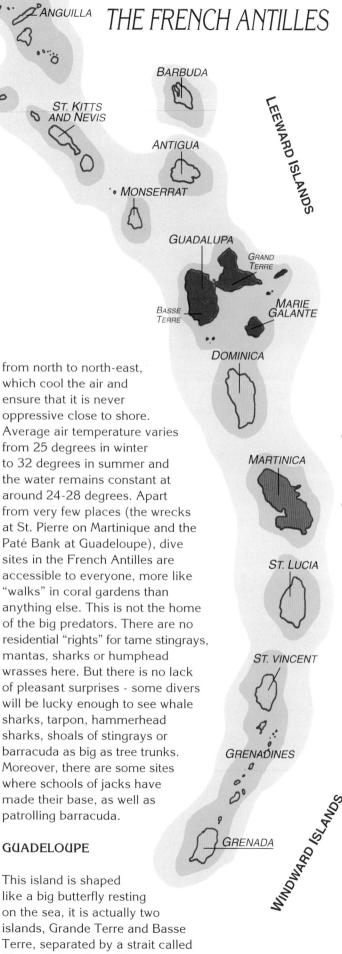

THE FRENCH ANTILLES

from north to north-east,
which cool the air and
ensure that it is never
oppressive close to shore.
Average air temperature varies
from 25 degrees in winter
to 32 degrees in summer and
the water remains constant at
around 24-28 degrees. Apart
from very few places (the wrecks
at St. Pierre on Martinique and the
Paté Bank at Guadeloupe), dive
sites in the French Antilles are
accessible to everyone, more like
"walks" in coral gardens than
anything else. This is not the home
of the big predators. There are no
residential "rights" for tame stingrays,
mantas, sharks or humphead
wrasses here. But there is no lack
of pleasant surprises - some divers
will be lucky enough to see whale
sharks, tarpon, hammerhead
sharks, shoals of stingrays or
barracuda as big as tree trunks.
Moreover, there are some sites
where schools of jacks have
made their base, as well as
patrolling barracuda.

GUADELOUPE

This island is shaped
like a big butterfly resting
on the sea, it is actually two
islands, Grande Terre and Basse
Terre, separated by a strait called
Riviere Salee. Grand Terre is a vast
plateau, only just over 100 metres
above sea level; Basse Terre,

A

B

despite its name, is actually a very mountainous island covered with tropical vegetation. Like Martinique, Guadeloupe has a windward shore, which is not really suitable for diving and a leeward, well-sheltered one, where the best diving centres are to be found (there are ten of them). Generally speaking the dives are not particularly difficult, except for the Paté Bank midway between Guadeloupe and Les Saintes. The most interesting sites are at depths of between 0 and 30 metres, with typical coralline fauna and flora and deep-water fish such as the jacks, but there are no rays or sharks. With visibility which is nearly always excellent at depths of between 10 and 40 metres, Guadeloupe is the ideal place to dive, for beginners or experts

C

D

E

F

C - The French Antilles have very varied countryside and rich vegetation as a result of the rain carried by the trade winds.

D - Sometimes tube sponges grow so close that they begin to look like the pipes of an enormous organ.

E - The blue of the water and the white sandy coastlines of the French Antilles can offer an easy access to the rich underwater world waiting to be explored.

F - Yellowtail snappers (Ocyurus chrysurus) are one of the most common fish found on the sea bottoms in the French Antilles.

alike, in absolute safety. Diving centres are continually being developed, especially in the area around the Ilets Pigeons, known as the Cousteau Reserve, which is renowned for its dive sites. The reef here descends vertically to a depth of 5-10 metres, at which point the seabed becomes a rocky platform to a depth of 15-20 metres, before dropping away again, from 20 to 45 metres. Each mooring buoy is the starting point for several evocatively-named dives: the Coral Garden, Jacks Reef, Hot Water Springs, Barracuda Point.

MARTINIQUE

The gentle, sheltered, leeward coast on the Caribbean side of the island is bathed by clear waters, while the windward, Atlantic shore has high rocky cliffs pummelled by the sea and beaches beaten by deep-sea waves which roll in from afar. The southern part of the island, drier and quite flat, is where the big sugar-cane plantations grow and most of the tourist facilities are concentrated on its white beaches. The north, on the other hand, offers a wilder, more mountainous landscape, characterised by dense tropical forest alternating with banana and pineapple plantations. Unlike the Caribbean shore, the Atlantic coast with its rough seas is not very popular with scuba divers, but the northern part of the island does have one exceptional, very deep, site - the St. Pierre wrecks, which resulted from the 1902 eruption of Montagne Pelée - and some impressive underwater walls. On the other hand, the more humid climate and the presence of freshwater inlets from streams greatly reduces underwater visibility. The Anses d'Arlets area in the south part of the island provides endless dive sites which are accessible to everyone. Another renowned diving point is the even more southerly Rocher du Diamant. One of the most extraordinary things about Martinique is the wealth of different sponges which grow there. Not only are they present all over, but there is a stunning variety of species and of colours: yellow organ pipes, brown drums opening up towards the surface, blue trees, opalescent vases trimmed in transparent lace: a joy to behold and an element of fundamental importance for the biotope.

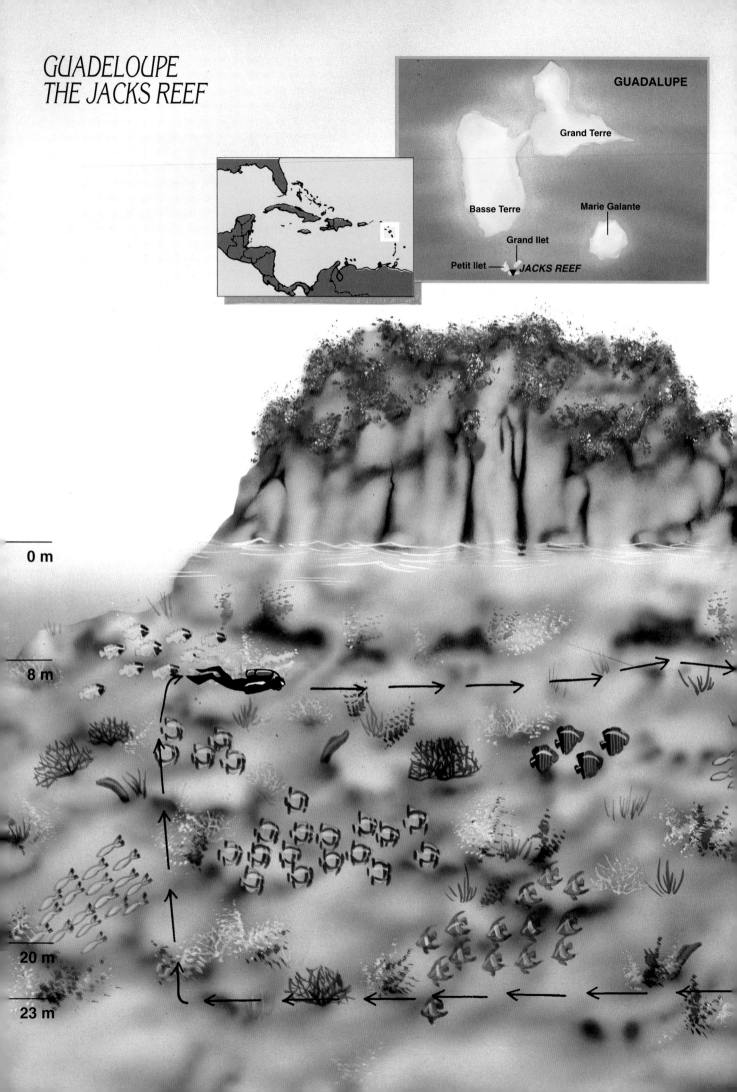

GUADELOUPE
THE JACKS REEF

GUADALUPE

Grand Terre

Basse Terre

Marie Galante

Grand Ilet

Petit Ilet — JACKS REEF

0 m

8 m

20 m

23 m

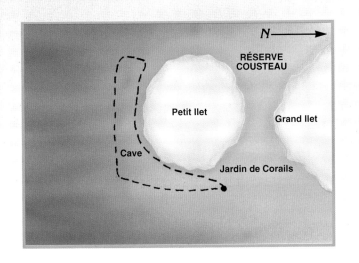

RÉSERVE COUSTEAU

N

Petit Ilet

Grand Ilet

Cave

Jardin de Corails

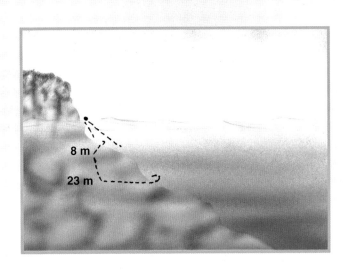

8 m

23 m

LOCALIZATION

The Jacks Reef is located on the south-east side of Petit Ilet, just in front of the coast. The boat is moored at the Jardin de Corail, in the pass that separates the two small islands. You can swim directly to the reef, just following the border between the sandy bottom and the reef itself.

You will see a kind of spur that is the best place to swim to, in order to observe the jacks. Even if the current is sometimes quite strong, generally the sea conditions are quire favourable. The silvery jacks swim in a compact group that follows the current: you are really in front of a great show!

A

B

C

D

A - The large schools of silvery jacks is the main attraction of this area.

B - A dense forest of sea plumes (Pseudopeterogorgia sp.). Although they bear some resemblance to deep-water black corals, they belong to the same family as the gorgonians.

C - Shoals containing hundreds of streamlined jacks can form an almost continuous wall around a diver.

D - A branch of the unique sea-rod gorgonians, large numbers of which dominate large areas of the sea bottom. When their polyps with eight feathered tentacles are completely open the gorgonians look as if they have been trimmed with bows.

THE DIVE

The boat moors in the Cousteau Reserve opposite Petit Ilet, at the Jardin de Corail - or Coral Garden - buoy, before descending to the sea-bed 6 metres down.

Move southwards, passing over the Jardin de Corail, before following the wall or crossing a sandy expanse on the sea-bed, 8 to 12 metres down.

This is where you stop and wait for the jacks to appear: anything from 5 to 300, it varies from day to day. Once on the edge of the wall, situated 100 metres from the buoy, follow it down to 15-22 metres heading in a westerly direction. 50 metres on you will come across an enormous sponge,

E - The big clefts in the reef make ideal habitats for the schools of blackbar soldierfish (Myripristis jacobus) which often allow divers to approach them.

F - The big vase sponges do not only get their name from their shape, but because fishes and invertebrates can find temporary shelter inside them.

G - A large French angelfish (Pomacanthus paru) swims close to the reef. It is difficult for any diver to remain aloof from the elegant beauty of this fish, one of the most beautiful found anywhere in the Caribbean.

H - The less illuminated areas of the reef and the clefts along the Petit Ilet wall are home to nocturnal fishes such as the squirrel fish.

I - The caves in the reef are home to numerous lobsters which are quite happy to have their photographs taken as long as divers keep at a safe distance.

1.5 metres tall and 1 metre wide. There are often porgies and Atlantic spadefish around.

The dive continues along the vertical wall for a further 100 metres before turning north for 50 metres to the Petit Ilet wall. A moltituide of sponges colour the wall which is strung with crannies where lobsters, mantis prawns, porcupine fish and morays shelter. Ascend the Petit Ilet wall on the left and you are back at the anchorage point to the east. Halfway back, (8 metres) the wall becomes particularly colourful and there are many different species of fish: yellowtail snappers *(Ocyurus chrysurus)*, French grunts, goggle eyes etc.

The dive continues at this depth until you reach a cave about 3 metres deep. It is quite safe to go in and watch the lobsters or the patterns made by the natural light as it filters in from on high. Continue for about 30 metres, above a plateau of fire coral, before returning to the Jardin de Corail where you can wait underneath the boat and continue to enjoy the dive.

F

G

H

E

I

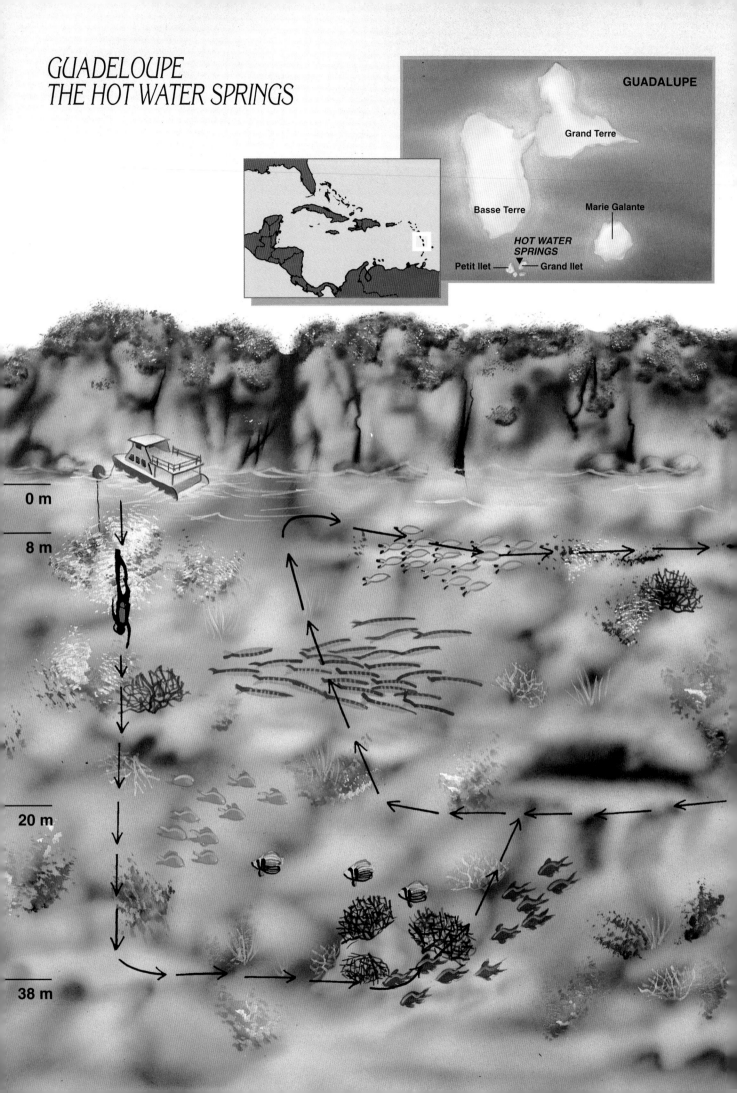

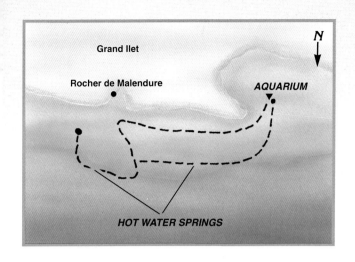

Grand Ilet

Rocher de Malendure

AQUARIUM

N

HOT WATER SPRINGS

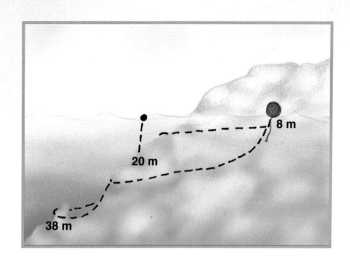

20 m

8 m

38 m

LOCATION

The spot where you can observe the hot water springs is located more or less in the middle of the north side of Grand Ilet. Sometimes you can notice a light current parallel to the shore, anyway it does not cause any difficulties at all. For expert divers the best solution is to let themselves drop just in front of the hot water springs and, at the end of the dive, swim back to the boat moored at the fixed buoy of the Aquarium.
It is anyway even possible to start the dive from the Aquarium, swimming the two way to and from the diving area.

THE DIVE

The boat is moored at Gran Ilet, in the Cousteau Reserve at Malendura, Basse-Terre. You enter the water on the west side of the island, where is located the marker buoy of the Aquarium, the depth at that point is 5 metres. Follow the edge of the wall at a depth of 20 metres for about 150 metres eastwards, until you reach a tiny cavity dug out of the wall which has made a small "sand bath" - at a depth of almost 23 metres. Stop here to see the scrolls and spirals the hot fresh water - it will burn your fingers - makes as it filters through the rock and the sand. This dive is suited to beginners. More experienced divers

A - These sea plumes sway in the water, moved by currents, so that their polyps can feed and oxygenate.

B - A large shoal of several kinds of grunts and snappers moves along the sea bed around the hot water springs looking for food and warmth.

C - The association between sponges and feather stars is often seen on parts of the sea bed where there are continuous currents, even weak ones, to provide both species an ideal habitat.

D - Some parts of the Grand Ilet reef are so rich in underwater life that a diver, whether his passion is photography or nature, could use an entire air tank in one point.

can do a drift dive in the current. As soon as you have entered the water from the boat, descend straight down the gently-sloping wall to 38 metres. Here there is a small sandy white beach, blackened where the hot water comes out. Swim westwards for 20 metres until you reach a clump of big black gorgonians and a magnificent coral outcrop which looks like rose petals. Then go gently back up the wall towards the hot water spring, for about 23 metres. Many different kinds of fish, like jacks and barracudas, ply the area around the hot-water springs looking for food. The dive continues with an ascent to a depth above the hot water springs (from 20 to 12 metres) to a platform which

is traversed southwards for 50 metres before reaching the edge of the Grand Ilet, where the sea-bed is characterised by the presence of large fissures which are rich in flora and fauna. Continue west for 150 metres, making your way back to the dive boat. During this crossing, between 8 and 5 metres, there is plenty to see and there are always surprises lying in wait. Finally you arrive at the Aquarium and its coralline masses, eaten away by the blue surgeons. You can wait here quite safely, watching the prawns, damselfish, butterflyfish and boxfish as they dawdle in the coral. There are often filefish too, which are accompanied by the ballet-dancing of the *Clepticus parrae*.

E - A school of jacks intercepts the light of the flash and the sun, creating a silvery band in the water.

F - Several different species of wrasses and serranids mix together and swim amongst the gorgonian fans looking for food.

G - The stoplight parrotfish (Sparisoma viride) *is one of the commonest of the parrotfish. This species undergoes a considerable colour change during its growth, as it changes sex female to male (in the photo).*

H - A large trunkfish (Lactophrys trigonus), *easily identified by its unusual shape and the hump on its back, moves in close to the reef searching for food.*

I - French grunts (Haemulon flavolineatum) *like to stay inactive for long periods in the more sheltered and shady part of the reef.*

J - A spotfin butterflyfish (Chaetodon ocellatus), *identified by the dark band which hides the position of its eyes from other predators.*

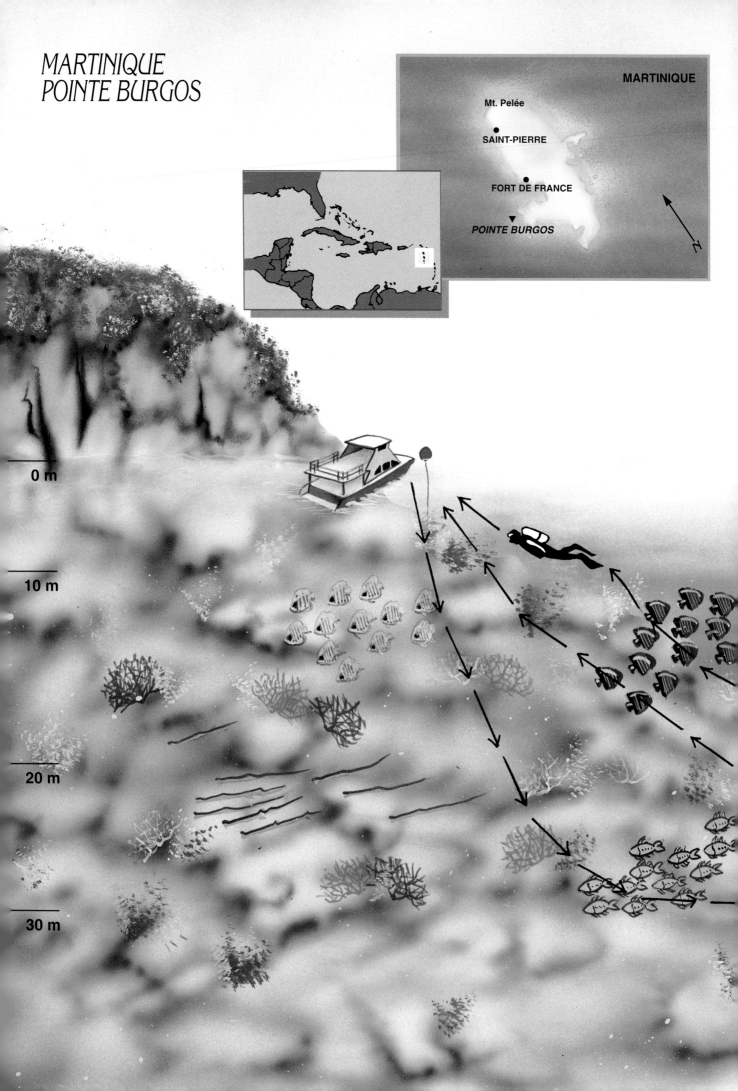

MARTINIQUE
POINTE BURGOS

MARTINIQUE

Mt. Pelée
SAINT-PIERRE

FORT DE FRANCE

▼ POINTE BURGOS

N

0 m

10 m

20 m

30 m

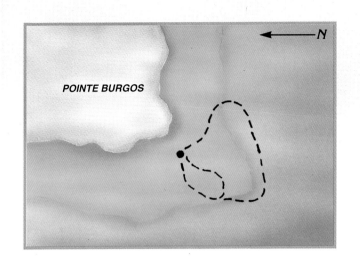

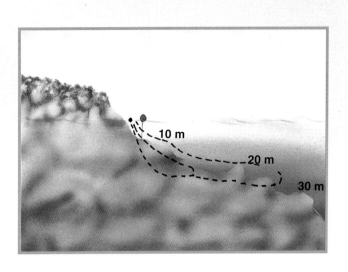

POINTE BURGOS

N

10 m

20 m

30 m

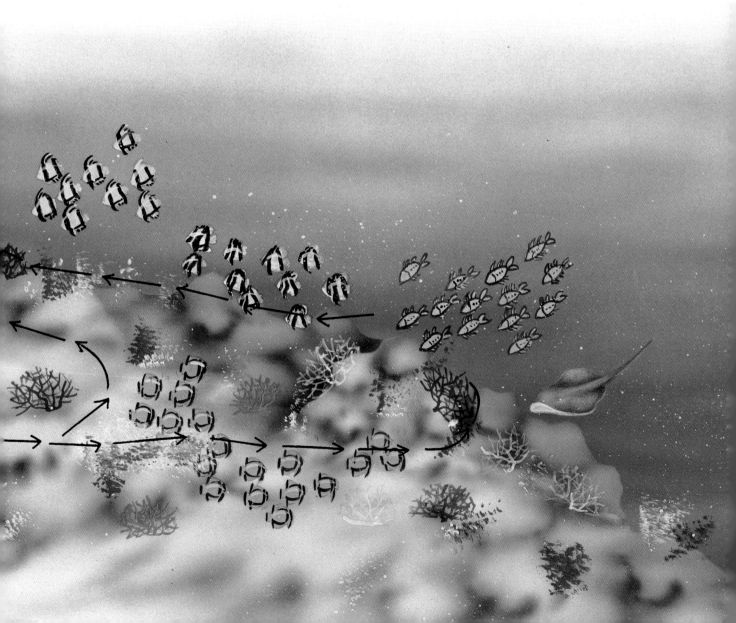

A - A small school of grey snappers (Lutjanus griseus) seeks protection at the base of a gigantic hard coral.

B - The double spiral tuft is the characteristic sign of the Christmas tree worm (Spirobranchus giganteus), which keeps its calcareous tube hidden amongst the coral.

LOCALIZATION

Pointe Burgos is famous for its school of Atlantic spadefish which are regular residents of the site and is an easy dive, ideal for beginners and more expert divers alike.
In most cases the absence of current ensures good visibility, which becomes excellent when the current increases.
Pointe Burgos is right after Pointe Lezarde, almost opposite the Rocher du Diamant. There is a permanent mooring buoy at 8 metres, about 50 metres off-shore.

D

A

B

C

THE DIVE

There are no problems down to a depth of 10-12 metres.
At this point the angle of the sea bed increases and there is a tongue of rock, covered in fissures, which descends to 18-20 metres.
This first part makes a more than adequate dive, as the area is home to schools of what the locals call *sorbes*, the snappers *(Lutjanus analis)*, and *gorettes*, the French grunts, *(Haemulon sciurus)* as well as a multitude of reef fish such as sergeant majors, trumpetfish and damselfish, which find shelter and food in the numerous corals growing around.
There are also masses of sponges, of all shapes and colours, one of the main attractions of diving in Martinique. However, you might choose to descend further to a depth of 25-30 metres and continue the dive out to sea, where a coral reef forms a peak rising back up to a depth of 22-23 metres.
You can run into anything and everything here: jacks, wrasses,

C - A Creole wrasse (Clepticus parrae) swimming close to a big sponge which is sheltering a large, dark-coloured, crinoid.

D - Crinoids often choose the big vase sponges as shelters; they feed by extending their thin, feathered arms.

E - A large shoal of jacks with a barracuda mixed in seems to swim towards the sun rays trapassing the surface of the sea.

F - The sergeant major (Abudefduf saxatilis), a pomacentrid, is one of the least shy of all fish and often approaches divers of its own accord.

G - A pair of barracuda is swimming close to the surface on the Pointe Burgos bottom.

H - This Atlantic spadefish (Chaetodipterus faber) is swimming along the base of the underwater wall where the polyps of small, solitary, hard corals grow like flowers.

I - The silhouette of a yellowtail snapper (Ocyurus chrysurus) appears in the blue.

splendid schools of spadefish *(Chaetodipterus faber).*
Continue downwards towards 32-33 metres and head south in the direction of an enormous wall which plunges from 35 to 100 metres. This is where the big predators hang out and you might meet rays or schools of jacks.
There has even been a reported sighting of a whale shark.
Sometimes you can see stingrays hidden under the sediment on the sea bed. The face of the underwater wall is itself worth observing closely: it is carpeted with *Montipora foliosa* corals, huge coral "flowers" with their "petals" stretched out towards the sun. On the way back to the boat, a stop at 3-4 metres is an opportunity to continue the dive along the sea bed where small grottoes alternate with sandy spaces. The light filtering through the surface of the water reinforces the impression of being in an underwater garden inhabited by snappers and damselfish which are periodically disturbed by one of the large barracuda that ply the area.

F

G

H

I

E

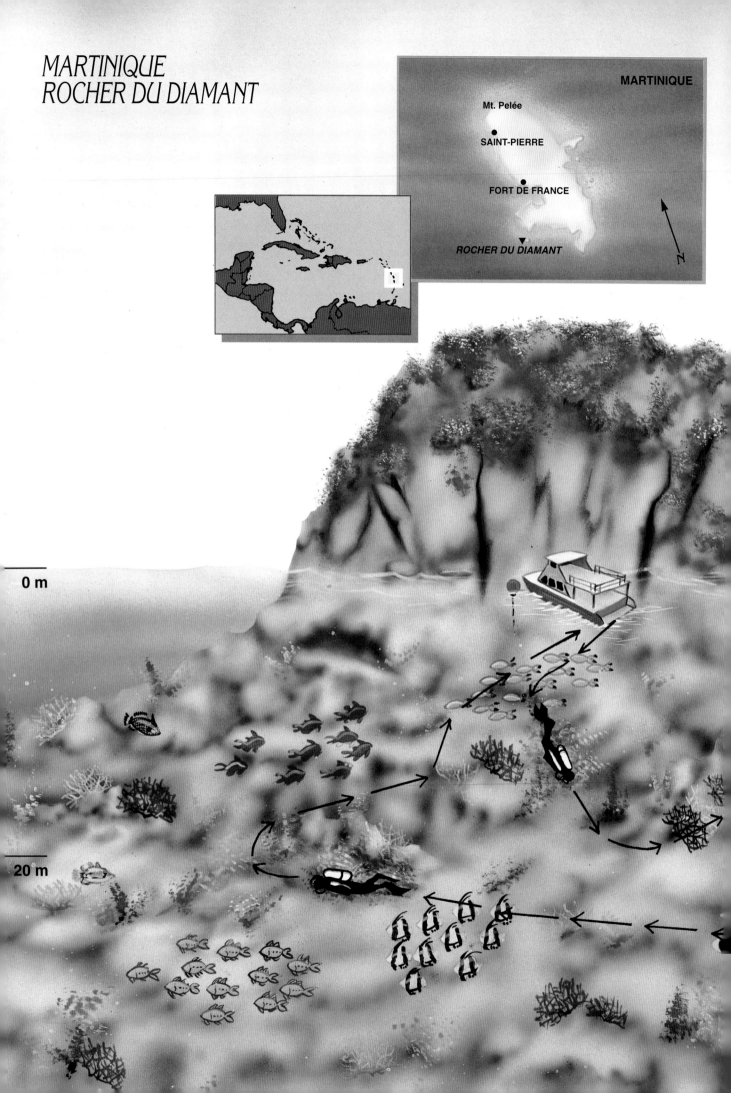

MARTINIQUE
ROCHER DU DIAMANT

MARTINIQUE

Mt. Pelée
SAINT-PIERRE

FORT DE FRANCE

ROCHER DU DIAMANT

N

0 m

20 m

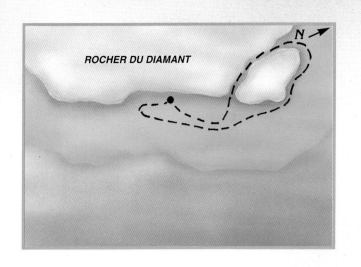

ROCHER DU DIAMANT

N

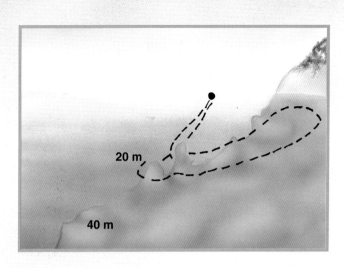

20 m

40 m

LOCALIZATION

This is a dive with a capital "D", one which promises unforgettable encounters, but it is also reserved for divers with some experience. The boat moors south/south-east of the Rocher du Diamant, using an anchorage tethered at a depth of 18 metres. Mornings are the best time to dive because of the depth, but also because this is the best time to see passing fish.

THE DIVE

The descent into the dark blue depths, right to the sea bed is carried out in the company of yellowtail snappers and jacks; then keeping at a constant depth of 18 metres, move off parallel to the Diamant. The next port of call is a cavern in the direction of the Rocher: here there are huge brown gorgonian sea fans to admire,

A - The huge outline of the Rocher du Diamant emerges from the waves like a fortress, with walls which plunge down to 50-60 metres.

B - A school of blackbar soldierfish (Myripristis jacobus) swims close to a big cleft in the rock.

C - A group of horse-eye jacks (Caranx latus) enlights with their silvery body the blue depths surrounding the Rocher du Diamant.

D - Sponges, gorgonians and hard corals grow only apparently in a caotic way, in fact these animals fight all the time in order to find the proper terrain to develope undisturbed.

E - A swarm of breams surrounds a diver filming a group of sponges growing above a colony of pencil coral (Madracis mirabilis) with dense, short, branches.

as they stretch out their branches into the caressing current and numerous lobsters to watch as they poke their antennae out of their hiding places. Further away a large ravine about twelve metres deep opens up in the Rocher du Diamant like an underwater cathedral, running for 50 metres. Safe from any outside aggression, purple corals, white gorgonians and an infinite number of coloured sponges cover the "cathedral" walls. At the end of the ravine you swim out into the turquoise waters of the open sea once more. The way back to the boat is by circling around the ravine and ascending from 12 to 0 metres along a vertical wall punctuated with small caves, fissures and plunging voids. Triggerfish, damselfish, wrasses - every possible species is represented. Expert scuba divers can do another, deeper, version of the dive. A quiet descent out to the open sea leads to a magnificent vertical wall plunging from 40 to 60 metres; it is full of caves which lead deeply and dangerously into the rock. Perfect for cave divers. The dive continues through a chimney which climbs back up to the top of the wall. With luck this dive can be a fascinating experience, you might see hammerhead sharks going by or, even more exceptionally, whale sharks. In fact, the Rocher du Diamant is one of the places

G

H

F

where you are most likely to see the bigger fishes.
In March and April humpbacks and sperm whales swim near the rock. A school of dolphins plies the island's leeward coast all the year round, while white-tailed eagles and tropic birds sweep the length and breadth of the skies. This is magic!

I

J

F - A small red hind (Epinephelus guttatus) looks curiously out of a crevice on the bottom.

G - The longspine squirrelfish (Holocentrus rufus) tends to spend the hours of daylight in the darker parts of the reef.

H - A pair of Atlantic spotted dolphins (Stenelle frontalis), a not uncommon encounter in the waters around the Rocher du Diamant, a point of passage for many of the big pelagic fish.

I - A large lobster caught unawares at the entrance to its lair at the base of the reef. Some Caribbean lobsters migrate long distances in the mating season.

J - The sea around the Rocher du Diamant is full of currents, making the waters ideal for the sighting of spotted eagle rays (Aetobatus narinari).

THE DUTCH ANTILLES
CURAÇAO

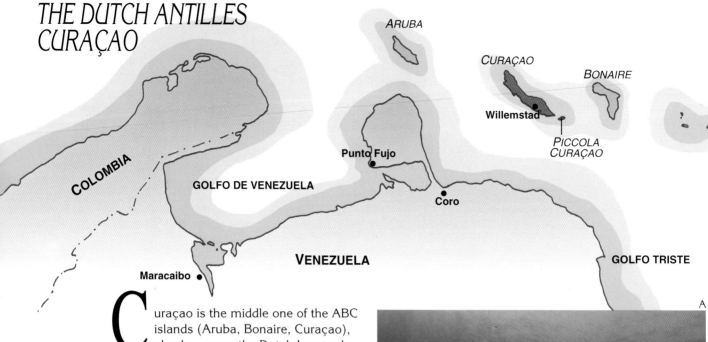

ARUBA

CURAÇAO

BONAIRE

Willemstad

PICCOLA CURAÇAO

COLOMBIA

Punto Fujo

GOLFO DE VENEZUELA

Coro

VENEZUELA

GOLFO TRISTE

Maracaibo

A - At Curaçao the coral platform is dominated by gorgonians of all types and sizes. There are candelabra and sea rod gorgonians alongside the classic fans.

Curaçao is the middle one of the ABC islands (Aruba, Bonaire, Curaçao), also known as the Dutch Leewards, situated in the southern part of the Caribbean opposite the south-American continent, just 60 kilometres from Venezuela.
With a total area of 444 square kilometres it is the biggest of the Dutch Antilles. To the south-west of Curaçao lies Little Curaçao, an uninhabited island which is 2.5 kilometres long and 750 metres wide, with a lighthouse.
Curaçao's climate is typically tropical, the sun shines virtually all the time and it is the north-east trades, which blow all the year round, that ensure a little cool relief. The mean annual temperature is 27.5 degrees centigrade.

HISTORY

The island was discovered in 1499 by Alonso de Ojeda, a sub-lieutenant travelling with Columbus. It was inhabited by the tall Arawak Indians and for this reason the Spaniards called it *Isla de los Gigantes* (the isle of giants).
Less than 20 years later the name Curaçao appeared for the first time on a Portuguese map, but even now the origin of the name is obscure. The most accredited theory is that after a short time the Spaniards renamed the island *Curazon* (heart). The Portuguese, who were masters in the art of mapmaking at the time, translated the term into their own language as *Curacau* or *Curaçao* although this word also has other

meanings in Portuguese.
The island belonged to the Spanish crown until 1634 when it was conquered by the Dutch.
From the end of the 17th century to the beginning of the 19th the British and the Dutch took turns in trying to conquer the island.
The French also got involved in no uncertain manner, but withdrew after being handsomely compensated.
In 1815 the island became definitively Dutch, although it was

B - This spotted trunkfish (Lactophrys bicaudalis) *shows the marks of a recent fight on its side.*

132

C - The lagoons of Little Curaçao are home to a large number of turtles who appreciate the calm waters with plenty of food.

D - A trumpetfish (Aulostomus maculatus) exploits its elongated form to hide amongst the sponges and the gorgonians.

in British hands at the time. The colonial status of the island and of the other Dutch Antilles was modified in 1954, when they gained independence from the colonial power, the Kingdom of the Netherlands.

The island's colonial part is jealously guarded. There are fortifications, plantation houses which belonged to the Dutch colonists and caves containing paintings by the native Arawaks.

Since the 1970s tourism has become one of the main pillars of the Antillean economy. Along the southern coast there are large, modern hotels and

E

D

F

the sea is always calm, unlike the northern coast, which is battered by huge, wild, waves.

Curaçao has a modern airport and an excellent infrastructure which recalls that of the old colonial power. It is a European island in the heart of the Tropics. There is a wide range of good restaurants and other places to eat; in addition to local cuisine, European, Chinese and Italian food is available. The St. Elisabeth Gasthuis, with 800 beds, is the most modern in the whole of the Caribbean, There is a modern depression chamber for underwater accidents and a 24-hour casualty department.

The island has facilities for all kinds of sport: golf, horse-riding, squash, tennis, fishing, cycling, fitness, jet-ski, water ski-ing, sailing, surfing, water-wheeling, snorkelling and, of course, diving. February is carnival month and the island's inhabitants really let themselves go for three entire days.

E - The rounded silhouette of the Atlantic spadefish (Chaetodipterus faber) and its striped livery make this fish easily identifiable.

F - In some places the French grunts (Haemulon flavolineatum) reach such numbers that they make a compact, colourful, curtain totally concealing the reef from the diver.

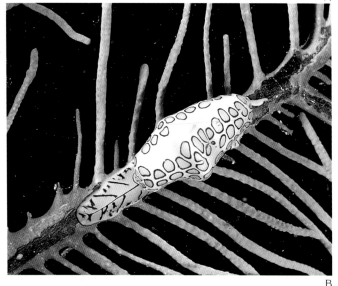

LITTLE CURAÇAO
A DIVING PARADISE

In addition to the splendid, untouched dive sites on Little Curaçao, there is also the most beautiful beach in the whole of Curaçao. All the diving centres organise day trips to this inhabited island which is only one square kilometres. in size. You can also get there by helicopter and do the return journey by boat. There is a reef off the coast of Little Curaçao which is virtually intact, and covered with enormous fan corals and gorgonians. The waters which bathe the island's shores are also filled

with the wrecks of ships which have gone aground here.

On the reef behind the navigation light there is the rusty wreck of the Dutch oil tanker *Bianca Maria Guidesman* which got stuck on the reef and is now being inexorably eaten by rust. The big holes in the bows and amidships make it interesting for photographers in particular. Apart from the single palm planted here in the past, the island is completely without vegetation as only cactus and lichens can survive under this baking sun. About halfway along the 1-kilometre beach is a cannon from the Dutch East Indian Company dating from the 18th century. The lagoon is scattered with anchors and chains from the ships which moored here around 300 years ago. In its own way this

A - These unique molluscs known as flamingo tongues (Cyphoma gibbosum) live in association with gorgonians on whose polyps they feed.

B - A grouper Cephalopholis fulva, can be observed here in one of its typical colouring.

C - Two grey angelfish (Pomacanthus arcuatus) face each other as if in a mirror, showing off their blue-bordered fins and yellow pectorals.

D - In the Seaquarium Animal Encounter it is possible to approach sharks and attract them with food, under the careful eye of an expert divemaster.

E - The compact petrified fans of the common sea fans (Gorgonia ventalina) can reach a height of two metres.

F - This photograph shows the rich underwater life of Curaçao, where sponges, gorgonians, hard corals and sea plumes colonize every rock formation.

G - These old coral ramifications, encrusted with sponges and other organisms, provide shelter to grunts (Haemulon sp.) and snappers (Lutjanus sp.), temporarily mixed together.

little island contributed to increasing the wealth of the colonists.

Once upon a time the island's hills were covered with green meadows, trees and plants. The Dutch brought horses on their sailing boats and brought them to graze on the island. Around 1880 a cunning Englishman obtained permission to mine the deep layer of phosphate created by the fermented guano. The colonists of Curaçao and Venezuela both claimed the substance as their own and it was not long before this splendid island was transformed into a dry, desolate, surface.

There is a lighthouse in the middle of the island. The keeper left his home underneath the tower when the rotating light was automated. There is a splendid view of the island from the light. A great number of turtles swim in the lagoon and several times during the year huge whales approach the island and can be seen from the edge of the drop-off. Numerous species of whale pass by here in the winter, including the sperm and the humpback.

Killer whales have been sighted more than once. Every year at the marine biology research institute at Carmabi they receive notice of at least five sightings.

DIVING IN CURAÇAO

All diving activities take place on the south coast because the trade winds make the north coast too rough. With over 100 dive sites, Curaçao can be included in a list of the most beautiful diving meccas in the Caribbean. There are three different zones; the section from Westpunt to the Kaap St. Marie lighthouse is called Banda Abao, the Centraal Curaçao diving area which is between Bullenbaai and the Princess Beach Hotel and the Curaçao Underwater Park, which runs from the Princess Beach Hotel to Oostpunt.

There are mooring buoys for boats in both the underwater Reserve and Banda Abao, in order to protect the splendid coral reef. The reef is close to the coast and the Centraal Curaçao dive sites can be reached by car. The coast shelves gently into quite shallow water and the drop-off starts just 50-100 metres

from the coast and plunges for hundreds of metres in several points. It is a typical coral barrier reef, with a wide variety of both hard and soft corals, gorgonians, big sponges, both shallow and deep-water fishes and numerous species of invertebrates.

Every dive promises something new and unexpected, like a shoal of Atlantic tarpon or a solitary hammerhead shark.

There are some really beautiful wrecks to visit on Curaçao, the biggest of which is the *Superior Producer* at Willemstad.

The Seaquarium has the wreck of the Dutch steamer *SS Orange Nassau* which went aground on the coral at the beginning of the century. The little *Towboat* rests in the Caracasbaai area.

This wreck is covered with splendid vegetation and must rank as one of the most beautiful in the Caribbean. Moving towards the Princess Beach Hotel, the wreck of the tug *Saba* lies in relatively shallow waters and the *Car Pile*, a heap of 1950s auto carcasses, close to Princess Beach Hotel, is also worth visiting.

In addition, there are magnificent anchors of old ships to be discovered all over, if you look carefully. You can dive off boats or straight from the shore in Curaçao. There are numerous well-organised dive centres on the island, practically every hotel has its own operation. They all belong to the CDOA, the association of all the Curaçao diving schools. Underwater harpoon fishing is absolutely forbidden throughout the island.

MUSHROOM FOREST

WESTPUNT

CURAÇAO

Santa Marta Baai

MUSHROOM
FOREST

WILLEMSTAD

Punt Kanon

0 m

10 m

15 m

NOORDPUNT

WESTPUNT

CURAÇAO

MUSHROOM ▼
FOREST

SANTA CRUZ

Santa Marta Baai

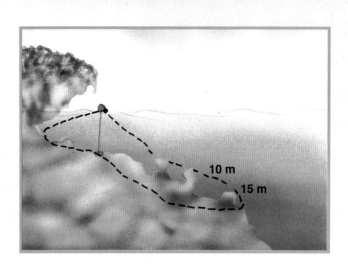

10 m

15 m

A

B

LOCALIZATION

There is a dive site not too far from the Coral Cliff Hotel at Banda Aboa, on the west side of the island, called Mushroom Forest. Mushroom Forest is one of the most beautiful and the most bizarre places I have ever dived.
It is a bay with mushroom-shaped coral banks several metres high. How and why this type of coral developed right here is still a mystery. A wide variety of fish and other marine animals live amongst the coral banks and it is not unusual to meet turtles.

A - A short distance from the surface the sea bed is characterised by these mushroom-shaped hard coral formations, where the "stalks" have probably been eroded by drilling sponges.

B - These colonies of boulder star coral, Montastrea *genus, cover large parts of the sea bed like petrified waterfalls, creating a unique landscape.*

C - The underwater scenery at Mushroom Forest is dominated by these dome-shaped coral formations which cover the surrounding rocks.

D - Seen from above in natural light the scenery of Mushroom Forest looks like a valley whose vegetation has been petrified and eroded by time.

E - The foureye butterflyfish (Chaetodon capistratus) *derives its unusual name to the livery worn by the young fish, with two ocellar marks on each flank.*

C

D

E

F

F - It is not known why these coral formations are so common in this zone alone.

G - A gigantic dome-like colony of brain coral (Diploria labyrinthiformis) *characterised by the deep ridges which protect the polyps and form an intricate design on the surface.*

H - A strange crab with spines and bristles camouflages itself amongst the coral which encrusts the sea bed.

I - In the picture can be seen a fairy basslet (Gramma loreto). *The males of this species hold the eggs in their mouth until it is time for them to hatch out.*

J - A spotted moray (Gymnothorax moringa) *peers out of its lair, where it stays all day, coming out at night to hunt.*

THE DIVE

The dive is done with an expert divemaster and starts in the Mushroom Forest. We fin about 100 metres from the mooring buoy towards the open sea where the water starts to get deep and the biggest mushrooms appear.
The mushroom-shape coral banks dominate the scene and we see big beaker corals and numerous colourful fish while swimming around them. Spiny lobsters and morays hide underneath the coral. Little sabre-toothed blennies, which hide in the empty homes of several kinds of worms, swim in and out of the brain coral's "labyrinth". The depth here is between 10-15

H

G

I

metres. At the end of the dive we have come back to the mooring buoy and swim towards the coast where we find a cave. It is quite safe to enter and admire the yellow tube corals which grow on the ceiling and the numerous little glass fish which swim close to the rocks. There are spiny lobsters and several kinds of prawns living there permanently too.
Of course, the cave can only be visited by anyone who has a powerful torch.

J

THE WRECK OF THE SUPERIOR PRODUCER S.A.

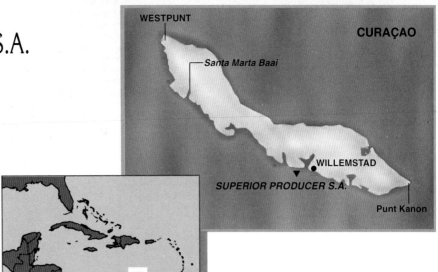

WESTPUNT

CURAÇAO

Santa Marta Baai

WILLEMSTAD

SUPERIOR PRODUCER S.A.

Punt Kanon

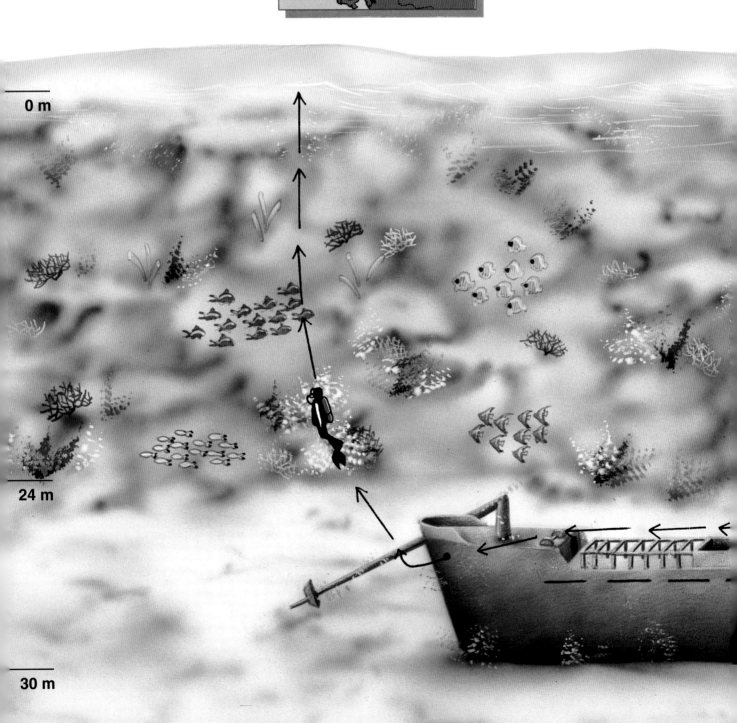

0 m

24 m

30 m

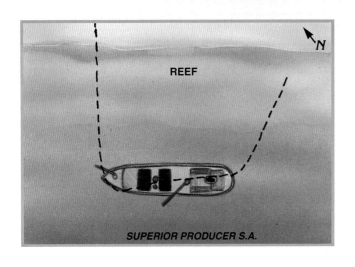

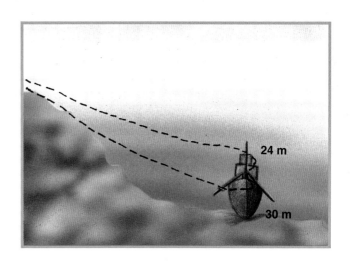

A - The dramatic moments of the accident of the Superior Producer S.A. here surrounded by several ships which came to her aid and tried to refloat her.

B - In this photograph can be seen members of the crew clustered on the port side on that dramatic 30 September 1977.

C - This image show the Superior Producer S.A. in its today final position. It can clearly be seen that during the shipwreck one of the cargo masts snapped like a toothpick.

D - The front end of the ship, like the whole wreck, is covered in splendid tube corals which open in the late afternoon and, of course, at night. It is like being in a magnificent garden.

E - The bows seen from on high together with part of the bridge and the superstructure.

F - This dramatic image can clearly show the wreck laying on the sand with the cargo mast broken and emerging from the blue depths.

G - This view shows the holds of the Superior Producer S.A. that, at the moment of the disaster, were piled high with bales of clothes, sheets, blankets, whisky etc.

H - The ship's structure has been transformed into an ideal substrate for hundreds of organisms which make colourful palettes out of the corroded metal.

A

B

C

D

LOCALIZATION

Diving on the *Superior Producer S.A.* is quite easy.
Boatdives are scheduled a few times by week by the various diving centre on Curaçao; very thrilling experience is diving from the helicopter which leaves from the platform opposite the Eden Roc Divecenter, but dives on the wreck can be made from shore as well.
The *Superior Producer* lies at the east side of the water factory, taking the road that leeds to the waterfort, you reach a mangrove forest and there is an opening in the forest where you can leave the car.

E

THE HISTORY

The *Superior Producer S.A.* was built in The Netherlands in the De Rietpol shipyard by Kramer and Booy N.V of Spaarndam, for Moerman of Rotterdam and was named *Andromeda*.
The cargo had been procured by Muller and Reitsma N.V., whose head office was also in Rotterdam.
The ship was launched on 10th August 1957, passed its sea trials on 8th November 1957 and was registered.
It was 49.5 metres long, 7.57 metres wide and drew 3.25 metres. Weighing 400 tonnes, its 500 HP 6-cylinder engine could haul it to a top speed of 10 knots.

In 1962 the ship was sold to the shipping company L. Remeeus N.V. and changed its name to *Superior Producer*. It was chartered to the Norfolk Lijn N.V Rotterdam. In 1973 it was sold to the Pan-Ven Line S.A. and renamed *Superior Producer S.A.* Up until it sank on 30th September 1977 in front of the Willemstad harbour, on the island of Curaçao, it continued to sail for this company. The story of the *Superior Producer S.A.* as a wreck starts in September 1977. The small merchant vessel sailed into the port of Willemstad on the island of Curaçao, but it was heading for the Isla de Margaritha in Venezuela to fuel up. It was already overloaded and the load was further increased at Curaçao.

The bridges and holds were piled high with bales of clothes, sheets, blankets, whisky and *Alkolada glacial*, the famous Curaçao perfume. When the *Superior Producer S.A.* left port on 30th September 1977 the sea was quite rough. The 30-knot wind was strong, even for Curaçao, where they are used to extremely violent winds. The pilot had disembarked before the ship was out of port. The ship had not even left the port when the wind started to push the ship around and at the first big wave the ship capsized, although it continued to float. Ships rushed to help the unlucky coaster which was towed away from the channel. The crew stayed on board the ship which was starting to tilt dangerously. Unsuccessful attempts were made to float the ship by removing part of the cargo, but it was no good. At 3.30 p.m. the *Superior Producer S.A.* disappeared into the waves and sank in a few minutes. The ten crew members had only to swim 200 metres to reach the shore safely. Only a few hours later divers had got lines on the ship and the coaster was towed 500 metres west towards the desalination plant because it was blocking access to the harbour. These divers spread the news that the wreck, which was lying on its keel on the sea bed at a depth of 30 metres and only 200 metres from the coast, was easy to reach. The numerous keen divers on Curaçao took an interest in it and the race to the wreck was on.

F

day the corals are closed but at twilight and during the night the wreck is covered with tube corals and is transformed into a yellow garden. The stairway behind the bridge makes a wonderful background and while I am looking for the best position something brushes my shoulders.

A great barracuda at least 1.5 metres long is swimming around the mast as if it wants to be photographed too. It lets me approach but unfortunately, despite by powerful grand-angle lens, it still looks very small. In the half-light of the bridge, which I go into, I find a big school of longspine squirrelfish *(Holocentrus rufus)*. Nothing at all remains of the furnishings. I look through the open

G

THE DIVE

You enter into the water at the waterline in corrispondence of some concrete blocks. You have to swim strait out towards the drop off. The best thing is to do this on the surface in order to spair your air because it is a long distance to swim underwater. After about 100 metres strait out from the shore you reach the edge of the reef, when you dive down and follow the sloping drop you will see the wreck about 50 metres from the reef, straight up her keel in the sand. The wreck is resting on its keel at 30 metres, parallel to the coral reef and not far from it. With the passing years it has been covered with magnificent corals. During the

H

portholes into the holds and the front end of the boat. The holds are empty although we do find something every now and again. The loading bays at the front end of the ship and a school of colourful Creole wrasse *(Clepticus parrae)* make a picture well worth photographing. The depth - the bridge is at 25 metres - means that the time at our disposal is almost up. Swimming over the sandy bottom I turn towards the reef and from there to the shore. One thing to think about is the current and on the other the waves. Normally there are breaking waves here at this dive site, be careful entering and leaving the water, the current can take you away from the wreck, do not spend to much time floating on the surface.

THE FISH OF THE CARIBBEAN

The area generally known as the Caribbean runs along the tropical coastlines of the American continents and continues through the archipelago stretching along the boundary between the Caribbean sea, on the inside, and the Atlantic Ocean on the outside. This band of islands is around 800 kilometres wide and almost 2,000 long, a modest total area if compared with the Pacific, where the Australian Great Barrier Reef alone takes up an only slightly smaller area. But this is one of the richest coral areas in the Atlantic, perhaps the only one which deserves the name, with more than 600 species of fishes and almost a hundred different corals, most of which originated in relatively recent times (15-10 million years ago) when the land which today forms Central America rose up and closed off all links with the Pacific.

These events and others which affected the Caribbean area certainly reduced the number of species and families, but on the other hand they permitted the evolution of unique populations. The Caribbean is dominated by the Caribbean current, which flows east to west and by a coastal counter-current, which affect each other reciprocally and create numerous internal vortices.

This current complex is of notable importance for marine life, as it carries the countless larvae of a huge range of animals from one point of the area to another, contributing to their diffusion and giving a reasonably uniform character to the whole of the Caribbean, which as divers will realise from their very first dive, is dominated by the sponges and sea-fans which take the place of the Alcyonaria found in the Red Sea and in Indo-Pacific waters. The Caribbean coral banks stretch from Florida to the Bahamas and on to Venezuela. A huge platform east of Florida stretches right to the Bahamas, which incorporate more than 3,000 islands, cays and reefs, creating a long barrier which is one of the largest in the Atlantic. The coral continues in the reefs off the long arc of islands from Cuba to Aruba. The coral barrier which runs parallel to the coastline of Belize is 250 miles long and considered the second most important in the world after the Australian one. The so-called "blue holes" are typical phenomena of this area - the remains of underwater caves whose vaults have collapsed, leaving broad abysses of an intense blue. Diving in the Caribbean means an encounter with a strange underwater world where, alongside corals which are not unlike those of the Indo-Pacific, you fill find huge sponges in incredible shapes and colours. Whether they look like huge elephant's ears, barrels, stove-pipes or elegant candelabras, whether they are pink, red or yellow, they all grow to sizes so enormous that they can hide one diver from another.

In view of their size it comes as no surprise that they become a kind of microcosm which attract the swarms of rays, bream and damselfish swimming around them, while inside there will often be sand stars, anemones, worms, crustaceans and fishes (gobies and blennies) which make their homes in the big oscula. Trumpetfish or scorpionfish lie in ambush in the shadows of the sponges, sometimes joined by the brightly-coloured fairy blassets (*Gramma loreto*), easily recognised by their fluorescent yellow and fuchsia colouring.

Along with the sponges, the walls of the Caribbean reefs have forests of gorgonians growing on them, from those with a regular pattern of ramifications (the fans of the *Venuses, Gorgonia flabellum*) to the much larger and more irregular ones such as the *Gorgonia ventalina* which can grow to a height of two metres; mixed with them, and gradually becoming more dominant as the depth increases, are the feathery, more fragile, black corals.

Depending on the reef's position its walls open up either into deep channels or the open sea and the sea-bed geometry is in each case intricate, full of holes and fissures which are home to numerous leopard, striped and green morays. The latter, of which there is a particular abundance in the Caribbean, have the unattractive, and totally undeserved, name of *Gymnothorax funebris*.

There are plenty of groupers in these dens too, red ones (*Cephalopholis*

144

fulva), striped ones (but it depends on their mood because they can change colour very fast) - *Epinephelus striatus* - better known as the Nassau grouper, right up to the gigantic *Epinephelus itajara* , unchallenged lords of the reef and of the submerged wrecks, visible from afar thanks to the transparency of these waters and, above all, their size, frequently well over two metres. Other, less fearsome, shade lovers are the squirrelfish and the soldierfish, seen against a background of huge shoals of glassfish whose scales reflect the flashes from underwater cameras inside the caves.

For the most part, the fish familes found in this part of the Atlantic will be familiar to anyone who has already dived in coral seas, but there is no lack of opportunities for interesting encounters and comparisons.

Everyone will be enchanted by the slow-moving grace of the French angelfish *(Pomacanthus paru)* or the grey angelfish *(Pomacanthus arcuatus)*, up to 50 cm long, especially as the latter seem to have no fear of divers, even approaching them spontaneously. The tranquil gait of these fish is in contrast with the rapid movements of butterfly fish such as the *Chaetodon capistratus*, perhaps the commonest fish in the area, recognisable by the ocellar marking near to the tail, which is two marks on young fish, hence the name four-eyed butterflyfish.

The *Chaetodon aculeatus* or long-nosed butterflyfish is much less commonly seen however, as it prefers the deep reefs.

It is perfectly built to swim in the tightest of coral fissures where it searches for invertebrates to feed on. Wherever you dive you will find the brightly-coloured Labridae with their classic darting movement, constantly in search for food. You will have no difficulty in spotting the crested porkfish *(Lachnolaimus maximus)* among them, looking rather bedraggled thanks to the long rays along its spine, nor the *Thalassoma bifasciatum* which carry out their courting rituals close to the surface during the early hours of the afternoon. But not all the fishes in the Caribbean live alone or in pairs.

There are fish which live in shoals such as the many kinds of snappers or the ubiquitous French grunters, which join up in their hundreds to form lively yellow and blue processions; or the big tarpons over two metres long, that can make an expedition to explore an old jetty memorable even if they are the only fish you see, sometimes even becoming a fixture on a dive, in view of their habit of taking up permanent residence in one place. The jacks are always there, forming silver walls with the darting barracuda, suddenly opening up to give precedence to sharks, including hammerheads, and the mantas, eagle-rays or the big sting-rays which live on the sandy bottoms. There is more life in these clearings and channels than might at first appear and there is a regular sequence of corals, rocks, sand and underwater meadows. Finally, a word of advice for the adventurous. Be sure to take the opportunity, between dives, to take a trip to a lagoon surrounded by mangroves. This unique environment, a halfway-house between land and sea, has considerable importance in the Caribbean, because the water between the roots provides a reproduction ground for an enormous number of species. Amongst sponges of all colours you can see oysters, crabs, jellyfish swimming upside down, young barracuda in training for life in more-dangerous waters - for them too - chasing the young of numerous other species, from angelfish to parrotfish to butterflyfish to ray's bream.

CARCHARHINIDAE FAMILY

Tiger shark
Galeocerdo cuvieri

This shark is recognisable by its short, wide nose and its caudal fin, whose upper lobe is bigger than the lower one. It is bluey-grey with dark vertical bars, which are more visible in young fish. It is extremely dangerous and will come right into coastal, even brackish, waters. It is seen along the outer reef walls and off-shore barriers. Grows up to 5.5 metres in length. Found in all the circumtropical seas.

Bull shark
Carcharinus leucas

Big-bodied with short, rounded nose and small eyes. The upper lobe of the caudal fin is larger than the lower one. Browny-grey on the back and lighter on the underside. Lives in shallow coastal waters and close to reefs and is considered dangerous. It grows up to 3.5 metres in length and is found in circumtropical waters.

GINGLYMOSTOMATIDAE FAMILY

Nurse shark
Gynglimostoma cirratum

Straight body flattened along the belly, with close-set dorsal fins. It has a small mouth on the underside of its head, with a couple of short barbels. Yellowy-grey colour. Lives on the sandy beds between the reefs, sheltered by the big corals and caves. Grows up to 4.3 metres in length. Found from Rhode Island to Brazil.

DASYATIDAE FAMILY

Southern stingray
Dasyatis americana

A ray with a lozenge-shaped body, sometimes more pronounced than others, with a pointed nose and slightly pointed pectoral fins. A line of tubercules runs down the centre of the back and it has a long sharp spine in the front half of the tail. Tends to bury itself in the sand when resting on the sea bed. It is grey-black in colour, the young being lighter than the adult specimens. It reaches a width of 1.5 metres. Found from New Jersey to Brazil.

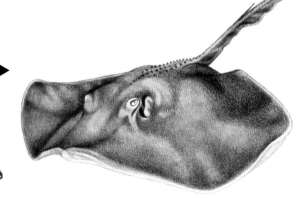

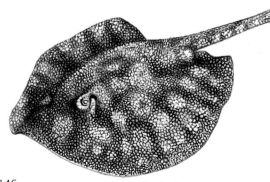

Yellow stingray
Urolophus jamaicensis

Ray with a disc-shaped body, a rounded nose and pectoral fin tips. The short tail has poisonous spines at the tip. Colouring is yellow-brown with dark markings of varying size. Lives on the sandy beds close to the reefs, where it buries itself. It can measure up to 76 centimetres in width. Found from North Carolina to Venezuela.

MYLIOBATIDAE FAMILY

Spotted eagle ray
Aetobatus narinari ▶

Ray with a lozenge-shaped body, big, pointed, wings and a pointed, convex, head. The tail is almost three times as long as the body and has toothed spines along it. The back is dark in colouring with numerous light spots. The spotted eagle ray lives in the deep reef channels, close to shady beds. It grows up to 2.5 metres in width. The species is found in circumtropical waters.

MURAENIDAE FAMILY

Green moray
Gymnothorax funebris

◀ This moray eel is easily recognisable by its greeny colour, which varies in intensity from specimen to specimen, but is always uniform. The green moray is a nocturnal animal but during the day it hides in the reef crevices, often in shallow water, and can be easily approached. It may attack if excessively provoked. It grows up to 2.3 metres in length. Found from Florida to Brazil.

Spotted moray
Gymnothorax moringa

This moray is common in shallow sea beds, often rich in vegetation, where it hides in crevices during the day, coming out at night to hunt. It is yellowy-white with numerous brown or reddy-black markings. It can grow up to 1.2 metres in length and is found from South Carolina to Brazil.

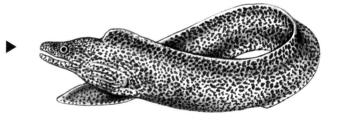

Purplemouth moray
Gymnothorax vicinus

This moray is recognisable by its yellowish eyes, its black-edged dorsal fin and its mouth, which is purple inside. ◀ Nocturnal, it lives on rocky sea beds and along reefs, including shallow ones. It grows up to 1.2 metres and is found from Florida to Brazil to the Canary Isles.

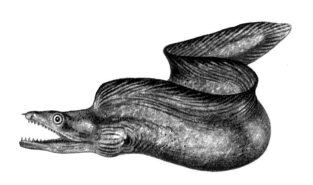

Chain moray
Echidna catenata

This eel has a powerful body, tall and compressed at the back, and a short head. The dorsal fin starts behind the branchial opening. Colouring is yellowish with a lighter, chain-shaped, pattern and the eyes are yellow. It prefers shallow rocky, coral sea-beds with abundant crevices where it can hide. Grows up ▶ to 50 centimetres. Found from Florida to Brazil.

CONGRIDAE FAMILY

Sand eel
Heteroconger halis

Elongated body and tapered head with large eyes and a small mouth. Grey-brown in colour. Lives in colonies on sandy beds where it stays buried all the time, leaving its mouth and part of its body outside. Grows up to 60 centimetres and is found throughout the Caribbean.

ALBULIDAE FAMILY

Bonefish
Albula vulpes

Tapered body with pointed nose and well-developed, downwards angling, mouth. The last ray on the dorsal and anal fins is filament-shaped. Tends to come into the coastal sandy beds with the tide. Found on coral sea beds with abundant sandy areas and reef channels. Grows up to 1 metre. Found from New Brunswick to Brazil.

ANTENNARIDAE FAMILY

Longlure frogfish
Antennarius multiocellatus

Deep-bodied, almost spherical fish, with a high dorsal fin and stubby pelvic and pectoral fins. The first spiny ray of the dorsal fin has evolved into a long filament for luring prey. Brilliantly camouflaged, it never moves until approached very closely. Colouring darkens if frightened. Has three distinctive blotches on the tail. Measures up to 14 centimetres. Found from Florida to the Caribbean.

MEGALOPIDAE FAMILY

Tarpon
Megalops atlanticus

Big, robust-bodied fish. Oblique, upward-angled mouth. Silvery body covered in large scales. The last ray of the dorsal fin is long and threadlike. Lives in surface waters where there is very little light. Measures up to 2.5 metres. Found from Virginia to Brazil.

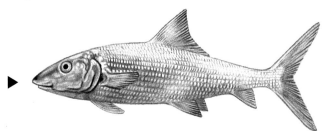

SYNODONTIDAE FAMILY

Lizardfish
Synodus intermedius

Robust, elongated body, flattened underbelly. Wide mouth showing its small but numerous teeth. Has a dark blotch on the operculum and yellowish lengthwise stripes along its sides. Lives on sandy beds in which it buries itself. Grows up to 55 centimetres, found from North Carolina to Brazil.

Ocellated frogfish
Antennarius ocellatus

Very similar to the previous fish, distinguished from it by three ocellar marks: one lateral, one dorsal and one caudal. Lives in rocky, coralline habitats as well as on sandy and muddy bottoms. Colour varies from brownish red to brownish yellow. Measures up to 38 centimetres. Found from North Carolina to the Caribbean.

OGCOCEPHALIDAE FAMILY

Spotted batfish
Ogcocephalus radiatus

Strangely-shaped fish, like a flattened disc with stubby pectoral fins and a tail. Its back is covered with small, dark, spots. It likes both rocky and sandy beds, tending to bury itself in the latter. Measures up to 38 centimetres, found in Florida and in the Bahamas.

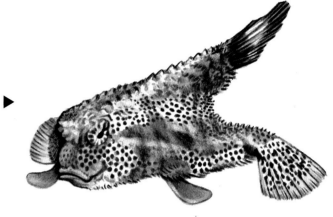

HOLOCENTRIDAE FAMILY

Longspine squirrelfish
Holocentrus rufus

Compressed, oval body; the front part of the dorsal fin has robust, white-tipped, spiny rays and the back part is exceptionally deep. During the daytime it hides in the reef crevices, coming out at night to hunt for mollusks, crustaceans and echinoderms. Measures up to 28 centimetres. Found from Bermuda to Venezuela.

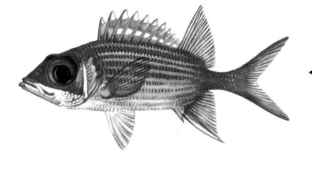

Squirrelfish
Holocentrus ascensionis

Very similar to the previous fish, distinguished mainly by its yellowish-green dorsal fin. Stays in the darker areas of the reef in the daytime. Likes shallow coral seabeds with abundant crevices and small caves. Measures up to 35 centimetres. Found from North Carolina to Brazil.

Blackbar soldierfish
Myripristis jacobus

Oval-bodied fish with a big head and large eyes. Red body with a black bar covering the rear edge of the opercula. Stays hidden in caves in the daytime where it swims upside down because of the light which reflects off the seabed. It measures up to 20 centimetres. Found from Georgia to Brazil right to the Cape Verde Islands.

FISTULARIDAE FAMILY

Blue-spotted cornetfish
Fistularia tabacaria

Elongated fish with tubular nose and terminal mouth. The two central rays of the tail fin are exceptionally elongated. Found near underwater meadows and reefs with sandy beds. Lives alone or in small groups. It grows up to 1.8 metres and is found from Nova Scotia to Brazil.

AULOSTOMATIDAE FAMILY

Trumpetfish
Aulostomus maculatus

Fish with an elongated body, tubular nose and terminal mouth. There is a thin barbel underneath its lower jaw. The dorsal fin consists of a series of separate spiny rays. It lives close to reefs where it camouflages itself by changing colour and swimming in an almost vertical position. It is a timid fish and one which is hard to approach. It measures up to 1 metre in length. Found from Florida to Brazil.

149

SYNGNATHIDAE FAMILY

Lined sea-horse
Hippocampus erectus

This fish's uniquely-shaped body is made up of bony rings, on which its head is set at an angle. It is found in areas rich in vegetation where it camouflages itself by anchoring itself to the algae with its prehensile tail. It grows up to 17 centimetres and is found from Nova Scotia to Argentina.

Fam. SCORPENIDI

Coral scorpionfish
Scorpaena plumieri

Powerfully-bodied scorpionfish with growths and appendices on its nose. It is greeny-brown with reddish shading. There are three dark vertical bars on the tail. The inside of the pectoral fins is dark with small white marks. This is one of the most common scorpionfish found on coral reefs, growing up to 40 centimetres. Found from New York to Brazil.

SERRANIDAE FAMILY

Jewfish
Epinephelus itajara

This is one of the biggest of the Atlantic groupers and has a wide, flat, head. It is greeny-grey in colour with small black marks. It usually makes its den in caves or wrecks and its sheer size - it grows up to 2.4 metres - makes it a potentially dangerous fish. Found from Florida to Brazil and in Africa from Senegal to Congo.

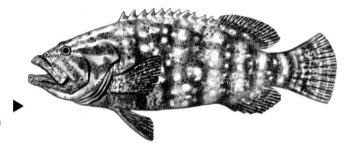

Red grouper
Epinephelus morio

Sturdy fish with a tapered body. The second spiny ray on the dorsal fin is bigger than the others. Concave caudal fin with pointed lobes in adult fish. Often stays immobile on the sea bed to camouflage itself. Measures up to 90 centimetres and is found from Massachusetts to Brazil.

Nassau grouper
Ephinephelus striatus

Grouper with tapered body and small pelvic fins. Common on coral sea beds where it rarely strays from the area immediately around its den. It changes colour rapidly if frightened or its interest is aroused. Shoals of thousands form in small areas for spawning. It grows up to 1 metre in length. Widespread from North Carolina to Brazil.

Graysby
Cephalophlois cruentatus

A small grouper with tapered body and a rounded edge to its tail. Its body is light-coloured with numerous reddish marks all over. It lives on coral beds from the surface down to depths of 60-70 metres. Grows up to 30 centimetres. Found from Florida to Brazil.

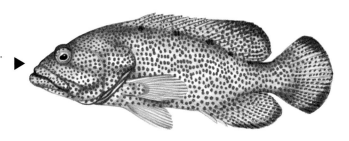

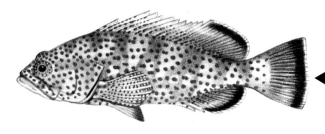

Red hind
Epinephelus guttatus

One of the commonest groupers to be found in shallow coral sea-beds, where it is often to be seen resting immobile on the bottom. Light-coloured body with reddish marks. Doral, anal and caudal fins have black edges. Measures up to 60 centimetres and is found from Florida to Brazil.

Coney
Cephalopholis fulva

Tapered body, whether straight-edged or slightly rounded the caudal fin, it always has distinct corners. Colouring tends to differ with depth. A gregarious species which prefers reefs abounding in crevices, from where it does not often stray. Allows divers to approach slowly. Grows up to 40 centimetres, it is found from Florida to Brazil.

Tiger grouper
Mycteroperca tigris

Grouper with tapered body and distinctive light-coloured vertical bars on its sides, which contribute to the tigerish looks. Its background colour tends towards reddish. Young fish are yellow. Lives in sheltered parts of the reef. Measures up to 85 centimetres and is found from Florida to Brazil.

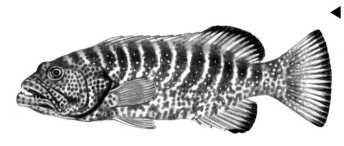

Black grouper
Mycteroperca bonaci

Long-body grouper Distinctive rounded edge to the dorsal and anal fins. Colour varies from reddish brown to black, with patches will also vary in intensity. The dorsal, anal and tail fins are black-edged. Lives on the reef, often moving into the open sea nearby. Measures up to 1.1 metres. Found from Massachusetts to Brazil.

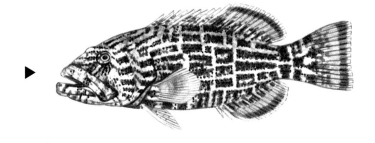

Sand perch
Diplectrum formosum

A small fish with an elongated, only slightly compressed, body. The pre-operculum has two groups of diverging spines. The fish is light-coloured with blue lengthwise stripes on its head and sides and lives in underwater meadowlands or coral, where it digs dens for itself. Measures up to 25 centimetres. Found from North Carolina to Uruguay.

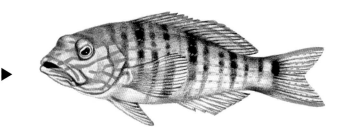

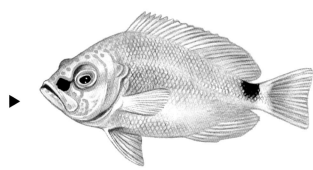

Greater soapfish
Rypticus saponaceus

This fish has a pointed front profile, flattened on the back of the head. The dorsal fin is set back and has a rounded rear edge. Lives in shallow water close to reefs and on sandy beds. If startled it secretes a mucous which is poisonous to other fish. Measures up to 33 centimetres. Found from Florida to Brazil and in the eastern Atlantic.

Butter Hamlet
Hypoplectrus unicolor

Deep, compressed, body. Lower edge of the pre-operculum is finely toothed. Has a distinct saddle-shaped mark on the caudal peduncle. Prefers coral reefs where it swims close to the seabed. Measures up to 13 centimetres. Found from Florida to Brazil.

Barred Hamlet
Hypoplectrus puella

Compressed body with slightly pointed snout. Brownish-yellow with a dark triangular blotch in the centre of each flank. Prefers rocky, shallower waters and coral reefs up to depths of 20-23 metres. Can be approached but is quick to flee into crevices for shelter. Measures up to 13 centimetres. Found from Florida to the Caribbean.

Indigo Hamlet
Hypoplectrus indigo

Similar to the previous species, from which it is distinguished by its bluish livery, with vertical white cars. Prefers coral seabeds, where it swims close to the bottom. Like the other species, this one too can be approached slowly. Measures up to 13 centimetres. Found from Florida to the Caymans to Belize.

Tobaccofish
Serranus tabacarius

Tapering body with a broad, horizontal, browny-orange stripe. Lives close to the seabed on the border between reefs and sandy beds or ones strewn with reef detritus. Tends to become gregarious at depths greater than 50 metres. Measures up to 18 centimetres. Found from Florida to Brazil.

Tigerfish
Serranus tigrinus

Small fish with an elongated, compressed body ending in a pointed snout. The opercula are spiny with toothed edges. As its name suggests it is marked with vertical, dark bars. The tips of the caudal lobes are yellowish. Lives on coral seabeds or underwater meadowlands. Measures up to 15 centimetres. Common in the Caribbean.

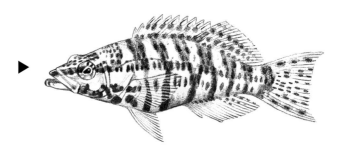

Peppermint bass
Liopropoma rubre

Small fish with tapering body and double dorsal fin. The tip of the dorsal, anal and tail fins are the same colour. The flanks have red stripes. Tends to stay hidden in crevices and hollows and is for this reason not often seen, although it is common. Measures up to 8 centimetres. Found from Florida to Venezuela.

GRAMMATIDAE FAMILY

Fairy basslet
Gramma loreto

Small fish with highly characteristic colouring, half purple and half yellow. Lives in small schools in hollows and crevices where it swims upside down because of the reflected light. Measures up to 8 centimetres. Found from Bermuda to Venezuela.

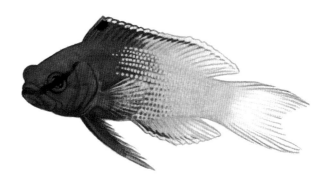

APOGONIDAE FAMILY

Spotted cardinalfish
Apogon maculatus

Small fish with a robust, oval body with a deep caudal peduncle. Bright red with a black spot on the operculum and at the base of the second dorsal fin. Prefers surface waters where it stays inside caves during the day. Measures up to 13 centimetres. Found from Florida to the Gulf of Mexico.

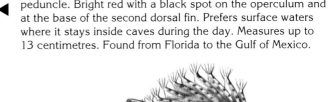

CIRRHITIDAE FAMILY

Redspotted hawkfish
Amblycirrhitus pinos

Small fish with a deep body and pointed nose. The spiny rays of the dorsal fin have fringed points. It has distinctive red spots on the nose, the back and the dorsal fin. Lives on reefs where it waits in ambush resting on the seabed. Measures up to 11 centimetres. Found from Florida to the Gulf of Mexico.

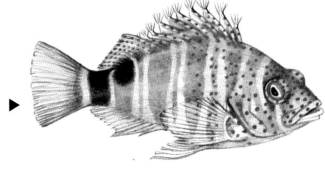

PRIACANTHIDAE FAMILY

Glasseye snapper
Heteropriacanthus cruentatus

Robust, compressed body with a square head and oblique mouth angled upwards. Very large eyes. Reddish with silvery vertical bars which disappear on the back. Prefers surface waters where it tends to inhabit the less illuminated areas during the day. Measures up to 30 centimetres. Found in circumtropical waters.

MALACANTHIDAE FAMILY

Sand tilefish
Malacanthus plumieri

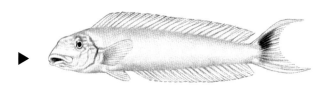

Elongated body with very large lips. Crescent-shaped tail
with pointed lobes. Yellowish blue with yellow and blue stripes
on the head. Tail is often yellow. Lives on sandy and rubble-
strewn seabeds where it digs itself a den. Measures up to
60 centimetres. Found from North Carolina to Brazil.

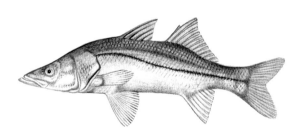

CENTROPOMIDAE FAMILY

Snook
Centropomus undecimalis

Robust body terminating in a pointed head, the dorsal fin has
a very angled profile. The lateral line is dark and continues
right to the rear edge of the tail. Lives in coastal waters where
there are plenty of mangroves. Measures up to 1.3 meters.
Found from South Carolina to Brazil.

CARANGIDAE FAMILY

Crevalle Jack
Caranx hippos

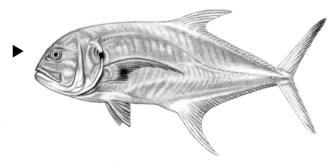

Has a deep, elongated body, very tapered and convex at the
front. Thin, characteristically forked, tail. The young fish are
gregarious and more common in coastal waters, while adult
specimens tend to be solitary. Commoner in open water and
along the outer edge of the reef. Measures up to 1 metre.
Found from Nova Scotia to Uruguay and in the eastern Atlantic.

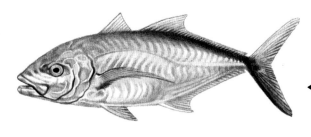

Bar jack
Carangoides ruber

Elongated, tapering, silvery body, marked by a dark band at the
base of the dorsal fin which stretches to the lower caudal lob.
Lives in shoals of variable size and often follows shoals of mullet
and sting-ray to feed on invertebrates they uncover. Measures
up to 60 centimetres. Found from New Jersey to Venezuela.

Rainbow fish
Elagatic bipinnulata

Elongated, spindle-shaped body with two light-blue horizontal
stripes separated by a green or yellowish streak. Common in
open water, this fish often moves in close to the outer slopes
of the reef. Lives in shoals and seems to be attracted by the
air bubbles produced by scuba-diving equipment. Measures
up to 1.2 metres. Found in all circumtropical waters.

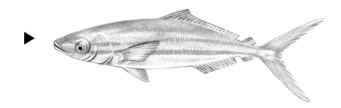

Horse-eye jack
Caranx latus

Relatively deep, compressed body. Its yellow tail distinguishes it from the other carangids. Lives in shoals in open water above the deepest reefs, often mixing with other carangids. Measures up to 70 centimetres. Found from New Jersey to Brazil.

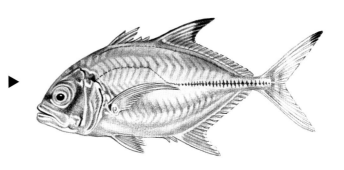

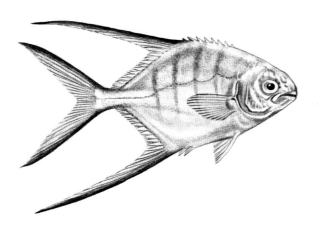

Palometa
Trachinotus goodei

Carangid with lozenge-shaped body, distinguished by large rays on the dorsal and anal fins. Silver livery with 3-5 vertical black streaks. Lives in coastal waters amongst coral formations. Measures up to 50 centimetres. Found from Massachusetts to Argentina.

LUTJANIDAE FAMILY

Yellowtail snapper
Ocyurus chrysurus

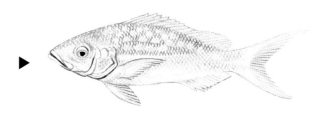

Elongated body with pronounced forked tail and pointed lobes. Purpley-blue colour with a horizontal yellow stripe and small spots. Swims alone or in small groups close to the reef or to meadowlands. More active at night. Measures up to 75 centimetres. Found from Massachusetts to Brazil.

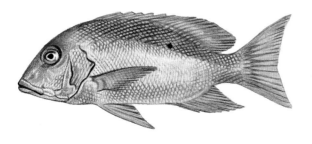

Mutton snapper
Lutjanus analis

Robust, deep body, olive-coloured with blackish streaks which are more marked in fish up to 40 centimetres. The adult fish prefer rocky and coral seabeds while the younger ones are more often to be found on sandy beds and in meadowlands. Measures up to 75 centimetres. Found from Massachusetts to Brazil.

Cubera snapper
Lutjanus cyanopterus

Tapered but robust body, greyish with reddish reflections at the front. Large lips. Prefers rather deep rocky and coral seabeds. Young fish are commoner along the shoreline. Measures up to 1.6 metres. Found from New Jersey to Brazil.

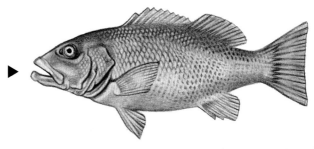

HAEMULIDAE FAMILY

Porkfish
Anisotremus virginicus

Compressed body, very deep at the front. The fish has two characteristic dark vertical bars on the head and a series of blue and yellow horizontal streaks. Swims alone or in small groups which are commoner above the reef during the day. The young act as cleaner fish. Measures up to 40 centimetres. Found from Florida to Brazil.

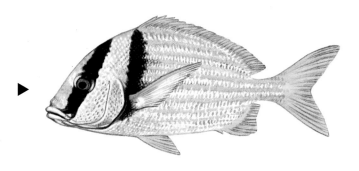

Bluestriped grunt
Haemulon sciurus

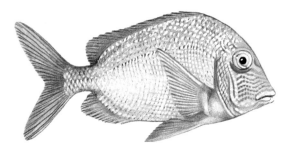

Deep, compressed body, the rear part of which is dark-coloured, including the dorsal and tail fins. Background colour is yellowish with numerous blue horizontal stripes. Forms large shoals near the coast on rocky or sand beds. Measures up to 45 centimetres. Found from South Carolina to Brazil.

French grunt
Haemulon flavolineatus

Deep body with pointed snout and small mouth. Yellowish with numerous blue streaks, horizontal above the lateral line and oblique below. Prefers coral seabeds where it forms shoals of up to a thousand fish. Likes poorly illuminated areas. Measures up to 30 centimetres. Found from South Carolina to Brazil.

SPARIDAE FAMILY

Saucereye porgy
Calamus calamus

Compressed body, deep at the front. Blunt-nosed. Bluish-grey colour with a rounded blue blotch between the eyes. Yellow corners to the mouth. Lives close to the sand beds in the reefs. Measures up to 40 centimetres. Found from North Carolina to Brazil.

SCIAENIDAE FAMILY

Reef croaker
Odontoscion dentex

Elongated, compressed body with a big, oblique, terminal mouth. Reddish body with a black blotch at the base of the pelvic fin. Prefers rocky habitats and shallow coral reefs, tending to stay in poorly-lit areas. Measures up to 25 centimetres. Found from Florida to Brazil.

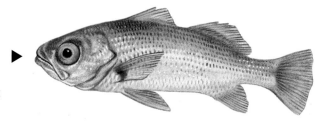

Jack-knife fish
Equetus lanceolatus

Deep front body section and very pointed rear section. Characteristically deep forward dorsal fin, especially in the young. Dark bar runs from the tip of the dorsal fin to the tail. Prefers the darker parts of reefs and hollows. Measures up to 25 centimetres. Found from South Carolina to Brazil.

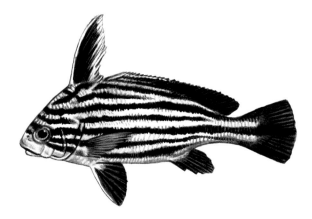

High hat
Pareques acuminatus

Deep-bodied at the front end, then stumpy with a well-defined dorsal fin and not so deep rear part. Reddish brown with longitudinal whitish stripes. Prefers surface waters close to rocky and coral bottoms, near caves and poorly-illuminated areas. Measures up to 23 centimetres. Found from South Carolina to Brazil.

MULLIDAE FAMILY

Yellow goatfish
Mulloidichthys martinicus

Tapered body, the snout has a slightly convex and pointed edge. Olive-coloured back with light-coloured flanks, bearing a horizontal yellow bar stretching right to the tail. Forms small shoals on the sandy beds close to reefs. Measures up to 40 centimetres. Found from the Caribbean to Capo Verde.

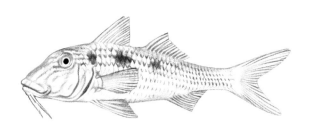

Spotted goatfish
Pseudopeneus maculatus

Tapered body with a slightly pointed snout. The edge of the operculum has a spine which is quite pronunced in some cases. There are three large blackish blotches on the sides of the body. Forms small groups of 4-6 fish to hunt. Grows up to 26 centimetres. Found from Florida to Brazil.

PEMPHERIDAE FAMILY

Glassfish
Pempheris schomburgki

Small fish with compressed, oval body, tapered at the rear. Silvery-pink colour, with a very long black-edged anal fin. Lives in shoals inside grottoes or in reef crevices, from which it comes out at night. Measures up to 16 centimetres. Found from Florida to Brazil.

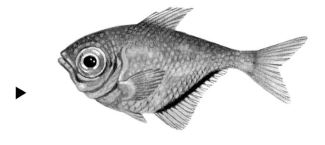

KIPHOSIDAE FAMILY

Bermuda chub
Kyphosus sectatrix

Deep, oval-shaped body with a small, terminal, mouth. Greyish in colour with thin bronze horizontal stripes. Tends to form shoals close to coral and rocky seabeds rich in algae. Measures up to 76 centimetres. Found from Massachusetts to Brazil.

EPHIPPIDAE FAMILY
Atlantic spadefish
Chaetodipterus faber

Very deep, compressed body; the lobes of the dorsal and anal fins are very elongated rearwards. Greyish with 4-5 dark, vertical, bands. Forms small school which swim in open waters some way from the reef. Sometimes spontaneously approaches divers. Grows up to 90 centimetres. Found from Massachusetts to Brazil.

CHAETODONTIDAE FAMILY
Foureye butterflyfish
Chaetodon capistratus

Butterflyfish with deep, compressed body with yellow fins and a small black spot on the rear edge of the dorsal fin. Tends to become dark at night-time. Usually swims in pairs close to reefs and rocky seabeds. Grows up to 20 centimetres. Found from Massachusetts to Brazil.

Reef butterflyfish
Chaetodon sedentarius

Deep, compressed body, almost vertical rear profile. Yellowish colouring, it has a dark, wide, band at the rear of its body, running from the dorsal to the anal fin. Prefers coral bottoms where it goes deep as 80-90 metres. Measures up to 15 centimetres. Found from North Carolina to Brazil.

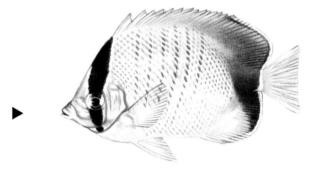

Spotfin butterflyfish
Chaetodon ocellatus

Deep, compressed body, with yellow fins and a small black mark on the rear edge of the dorsal fin. Tends to turn a darker colour at night. Generally swims in pairs close to reefs and rocky bottoms. Maximum size 20 centimetres. Found from Massachusetts to Brazil.

Longsnout butterflyfish
Chaetodon aculeatus

Compressed, very deep body thanks to the dorsal fin, which has well-developed spiny rays. Long, pointed snout. Solitary, preferring the deepest coral seabeds and reef crevices where it takes shelter if frightened. Measures up to 10 centimetres. Found from Florida to Venezuela.

Banded butterflysifh
Chaetodon striatus

Deep, compressed body, whitish in colour with 3 dark slanting bars, the first of which hides the eye. Young fish have an ocellar marking on the caudal peduncle. Lives alone or in pairs, close to the coral. Measures up to 16 centimetres. Found from Massachusetts to Brazil.

POMACANTHIDAE FAMILY

Grey angelfish
Pomacanthus arcuatus

Angelfish with deep, compressed body; the dorsal and caudal lobes are pointed at the rear. The tail fin has a straight trailing edge. Greyish-brown in colour, with a very pale mouth. Lives alone or in pairs in the richest areas of the reef. Measures up to 50 centimetres. Found from Bermuda to Brazil.

French angelfish
Pomacanthus paru

Angelfish with rounded, compressed body; rear lobes of the dorsal and anal fins are very pointed. Blackish in colour with yellow markings on the snout and the pectoral fins. Prefers the parts of the reef closest to the surface, rich in gorgonians. Measures up to 30 centimetres. Found from Florida to Brazil.

Rock beauty
Holacanthus tricolor

Distinctively-coloured butterflyfish: yellow front-body and tail sections, black central section and blue mouth. Pointed lobes to dorsal, anal and caudal fins. Extremely territoral, it normally stays close to its own area of the reef. Measures up to 20 centimetres. Fround from Georgia to Brazil.

Blue angelfish
Holocanthus bermudensis

Angelfish with deep, compressed body; the rear lobes of the dorsal and anal fins very pointed and extend backwards past the trailing edge of the caudal fin. Blue with yellow borders to the fins. Prefers the areas of the reef closest to the surface. Measures up to 38 centimetres. Found from Florida to Yucatan.

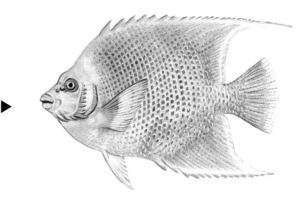

Queen angelfish
Holacanthus ciliaris

Angelfish with deep, compressed body; the rear lobes of the dorsal and anal fins very pointed and extend backwards past the trailing edge of the caudal fin. Yellow, closely spotted with blue on the sides and a blotch of the same colour on the head. Lives on the parts of the reef closest to the surface and the deepest parts (over 50 metres). Measures up to 45 centimetres. Found from Bermuda to Brazil.

Cherubfish
Centropyge argi

Small, oval-bodied angelfish, with yellow markings on the head and part of the back, and blue sides, belly and tail. Prefers the deepest parts of the coral bed, usually over 30 metres, where it sometimes forms small groups. Measures up to 8 centimetres. Found from Bermuda to Venezuela.

POMACENTRIDAE FAMILY

Blue chromis
Chromis cyanea

Small, oval-bodied fish with deeply cleft tail fin. Bluish with black-edged caudal lobes. Quite common around the reef, where it forms shoals. Measures up to 13 centimetres. Found from Florida to Venezuela.

Brown chromis
Chromis multilineata

Grey, swarthy-coloured fish with a black spot at the base of the pectoral fins and yellow tips to the dorsal fin and the caudal lobes. Lives in groups above coral formations, Measures up to 17 centimetres. Found from Florida to Brazil.

Beaugregory
Stegastes leucostictos

Small fish, slightly oval in shape, forked tail with rounded lobes. Brownish in colour with a lighter or yellowish tail. Territorial species, prefers sandy seabeds or ones rich in algae and detritus. Measures up to 10 centimetres. Found from Maine to Brazil.

Bi-colour damselfish
Stegastes partitus

Small fish with a compressed, oval-shaped body and a small, terminal, mouth. Dark-coloured front section to the body and white at the back. Lives close to the higher parts of the reef, where it establishes its territory which it defends from other fishes of the same species. Measures up to 12 centimetres. Found from Florida to the Gulf of Mexico.

Three-spot damselfish
Stegastes planifrons

Small fish with compressed, oval body and small terminal
mouth. Dark in colour with yellow-rimmed eyes and black spots
at the base of the pectoral fins and the caudal peduncle. Lives
close to the parts of the reef closest to the surface, which are
richer in algae, where it establishes its own territory and defends
it tenaciously from all comers, including divers. Measures up
to 12 centimetres. Found from Florida to the Gulf of Mexico.

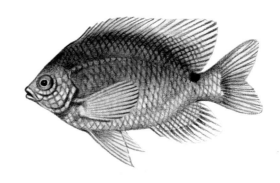

Sergeant major
Abdudefduf saxatilis

Compressed, ovoid, deep body covered with rough scales,
which extend to the fins too. Silvery white with dark vertical
bars and a yellow stripe at the base of the dorsal fin. Lives in
shoals in the parts of the reef closest to the surface. Measures
up to 20 centimetres. Found from Rhode Island to Uruguay.

Yellowtail damselfish
Microspatodon chrysurus

Small fish with a robust, brownish body, with small blue
markings and a distinctive yellow tail. The young fish tend to
stay amongst the branches of the fire corals, sometimes as
cleaner fish. Adults occupy small territories in the parts of the
reef closest to the surface. Measures up to 21 centimetres.
Found from Florida to Venezuela.

LABRIDAE FAMILY

Spanish hogfish
Bodianus rufus

Fish with robust body and pointed head. It has a purple back
and the rest of the body is yellowish. Swims continuously close
to the seabed, showing no fear at all, not even of divers.
Measures up to 40 centimetres. Found from Florida to Brazil.

Spotfin hogfish
Bodianus pulchellus

One of the Labridae, with a robust body and pointed snout.
The dorsal and anal fins have pointed rear lobes. The adult fish
are almost totally red except for the tail and part of the caudal
fin, which are yellow. Generally commoner on coral reefs over
20 metres down. Measures up to 20 centimetres. Found from
Florida to Brazil.

Hogfish
Lachnolaimus maximus

Fairly large member of the Labridae family with a pointed head. Recognisable principally by the first rays of the dorsal fin, which are very developed. Whitish, with a dark bar along the back, stretching from the mouth to the tail. Prefers sandy seabeds where itlikes to dig for its prey. Measures up to 90 centimetres. Found from North Carolina to Brazil.

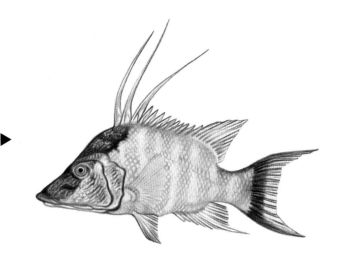

Bluehead wrasse
Thalassoma bifasciatum

Elongated, compressed body, with colouring which varies greatly according to age. In adults the body is greeny at the rear and bluish at the front with black and white stripes in between. The young fish are yellowish. It is found in a great number of different habitats. Measures up to 18 centimetres. Found from Florida to Venezuela.

Puddingwife
Halichoeres radiatus

Very deep body, blue-greenish in colour, with yellow-edged caudal fin. This is an uncommon fish and is hard to approach, as it swims continuously and is also very suspicious. Measures up to 50 centimetres. Found from North Carolina to Brazil.

Slippery dick
Halichoeres bivittatus

Labrid with deep, tapering body with a large caudal fin. Extremely variable colouring, but prevalently greenish. A horizontal dark band runs along the sides. The caudal fin lobes have dark tips. It is found in various different habitats, from coral reefs to sandy seabeds to underwater meadows. Measures up to 26 centimetres. Found from North Carolina to Brazil.

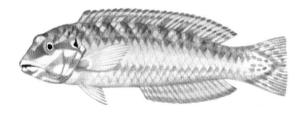

Creole wrasse
Clepticus parrae

Large Labridae with tapering body. The lobes of the dorsal and anal fins are pointed and the tail is slightly lunar-shaped. Adult fish are dark purple, with a yellowish rear part and a pale mout. It prefers the deepest parts of the reef where it forms large shoals before sunset. Measures up to 30 centimetres. Found from North Carolina to the Gulf of Mexico.

SCARIDAE FAMILY

Blue parrotfish
Scarus coeruleus

Tapered, robust, body. Adult males have a characteristic frontal bump which modifies the front profile of the snout. Mainly blue in colour. Feeds principally on algae and for this reason it moves swiftly from one part of the reef to another. Measures up to 90 centimetres. Found from Maryland to Brazil.

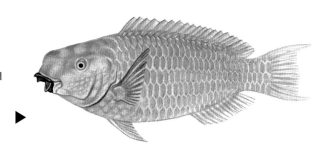

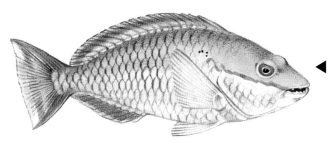

Queen parrotfish
Scarus vetula

Blue-green parrotfish with scales edged in pinky-orange. The nose has broad blue stripes around the mouth and close to the eyes. Lives on coral reefs up to 25 metres in depth and measures up to 60 centimetres. Found from Florida to Argentina.

Spotlight parrotfish
Sparisoma viride

Mainly green in colour. With yellowy-orange slanting bars on its head and on the caudal fin and a yellow mark on the operculum. Reasonably common where coral seabeds alternate with areas rich in algae. Measures up to 50 centimetres. Found from Florida to Brazil.

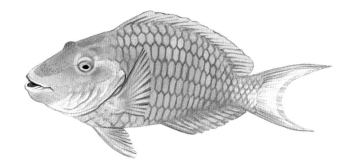

Red-banded parrotfish
Sparisoma aurofrenatum

Green parrotfish with red and orange shading. Has an orange bar at each side of the mouth and fins shaded with purple. Prefers reefs where there is an abundance of algae. Measures up to 35 centimetres. Found from Florida to Brazil.

OPISTHOGNATHIDAE FAMILY

Yellowhead jawfish
Opistognathus aurifrons

Small, bottom-dwelling fish with elongated, tapering body ending in a short but powerful head, with large eyes. Colouring is blue with a yellowish head. Lives on the bottom of the ocean close to a den it digs itself, ready to take shelter. Measures up to 10 centimetres. Found from Florida to Venezuela.

SPHYRAENIDAE FAMILY

Great barracuda
Sphyraena barracuda

Tapering, sub-cylindrical body with a long, pointed snout and prominent lower jaw. The two dorsal fins are clearly separate. The caudal fin is slightly lunar-shaped, with pointed lobes. Colouring is silvery with dark vertical bands and small spots near the caudal fin. Lives in coastal waters above coral, sandy or meadowland seabeds. Measures up to 2 metres. Found in all circumtropical waters.

SCOMBRIDAE FAMILY

Cero
Scomberomorus regalis

Very tapering body, caudal peduncle has numerous small dorsal and pelvic fins. Characteristic forked tail. Silver body with a series of dark blotches surrounding a gold, horizontal, stripe. Lives in open waters along the outer slopes of the reef. Measures up to 1.2 metres. Found from Massachusetts to Brazil.

BLENNIDAE FAMILY

Red-mouthed blenny
Ophioblennius atlanticus

Blenny with compressed body and blunt nose. The mouth has distinctive big lips. Dark-coloured with yellow or pink shading on the pectoral and caudal fins. A territorial fish, it prefers rocky seabeds and the parts of the reef closest to the surface. Measures up to 13 centimetres. Found from North Carolina to Brazil.

GOBIDAE FAMILY

Neon goby
Gobiosoma oceanops

Small goby, easily recognisable by its dark colouring, on which two fluorescent-blue horizontal stripes stand out. Cleaner fish, which forms groups with others of its species in the characteristic "service stations". Measures up to 5 centimetres. Found from Florida to Honduras.

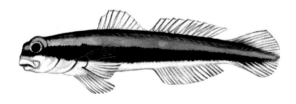

Cleaner goby
Gobiosoma genie

Small goby with a dark-coloured back and pale underside, with black streaks and a yellow-V-shaped mark between the eyes. Cleaner fish which forms shoals in certain particular areas of the reef. Measures up to 4 centimetres. Found in the Caribbean.

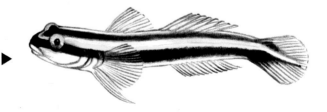

ACANTHURIDAE FAMILY

Surgeonfish
Acanthurus chirurgus

Surgeonfish with deep, compressed, body with a distinctive set of dark vertical bars, sometimes more clearly visible than others. This species usually lives alone, or with other surgeonfish, close to the reef. Measures up to 25 centimetres. Fround from Massachusetts to Brazil.

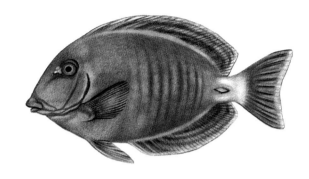

Surgeonfish
Acanthurus chirurgus

Surgeonfish with deep, compressed, body with a distinctive set of dark vertical bars, sometimes more clearly visible than others. This species usually lives alone, or with other surgeonfish, close to the reef. Measures up to 25 centimetres. Fround from Massachusetts to Brazil.

Bahia surgeonfish
Acanthurus bahianus

Surgeonfish with colouring varying from bluey grey to dark brown. Light-coloured spokes surround the eyes. Prefers flat or slightly-sloping coral seabeds. Measures up to 35 centimetres. Found from Massacusetts to Brazil.

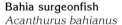

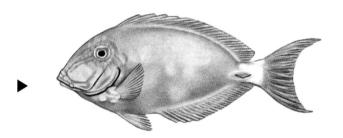

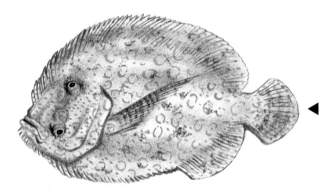

BOTHIDAE FAMILY

Ocellated turbot
Bothus lunatus

Identifiable by the series of ocellar spots on the body and the small bluish marks on the fins. Has a very elongated pelvic fin which is often kept erect. Lives on sandy seabeds or ones covered in detritus, where its ability to change colour enables it to camouflage itself and hide. Measures up to 40 centimetres. Found from Florida to Brazil.

Fam. BALISTIDI

Ocellated turbot
Bothus lunatus

Identifiable by the series of ocellar spots on the body and the small bluish marks on the fins. Has a very elongated pelvic fin which is often kept erect. Lives on sandy seabeds or ones covered in detritus, where its ability to change colour enables it to camouflage itself and hide. Measures up to 40 centimetres. Found from Florida to Brazil.

Grey triggerfish
Balistes capriscus

Greyish triggerfish, with small bluish spots on the back and fins.
Lives alone or in small groups near rocky seabeds or ones
which are rich in vegetation. Measures up to 30 centimetres.
Found from Nova Scotia to Argentina.

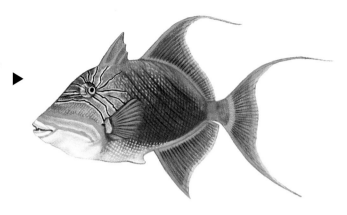

Black durgon
Melichthys niger

Bluish-black body with bluish stripes at the base of the dorsal
and anal fins. Lives in small groups along the outer reef wall, to
depths of 60 metres. Measures up to 50 centimetres. Found in
circumtropical seas.

argasso triggerfish
Xanthichthys ringens

Bright blue triggerfish with compressed, oval-shaped body,
with three opercular black streaks and a number of dark,
horizontal, bands made up of small markings. Prefers the
deepest parts of the reef. The young fish often live amongst
the floating sargasso. Measures up to 25 centimetres. Found
from North Carolina to Brazil.

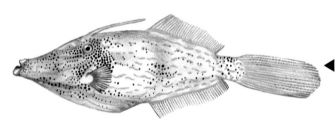

MONACANTHIDAE FAMILY
Scrawled filefish
Aluteres scriptus

Tapered body with pointed snout and broad tail. Colouring
characterised by irregular streaks and small blue markings.
A solitary fish, it lives in both lagoons and along the outer reef
wall, from where it heads for the open sea. Measures up to 1.1
metres. Common in circumtropical seas.

OSTRACIIDAE FAMILY
Smooth trunkfish
Lactrophrys triqueter

Fish with a triangular-shaped silhouette. Has large hexagonal
bony scales. Dark with numerous lighter-coloured marks.
Usually a solitary fish, it does sometimes form small groups.
Prefers coral seabeds although can be found too on sandy ones.
Measures up to 30 centimetres. Found from Massachusetts
to Brazil.

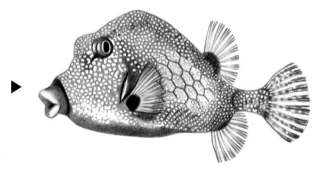

166

Variegated trunkfish
Lactophrys quadricornis

Fish with a triangular-shaped silhouette with a large caudal peduncle. Yellowish in colour with numerous blue streaks and marks. Usually a solitary fish, It prefers coral seabeds and meadowlands where it camouflages itself by changing colour. Measures up to 38 cetrimetres. Found from Massachusetts to Brazil.

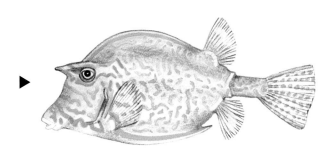

TETRAODONTIDAE FAMILY

Longnose pufferfish
Canthigaster rostrata

Small pufferfish with a very pointed nose and a small, terminal, mouth. Dark colouring on the back and yellowish along the sides. Blue streaks and marks around the eyes, close to the mouth and on the tail. Prefers coral seabeds and meadowlands. Measures up to 11 centimetres. Found from Florida to Brazil.

Bandtail pufferfish
Sphoeroides spengleri

Elongated body, rounded at the front. The large nostrils are easily spotted on the head. A horizontal series of marks runs along the sides below the lateral line. This fish nearly always swims close to the seabed, whether meadowlands, coral or detritus-strewn. Measures up to 18 centimetres. Found from Massachusetts to Brazil.

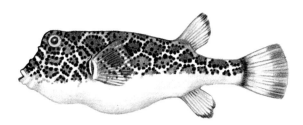

Chequered pufferfish
Sphoeroides testudineus

Round, spindle-shaped body, marked with light-coloured geometrical lines making a kind of grid. Prefers coastal bays, rocks and meadowlands. Not often found close to reefs. Measures up to 30 centimetres. Found from Bermuda to Brazil.

DIODONTIDE FAMILY
Burrfish
Diodon hystrix

Tapered body but has a large, rounded front end. Goggle eyes. The mouth has a single dental plate in each jaw. The skin is covered in spines which become erect when the animal swells up. During the day it tends to stay in caves or other poorly-illuminated areas of the reef. Measures up to 90 centimetres. Found in all circumtropical waters.

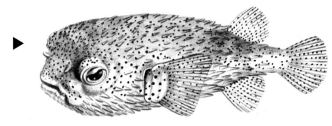

168 *A group of Atlantic spotted dolphins swims close to the sandy sea bed at Bahama Bank.*

Cover This picture shows the rich Caribbean sea bed where corals, gorgonians and sponges compete for living space. Photograph by Kurt Amsler

Back cover - top A grey angelfish (Pomacanthus arcuatus) seems to observe the photographer with curiosity. Photograph by Kurt Amsler

Back cover - bottom Two divers explore the Black Caves, lovely underwater grottoes in Honduras. Photograph by Kurt Amsler

The author, Kurt Amsler, thanks: his wife Isabelle Amsler, Christopher J. Allison, Renate Bernd, Joe M. Clark, John Englander, Chris Ery, Cathy Church, Rebecca Fitzgerald, Roger Fivat, Stephen Frink, Maurits Groen, Doris Hagenbucher, Bill Horn, Jacques Imbert, Ben Rose, Marco Rosenfelder, Ron Reed, Kenneth G. Thompson, Divemaster Kevin, Charles Novalez, Capt. Wesley, Frank Wirth, Aqua Safari, Crew of Seafever, Ocean Touren, Ocean Divers, Crew of Rembrandt van Rijn, Unexso.

PHOTOGRAPHIC CREDITS

Kurt Amsler: pages 1, 2-3, 6 (A, C), 7, 8, 9, 10, 11, 12, 13, 16, 17, 20, 21, 24, 25, 26, 27, 34 (C, D), 35, 38, 39, 54, 55, 58, 59, 62, 63, 66, 67, 68, 69, 72, 73, 76, 77, 80, 81, 84, 85, 86, 87, 90, 91, 100, 101, 104, 105, 108, 109, 112, 113, 118 (A, C), 119 (E, G, H, I), 122 (B, D, E), 123, 126, (A, B, C), 127, 130, 131 (F, G, H, J), 132, 133, 134 (A, B, C, D), 135, 138 (A, B, C, D, F), 139 (H, I, J); Marcello Bertinetti/Archivio White Star: pages 6 B, 114 A, 115 E; Daniel Deflorin: pages 6 D, 59 F, 114 B, 115 (C, D, F), 118 (B, D), 119 F, 122 (A, C), 126 D; Eleonora De Sabata: pages 40 A, 44 (A, B, C, D), 45, 48, 49, 52, 53; Stephen Frink/Archive Kurt Amsler: pages 30, 31, 34(A, B); Andrea and Antonella Ferrari: pages 40 (B, C), 41, 44 E, 52, 53, 68, 69; John Neuschwander: pages 134 D, 139 G, 142 (A, B, C, E), 143 (G, H); Dietmar Reimer/Archive Curaçao Toeristen Bureau Benelux, Rotterdam: page 142 D.

GW00600691

Text © 2012 by Jean Moss
Photographs © 2012 by Alexandra Grablewski
Illustrations © 2012 by The Taunton Press, Inc.
Charts & Schematics © 2012 by Jean Moss

The material was previously published in the
book *Sweet Shawlettes: 25 Irresistible Patterns
for Knitting Cowls, Capelets, and More*
(ISBN 978-1-60085-400-2)
First published in this format 2014

The Taunton Press
Inspiration for hands-on living®

The Taunton Press, Inc., 63 South Main Street
PO Box 5506, Newtown, CT 06470-5506
e-mail: tp@taunton.com

Cover design: Kimberly Adis
Interior design: Alison Wilkes
Illustrator: Jean Moss and Christine Erikson
Photographer: Alexandra Grablewski

Threads® is a trademark of The Taunton Press,
Inc., registered in the U.S. Patent and Trademark
Office.

The following names/manufacturers appearing in
Mini Scarves & Wraps are trademarks: Bergere de
France®, Berroco® Glacé™, Berroco Metallica
FX®, Rowan®.

Library of Congress Cataloging-in-Publication Data

Moss, Jean (Knitwear designer)
 Mini scarves & wraps : 6 easy projects to knit and
wear / Jean Moss.
    pages cm
 ISBN 978-1-62710-959-8
 1. Knitting--Patterns. 2. Scarves. I. Title. II. Title:
Mini scarbes and wraps.
 TT825.M68323 2014
 746.43'2--dc23
                                  2014025347
Printed in the United States of America
10 9 8 7 6 5 4 3 2 1

Contents

Garland Necklet

Get a touch of Venetian pizzazz with this necklet of flowers—a versatile addition to any wardrobe. Although the yarn I've used came out of my stash, many other fancy yarns will do. This is a great project for knitting up a quick gift, with no fuss about gauge or yarns. Just find your own mix of texture, luster, and glitz, and get out there and sparkle!

SKILL LEVEL
Easy

FINISHED MEASUREMENTS
65 in. (165 cm) long

YARN
Colorway 1 (p. 4)
Bergere de France® Tulle
172 yd. (160 m) per 50 g ball:
1 ball each Pink (A) and Green (C)
Rowan® Mulberry Silk
164 yd. (150 m) per 50 g hank:
1 hank Magenta (B)
Berroco® Glacé™
75 yd. (69 m) per 50 g hank:
1 hank 2846 (D)
Colinette Zanziba
103 yd. (94 m) per 100 g hank:
1 hank Bright Charcoal (E)

Colorway 2 (opposite)
Rowan Pure Silk DK
137 yd. (125 m) per 50 g ball:
1 ball Firefly 162 (A)
Louisa Harding Sari Ribbon
66 yd. (60 m) per 50 g ball:
1 ball Flame (B)
Berroco Metallic FX®
85 yd. (78 m) per 25 g hank:
1 hank Gold 1001 (C)
Rowan Shimmer

191 yd. (175 m) per 25 g ball:
1 ball Jet 95 (D)
Rowan Chunky Chenille
151 yd. (140 m) per 100 g ball:
1 ball Parchment 383 (E)
From my stash
Unlabeled viscose ribbon
1 ball Burgundy (F)

NOTIONS
1 pair size 3 U.S. (3.25 mm)
double-pointed needles for Colorway 1 (B)
and Colorway 2 (D)
1 pair size 6 U.S. (4 mm) double-pointed
needles for Colorway 2 (A)
1 pair size 8 U.S. (5 mm) double-pointed
needles for Colorway 1 (D) and Colorway 2 (C),
(E), and (F)
1 pair size 10 U.S. (7 mm) double-pointed
needles for Colorway 1 (A) and (C)
and Colorway 2 (E)
1 pair size 11 U.S. (8 mm) double-pointed
needles for Colorway 2 (B)
Tapestry needle

GAUGE
For once, gauge is not important!

continued on p. 5

TO MAKE NECKLET

Work 2 lengths of I-cord (p. 28), one each in (C) and (D) to measure 65 in. (165 cm) when braided. To do this, make each cord slightly longer than the given length and then sew together at one end the 2 cords plus either 1 strand of (E), if using Colorway 1, or 3 strands of (E), if using Colorway 2. Braid the 3 strands until the correct length is achieved. Fasten off and sew together at the end to secure the braid.

For Colorway 1 (opposite)
Make 5 cabbage roses in (B) and 3 florets in (A).

For Colorway 2 (p. 3)
Make 3 cabbage roses in (F), 2 in (A), and 3 florets in (B).

Cabbage Rose

Cast on 10 sts.
Row 1 Knit.
Row 2 Purl.
Row 3 Knit in front and back of every stitch. To do so, knit the next st but do not take the st off LH needle. Knit the st again through the back loop and then slip the original st off LH needle—20 sts.
Row 4 Purl.
Row 5 Knit in front and back of every st—40 sts.
Row 6 Purl.
Row 7 Knit in front and back of every st—80 sts.
Row 8 Purl.
Cast off. Twist into a rose shape and secure with the end of knitting.

Florets

Loosely cast on 21 sts. Work 4 rows in Stockinette St. Pass all sts one at a time over the 1st st, then fasten off. Roll the cast-on edge into the cast-off edge by making 1 twist to form a floret, then sew into place.

FINISHING

Using the tapestry needle, neatly sew the finished pieces to the cord (D) at the following intervals, as shown on the schematic:
Sew 1 floret at each end.
Sew 1 rose about 5 in. (12.7 cm) from each end.
Then at one end only, beginning about 5 in. (12.7 cm) from the last sewn rose, sew 1 rose, 1 floret, and 2 more roses all evenly spaced about 5 in. (12.7 cm) apart.

Garland Schematic

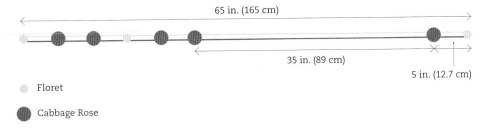

65 in. (165 cm)

35 in. (89 cm)

5 in. (12.7 cm)

⫘ Floret

● Cabbage Rose

In colorway 2 (p. 3), a strand of jet yarn winds through the design and highlights the braided cord; in colorway 1 (opposite), a hint of pale green complements brilliant magenta and pale pink cabbage roses.

Evergreen Scarf

This leafy scarf keeps you warm and stylish on the chilliest days, but the cashmerino yarn is light enough to take you through the spring, too. The bulk of the knitting is garter stitch, reversible, and stress-free. Make the scarf your own by playing around with variations on the leaves. Keep the stitchwork simple with just one type of leaf, or use all three patterns in different colors as I did. You could also try striping the garter stitch for a scarf as colorful as the leaves. The choice is yours!

SKILL LEVEL
Easy

FINISHED MEASUREMENTS
Small: 2 in. (5 cm) wide, 52 in. (132 cm) long
Large: 2 in. (5 cm) wide, 68 in. (173 cm) long

YARN
Rowan Cashsoft DK
126 yd. (115 m) per 50 g ball:
2 balls Lime 509 (A)
1 ball Spruce 541 (B)
1 ball Cashew 522 (C)

NOTIONS
1 pair size 6 U.S. (4 mm) needles
or size to obtain gauge
Size D-3 (3.25 mm) crochet hook
Stitch holder
Tapestry needle

GAUGE
24 sts and 48 rows = 4 in. (10 cm) in Garter Stitch (p. 28)

Note
Slip the first stitch and knit into the back of the last stitch on every row to make a neat selvage.

TO MAKE SCARF
Fringe 1
Using (A), cast on 6 sts and, working in Garter St. throughout, cont until work measures 11½ in. (29 cm), ending on a WS row. Place stitches on the holder.

Fringe 2
Using (A), cast on 6 sts and, working in Garter St. throughout, cont until work measures 8½ in. (21.5 cm), ending on a WS row.
Next row (RS) Work across all 6 sts of Fringe 2, and then all 6 sts of Fringe 1—12 sts.
Cont until work measures 28 in. (71 cm) from the top of the fringes to make a scarf that wraps once around the neck, or 44 in. (112 cm) to make a scarf that wraps twice.
Cont to work the scarf as follows:
Work across the first 6 sts (Fringe 1), then join a new ball of yarn and work to the end (Fringe 2).
Working the 2 pieces separately, when Fringe 2 measures 8½ in. (21.5 cm), ending on a RS row, cast off.
Cont working Fringe 1 until the total length measures 11½ in. (29 cm), ending on a WS row. Cast off.

FINISHING
Using the tapestry needle, securely weave in ends.

continued on p. 9

Large Stockinette Stitch Leaf (Make 10)

Using (B), cast on 5 sts.

Row 1 (RS) K2, yo, k1, yo, k2—7 sts.

Row 2 (and all WS rows) Purl.

Row 3 K3, yo, k1, yo, k3—9 sts.

Row 5 K4, yo, k1, yo, k4—11 sts.

Row 7 Ssk, k7, k2tog—9 sts.

Row 9 Ssk, k5, k2tog—7 sts.

Row 11 Ssk, k3, k2tog—5 sts.

Row 13 Ssk, k1, k2tog—3 sts.

Row 15 Sl 1, k2tog, psso—1 st.

Fasten off rem st.

Small Stockinette Stitch Leaf (Make 8)

Using (C), cast on 5 sts.

Row 1 (RS) K2, yo, k1, yo, k2—7 sts.

Row 2 (and all WS rows) Purl.

Row 3 Ssk, k3, k2tog—5 sts.

Row 5 Ssk, k1, k2tog—3 sts.

Row 7 Sl 1, k2tog, psso—1 st.

Fasten off rem st.

Garter Stitch Leaf (Make 10)

Note: M1 by knitting into the st below the next st and, without slipping the made st off the needle, knit into next st.

Using (A), cast on 9 sts.

Row 1 K3, sl2tog kwise, k1, p2sso, k3—7 sts.

Row 2 K1, m1, k2, p1, k2, m1, k1—9 sts.

Row 3 K3, sl2tog kwise, k1, p2sso, k3—7 sts.

Row 4 K1, m1, k2, p1, k2, m1, k1—9 sts.

Row 5 K3, sl2tog kwise, k1, p2sso, k3—7 sts.

Row 6 K3, p1, k3.

Row 7 K2, sl2tog kwise, k1, p2sso, k2—5 sts.

Row 8 K2, p1, k2.

Row 9 K1, sl2tog kwise, k1, p2sso, k1—3 sts.

Row 10 K1, p1, k1.

Row 11 Sl2tog kwise, k1, p2sso—1 st.

Fasten off rem st.

Using the crochet hook, make 28 single crochet chains (see p. 28), each about 2 in. (5 cm) long. Attach one end of each chain to the Scarf and the other end to a leaf, as shown on the schematic.

Evergreen Schematic

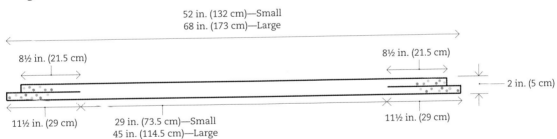

52 in. (132 cm)—Small
68 in. (173 cm)—Large

8½ in. (21.5 cm)

8½ in. (21.5 cm)

2 in. (5 cm)

11½ in. (29 cm)

29 in. (73.5 cm)—Small
45 in. (114.5 cm)—Large

11½ in. (29 cm)

- Garter Stitch Leaf in (A)

- Large Stockinette Stitch Leaf in (B)

- Small Stockinette Stitch Leaf in (C)

Penumbra Cowl

Add a touch of magic to your knitting with this simple Japanese technique—shadow knitting. Alternate rows of light and shade, throw in a few sculptured stitches, and *presto*, an illusion occurs, tricking the eye into believing the colors are changing. I'm a big fan of pop art, and shadow knitting is a wonderful tool for creating bold optical knits. Wool/cotton yarn ensures fabulous stitch definition.

SKILL LEVEL
Intermediate

FINISHED MEASUREMENTS
12½ in. (31.7 cm) high, 25 in. (63.5 cm) around

YARN
Rowan Wool Cotton
123 yd. (113 m) per 50 g ball:
2 balls Inky 908 (A)
2 balls Antique 900 (B)

NOTIONS
Size 6 U.S. (4 mm) circular needle
or size to obtain gauge
Stitch marker
Tapestry needle

GAUGE
20 sts and 40 rows = 4 in. (10 cm) in Penumbra Chart pattern

TO MAKE COWL
Using yarn (A), cast on 124 sts and place marker. Join in the round, taking care not to twist the sts.
Work 6 rows of Garter St. in the round (p. 28), knitting and purling alternate rounds.
Attach yarn (B) and work the Penumbra Chart, rep the 31 sts 4 times on every round.
Work all 44 rounds twice, then work the first 22 rounds once.
Using yarn (A) only, work 6 rows in Garter St., knitting and purling alternate rounds.
Cast off as follows: K1, *pass this st back to the LH needle and k2tog; rep from * across row.

FINISHING
Using the tapestry needle, securely weave in ends.

continued on p. 13

Penumbra Chart

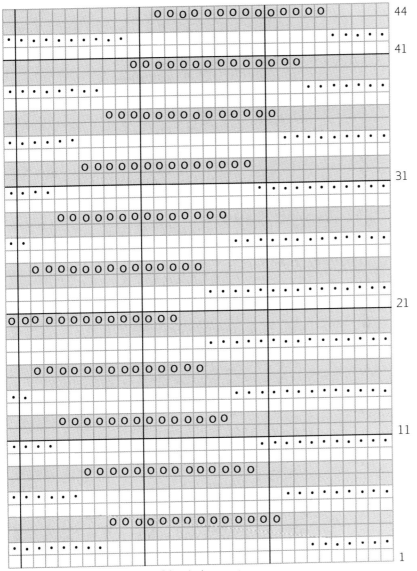

44

41

31

21

11

1

31-stitch repeat

The NB Chart is read from right to left on all rounds.

☐ K, using (B)

▨ K, using (A)

⦁ P, using (B)

O P, using (A)

Penumbra Schematic

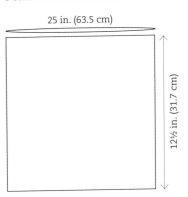

25 in. (63.5 cm)

12½ in. (31.7 cm)

At first glance, this appears to be a simple striped cowl. But look again and you'll see wide zigzags running top to bottom through the pattern.

Harlequin Cape

Hone your entrelac skills on this snug cape—which easily transforms into a collar. I chose Rowan's Colourscape yarn so that I could sit back and enjoy knitting the entrelac blocks knowing the colors would take care of themselves. Other handpaints should perform just as well, as long as you work a swatch first. You can then watch and wonder as you knit—the hues changing gradually before your eyes and fitting the blocks like magic!

SKILL LEVEL
Intermediate

FINISHED MEASUREMENTS
40 in. (101.6 cm) wide, 7 in. (18 cm) long

YARN
Rowan Colourscape Chunky
175 yd. (160 m) per 100 g skein:
2 skeins Carnival 430

NOTIONS
1 pair size 10½ U.S. (7 mm) needles
or size to obtain gauge
Size H-8 U.S. (5 mm) crochet hook
Large button

GAUGE
14 sts and 18 rows = 4 in. (10 cm) in
Stockinette Stitch (p. 29)

TO MAKE CAPE
Loosely cast on 88 sts and work in entrelac as follows:

Base triangles
First base triangle *P2, turn, k2, turn, p3, turn.
Cont in this way, purling 1 st more from the left needle each time, until there are 8 sts on the RH needle.
Do not turn.
Rep from * 10 times—11 base triangles.

First row of blocks
First edging triangle K2, turn, p2, turn, kfb, then skpo, turn, p3, turn, kfb, k1, then skpo, turn, p4, turn.
Cont in this way, dec 1 st from the base triangles on knit rows each time until kfb, k5, skpo has been worked.
Do not turn; leave these 8 sts.
Blocks *Pick up and knit 8 sts from the row ends of the first base triangle, turn, p8, turn, k7, skpo, turn, p8.
Cont in this way until all sts of the first base triangle have been decreased. Do not turn.
Rep from * for 9 more blocks across the row, picking up sts between the base triangles.
Second edging triangle Pick up and knit 8 sts from the row ends of the last base triangle, turn, p2tog, p6, turn, k7, turn. P2tog, p5, turn, k6.
Cont in this way, dec at the beg of every purl row until 1 st rem, turn, slip st onto the RH needle.

continued on p. 16

Whether neatly centered or worn to one side, a large, square button will highlight the woven-band effect of the entrelac technique.

Second row of blocks (no side triangles)
Blocks *P1, pick up and purl 7 sts, turn, k8, turn. P7, p2tog, turn, k8.

Cont in this way until all sts of the first row block have been decreased. Do not turn.

Work 10 more blocks in this way, picking up 8 sts.

Third row of blocks
Work as for the first row of blocks, working into the second row of blocks instead of into the base triangles.

Closing triangles
P1, *pick up and purl 7 sts from row-ends of the first side triangle, turn, k8, turn. P2tog, p5, p2tog, turn, k7, turn. P2tog, p4, p2tog, turn, k6, turn.

Cont in this way until *turn, k2* has been worked, turn, p1, p2tog, turn, k2, turn, p3tog—1 st rem.

Rep from * to complete the other 10 closing triangles.

Fasten off rem st.

FINISHING
Securely weave in ends.

Press lightly (p. 28) on the WS.

Attach the button along the cast-on edge as desired. Using the crochet hook, make a single crochet chain (p. 28) about 4 in. (10 cm) long. Bend the chain into a loop, and attach it to the side edge of the Cape at the apex of the first base triangle.

Harlequin Schematic

40 in. (101.6 cm)

7 in. (18 cm)

Thoughts on Color

Color has a powerful effect on our everyday lives. Here are some fun tips for choosing just the right color.

Red is a symbol of protection and caution in many cultures. It is powerful and passionate.

Blue is at once uplifting, relaxing, serene, and inspiring.

Yellow is the brightest color in the spectrum. It lifts the spirits and brings a sense of joy.

Green is nature's hallmark, said to encourage good fortune and healing.

Purple is a symbol of royalty, wealth, ritual, creativity, and eccentricity.

Neutrals, such as ivory, taupe, and buff, borrow their hue from the natural world and are symbolic of wholeness and unity.

Metallics, such as silver, gold, bronze, and copper, bring life and oomph to the world around us, and in many cultures are thought to deflect the "evil eye" and inspire creativity.

Double-wrapped, the Harlequin Cape easily converts to a collar that will keep your neck warm and cozy on cold days.

Ceilidh Shawlette

I love to dance and I've always adored tartans—and this shawlette is inspired
by both, taking its name from the Gaelic word for *party*. As a child growing up in
a Lancashire mill town, I wore a kilt every winter—a bold splash of color during those
cold, gray days. There's something joyous about the way a kilt swings, giving the
wearer built-in sashay. If you're lucky enough to have your own clan plaid, just recolor
the chart to match. The tweedy and sumptuous alpaca yarn is light yet warm, making
this shawlette the perfect piece to wear to the next ceilidh!

SKILL LEVEL
Experienced

FINISHED MEASUREMENTS
26 in. (66 cm) wide at shoulder, 10 in.
(25.5 cm) long without collar

YARN
Rowan Lima
109 yd. (100 m) per 50 g ball:
4 balls Machu Picchu 885 (A)
1 ball each Titicaca 883 (B),
Guatemala 892 (C), La Paz 891 (D),
Puno 886 (F), and Nazca 887 (G)
2 balls Chile 882 (E)

NOTIONS
1 pair size 9 U.S. (5.5 mm) needles
or size to obtain gauge
Size 7 U.S. (4.5 mm) circular needle
Size 8 U.S. (5 mm) circular needle
Size G-6 U.S. (4 mm) crochet hook
Stitch markers
Tapestry needle

GAUGE
20 sts and 26 rows = 4 in. (10 cm) in Ceilidh Chart pattern

Note
For information on knitting intarsia, see p. 28.

TO MAKE SHAWLETTE
Using size 9 U.S. (5.5 mm) needles and yarn (A),
cast on 51 sts.
Work all 30 rows of the Ceilidh Chart, centering the
chart as follows:
RS rows Work the last 5 sts of the chart, work all
20 sts twice, work the first 6 sts.
WS rows Work the last 6 sts of the chart, work all
20 sts twice, work the first 5 sts.
Cont in this way until the piece measures 46 in.
(117 cm).
Cast off.

FINISHING
Place markers 10 in. (25.5 cm) from the cast-on and cast-
off edges along top side edge.
Position the shawl's cast-off edge on a flat surface
in front of you. Arrange the shawl's length counter-
clockwise, so that the cast-on edge completely overlaps
the cast-off edge, ending along its side edge, forming a

continued on p. 20

Ceilidh Chart

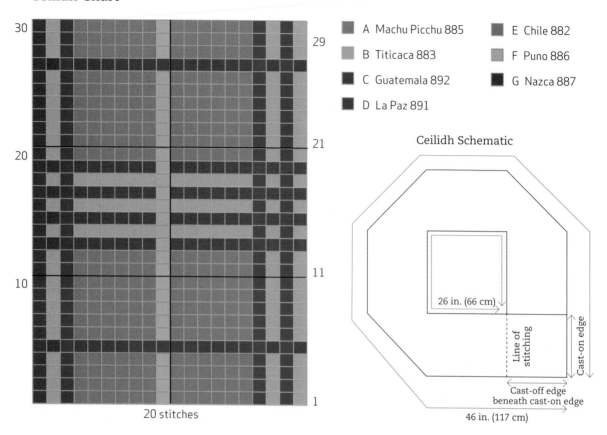

30

29

20

21

10

11

1

20 stitches

A Machu Picchu 885

B Titicaca 883

C Guatemala 892

D La Paz 891

E Chile 882

F Puno 886

G Nazca 887

Ceilidh Schematic

26 in. (66 cm)

Line of stitching

Cast-on edge

Cast-off edge
beneath cast-on edge

46 in. (117 cm)

circle shape, as indicated on the schematic (above). Using the tapestry needle, slip stitch along the inside edge where the two ends overlap to join the ends into a circle.

Collar
Using size 7 U.S. (4.5 mm) circular needle and yarn (A), pick up and knit 150 sts around the inner neckline, beginning at the center back with RS facing.
Round 1 *K1, p1; rep from * around.
Rep this round until the collar measures 6½ in. (16.5 cm).
Change to size 8 U.S. (5 mm) circular needle and cont as set until the collar measures 13¾ in. (35 cm), then change to yarn (E) and work 1 row. Loosely cast off in rib.

Using yarn (A), with RS facing, work 1 row of single crochet (p. 28) as follows:
1. Through two thicknesses of cast-on edge and last 10 in. (25.5 cm) of shawl.
2. Through two thicknesses along cast-off edge and first 10 in. (25.5 cm) of shawl.
3. Through one thickness around inside edge of shawl.
4. Through one thickness from start of cast-on edge along side edge for 6 in. (15.2 cm) then through two thicknesses over remaining 4 in. (10 cm).
Using the tapestry needle, weave the ends into like colors. Press lightly (p. 28) on the WS, avoiding the ribbing.

On the final crocheted
seam from side edge to
neck, leave the first 6 in.
(15 cm) open so that the
end hangs down. Hold
this flap in place with
a traditional kilt pin—
choices range from the
very basic to ornate family
crests and Celtic symbols.

Treasure Jabot

Bowl your friends over in this stunning pure silk jabot. Originally made of cambric or lace, the jabot has had many incarnations over hundreds of years, from military and traditional Scottish dress to neckwear for judges—and also pirates. I love pattern-on-pattern, and entrelac works well with frills to emphasize texture. However, despite looking intricate, this pattern is a straightforward knit once you get the hang of entrelac. The frills are a movable feast; I've got three, but you can knit more or less, depending on how frivolous you're feeling.

SKILL LEVEL
Intermediate

FINISHED MEASUREMENTS
3 in. (7.5 cm) high, 39 in. (100 cm) wide without frills, 46 in. (117 cm) with frills

YARN
Rowan Pure Silk DK
137 yd. (125 m) per 50 g ball:
2 balls Firefly 162

NOTIONS
1 pair size 5 U.S. (3.75 mm) needles, *or size to obtain gauge,* plus 1 extra needle
Size F-5 U.S. (3.25 mm) crochet hook
2 stitch holders

GAUGE
24 sts and 28 rows = 4 in. (10 cm) in Stockinette Stitch (p. 29)

TO MAKE JABOT
Loosely cast on 132 sts and work in entrelac as follows:

Base triangles
First base triangle *P2, turn, k2, turn, p3, turn.
Cont in this way, purling 1 st more from the LH needle each time, until there are 6 sts on the RH needle.
Do not turn. Rep from * 21 times—22 base triangles.

First row of blocks
First edging triangle K2, turn, p2 turn, kfb, then skpo, turn, p3, turn, kfb, k1, then skpo, turn, p4, turn.
Cont in this way, dec 1 st from the base triangles on knit rows each time until *kfb, k3, skpo* has been worked. Do not turn; leave these 6 sts.
Blocks *Pick up and knit 6 sts from the row ends of the 1st base triangle, turn, p6, turn, k5, skpo, turn, p6.
Cont in this way until all sts of the 1st base triangle have been decreased. Do not turn. Rep from * for 20 more blocks across the row, picking up sts between the base triangles.

continued on p. 25

For a touch of classic style, consider adding a vintage gold tiepin horizontally across the top of the frills.

24

Second edging triangle Pick up and k6 sts from the row ends of the last base triangle, turn, p2tog, p4, turn, k5, turn. P2tog, p3, turn, k4.
Cont in this way, dec at the beg of every purl row until 1 st rem, turn, slip st onto the RH needle.

Second Row of Blocks (No Side Triangles)
Blocks *P1, pick up and purl 5 sts, turn, k6, turn. P5, p2tog, turn, k6.
Cont in this way until all sts of the 1st row of blocks have been decreased. Do not turn. Work 21 more blocks in this way, picking up 6 sts.

Third Row of Blocks
Work as for 1st row (including edging triangles), working into the 2nd row of blocks instead of into the base triangles.

Closing Triangles
P1, *pick up and purl 5 sts from row-ends of the 1st side triangle, turn, k6, turn. P2tog, p3, p2tog, turn, k5, turn. P2tog, p2, p2tog, turn, k4, turn.
Cont in this way until *turn, k2* has been worked, turn, p1, p2tog, turn, k2, turn, p3tog—1 st rem.
Rep from * to complete the other 21 closing triangles.
Fasten off rem st.

Frills (Make 2)
**Cast on 50 sts and knit 2 rows. Then work 8 rows in Stockinette St.
Next row K1, *k3tog; rep from * to last st, k1—18 sts. **
Cont working these sts for a further 8 rows in Stockinette St., then leave on holder.
Rep from ** to **, then place the 2nd frill on top of the 1st frill and, using the 3rd needle, purl the front and back needles together on the next row—18 sts.
Cont working these sts for a further 8 rows in Stockinette St., then leave on holder.
Rep from ** to ** once more, then place the new frill on top of first 2 frills and join together as before, using 3 needles—18 sts.
With RS facing, pick up and knit 18 sts along the side edge of Jabot. Then place together the right sides of a joined frill and jabot and work a Three-Needle Bind-Off (p. 29). Attach the other frill to other end in the same way.

FINISHING
Securely weave in ends. Press lightly (p. 28) on the WS.
With RS facing, work 1 row of single crochet (p. 28) along the cast-on and cast-off edges.

Treasure Schematic

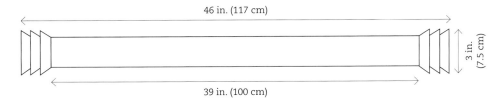

46 in. (117 cm)

3 in. (7.5 cm)

39 in. (100 cm)

Knitting Abbreviations

alt alternate

approx approximately

beg beginning

ch chain (single crochet)

cm centimeter(s)

cn cable needle

cont continue

dec decrease

ev every

g gram(s)

in. inch(es)

inc increase

k knit

k2tog knit 2 sts together

k3tog knit 3 sts together

kfb knit st in front and back

kwise knitwise

LH left hand

m meter(s)

mm millimeter(s)

p purl

p2tog purl 2 sts together

p2tog-b p1, return this st to LH needle, then with point of RH needle, pass next st over and off needle; then slip st back to RH needle

p3tog purl 3 sts together

pm place marker

psso pass slipped st over

rem remaining

rep repeat

RH right hand

RS right side

s2kpo sl2tog kwise, k1, pass 2 slipped sts over

sk skip

sk2po slip 1 st wyib, k2tog, psso

skpo slip 1 st, k1, pass the slipped st over

sl slip

sl2tog slip 2 sts together

ssk (slip, slip, knit)—slip next 2 sts knitwise, one at a time, to RH needle. Insert tip of LH needle into fronts of these sts from left to right and knit them together.

st(s) stitch(es)

tbl through back loop

tog together

w & t wrap yarn and turn work

WS wrong side

wyib with yarn in back

yd. yard(s)

yo yarn over needle to make 1 st

Needle and Hook Sizing

Knitting Needles

Millimeter Range	U.S. Size Range
2.25 mm	1
2.75 mm	2
3.25 mm	3
3.5 mm	4
3.75 mm	5
4 mm	6
4.5 mm	7
5 mm	8
5.5 mm	9
6 mm	10
6.5 mm	10½
8 mm	11
9 mm	13
10 mm	15
12.75 mm	17
15 mm	19
19 mm	35
25 mm	50

Crochet Hooks

Millimeter Range	U.S. Size Range
2.25 mm	B-1
2.75 mm	C-2
3.25 mm	D-3
3.5 mm	E-4
3.75 mm	F-5
4 mm	G-6
4.5 mm	7
5 mm	H-8
5.5 mm	I-9
6 mm	J-10
6.5 mm	K-10½
8 mm	L-11
9 mm	M/N-13
10 mm	N/P-15
15 mm	P/Q
16 mm	Q
19 mm	S

Special Stitches

Blocking and Pressing

Never underestimate the power of blocking and pressing! Small mistakes often become invisible when a piece is well presented. Some projects need pressing more than others, so I've included specific instructions to press in some projects.

Before blocking, neaten the selvages by sewing or weaving in all the ends along the sides or along color joins where appropriate. Then, using pins, block each piece of knitting to shape—this also gives you an opportunity to check the measurements. Gently press each piece on the WS, omitting ribbing, using a warm iron and a damp pressing cloth. Take special care with the edges.

Garter Stitch

Knit all rows or purl all rows.

I-Cord

Cast on 3 sts using a double-pointed needle, *slide these sts to the other end of the needle, then knit them using the yarn brought around from the other end. Rep from * to end.

Intarsia

A way of getting as many colors as you're able to handle into one row, this technique was once called picture knitting. It can create wonderful designs and it's not difficult, per se, but it can be fiddly and therefore off-putting to new knitters.

If the design has a background color, use separate balls of yarn for each of the contrast colors, stranding or weaving the main color behind. This cuts down on the number of ends to weave in later and gives the contrast colors a slightly raised effect, which helps define the pattern.

For intarsia with random shapes, use a separate length of yarn for each color every time it occurs, twisting the two colors around each other at the start and finish to avoid creating holes in the knitting. To eliminate tangles, wrap each length around a bobbin and let it dangle on the back of the work or use short lengths of yarn (no longer than 24 in. (61 cm) and straighten at the end of each row.

Single Crochet (U.K. Double Crochet)

I often use crochet to finish off a shawlette. In this booklet, I use the U.S. term *single crochet;* U.K. knitters should remember that terminology for basic crochet stitches like single crochet and double crochet in the U.S. translates into double crochet and treble crochet, respectively, in the U.K.

Make a slip knot to begin.

Insert the hook into the next st.

Yo and pull a loop through the next st indicated in the pattern—2 loops are on the hook.

Yo and pull a loop through both loops on the hook, 1 single crochet completed.

Rep steps 1–3 as instructed in the pattern. (Illustration on the facing page.)

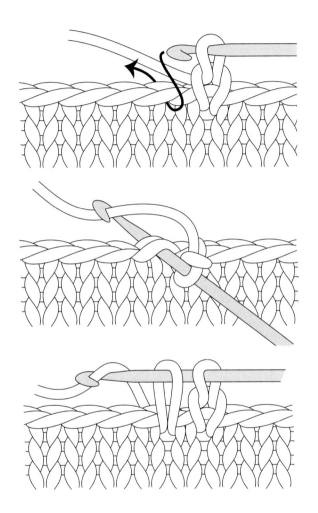

Stockinette Stitch

Knit on RS rows and purl on WS rows.

Three-Needle Bind-Off

This is a neat way of joining seams on the inside or decoratively on the outside, especially if the shoulder shaping uses short rows.

Place the work RS together, with the back sts on 1 needle and front sts on another. *Work 2 tog (1 from front needle and 1 from back needle). Rep from * once.

Cast off the first st over the second st. Continue to work 2 sts tog (1 front st and 1 back st) and cast off across. (Illustration below.)

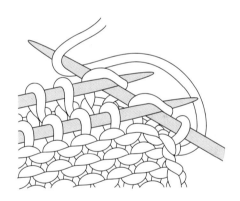

Standard Yarn Weights

Yarn Weight Symbol and Category Name	Super Fine 1	Fine 2	Light 3	Medium 4	Bulky 5	Super Bulky 6
Types of yarn in category	Sock, fingering, baby	Sport, baby	DK, light worsted	Worsted, afghan, Aran	Chunky, craft, rug	Bulky, roving
Knit gauge range in St st in 4 in.*	27–32 sts	23–26 sts	21–24 sts	16–20 sts	12–15 sts	6–11 sts
Recommended metric needle size	2.25–3.25 mm	3.25–3.75 mm	3.75–4.5 mm	4.5–5.5 mm	5.5–8 mm	8 mm and larger
Recommended U.S. needle size	1–3	3–5	5–7	7–9	9–11	11 and larger
Crochet gauge range in sc in 4 in.*	21–31 sts	16–20 sts	12–17 sts	11–14 sts	8–11 sts	5–9 sts
Recommended metric hook size	2.25–3.5 mm	3.5–4.5 mm	4.5–5.5 mm	5.5–6.5 mm	6.5–9 mm	9 mm and larger
Recommended U.S. hook size	B/1–E/4	E/4–7	7–I/9	I/9–K/10.5	K/10.5–M/13	M/13 and larger

*The information in this table reflects the most commonly used gauges and needle or hook sizes for the specific yarn categories.

Look for these other *Threads* Selects booklets at www.tauntonstore.com and wherever crafts are sold.

Prairie Girl Gifts
EAN: 9781621139492
8½ x 10⅞, 32 pages
Product# 078030
$9.95 U.S., $9.95 Can.

Pet Projects to Knit
EAN: 9781627100991
8½ x 10⅞, 32 pages
Product# 078034
$9.95 U.S., $9.95 Can.

Cute Pets to Knit
EAN: 9781627107747
8½ x 10⅞, 32 pages
Product# 078043
$9.95 U.S., $9.95 Can.

Button Jewelry
EAN: 9781627107808
8½ x 10⅞, 32 pages
Product# 078040
$9.95 U.S., $9.95 Can.

Bead Necklaces
EAN: 9781621137641
8½ x 10⅞, 32 pages
Product# 078002
$9.95 U.S., $9.95 Can.

Drop Earrings
EAN: 9781621137658
8½ x 10⅞, 32 pages
Product# 078003
$9.95 U.S., $9.95 Can.

Bead Bracelets
EAN: 9781621139515
8½ x 10⅞, 32 pages
Product# 078028
$9.95 U.S., $9.95 Can.

Crocheted Hearts & Flowers
EAN: 9781627107761
8½ x 10⅞, 32 pages
Product# 078044
$9.95 U.S., $9.95 Can.

Easy-to-Sew Flowers
EAN: 9781621138259
8½ x 10⅞, 32 pages
Product# 078017
$9.95 U.S., $9.95 Can.

Easy-to-Sew Tote Bags
EAN: 9781621138297
8½ x 10⅞, 32 pages
Product# 078021
$9.95 U.S., $9.95 Can.

Easy-to-Sew Gifts
EAN: 9781621138310
8½ x 10⅞, 32 pages
Product# 078023
$9.95 U.S., $9.95 Can.

Beaded Gifts
EAN: 9781627107730
8½ x 10⅞, 32 pages
Product# 078039
$9.95 U.S., $9.95 Can.

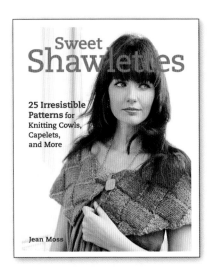
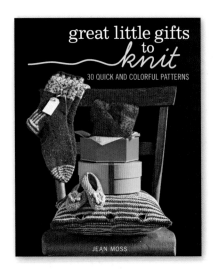

GW00600694

20
GREATEST HITS

THE
BEATLES

Wise Publications
London/New York/Sydney

Exclusive Distributors:
Music Sales Limited
8/9 Frith Street, London W1V 5TZ, England
Music Sales Pty. Limited
120 Rothschild Avenue, Rosebery, NSW 2018, Australia

This book © Copyright 1982 by
Wise Publications
ISBN 0-7119-02097
Order No. NO 18269

Love Me Do.

John Lennon and Paul McCartney.

From Me To You.

John Lennon and Paul McCartney.

Medium tempo, with a beat

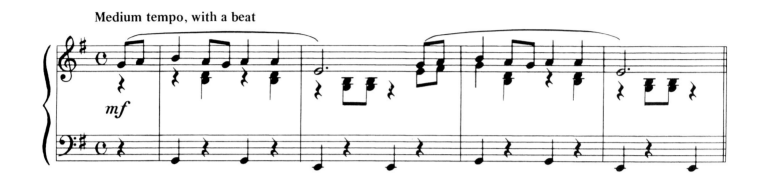

If there's an-y-thing that you want, If there's an-y-thing I can

do, Just call on me ___ and I'll send it a-long ___ with love, ___

lips that long to kiss_ you,_____ and keep you sat-is-fied. If there's

an-y-thing that you want, If there's an-y-thing I can do, just

call on me_ and I'll send it a-long_ with love,_ from me_ to you._

1. G Em
_____ If there's _____

2. G Em

She Loves You.

John Lennon and Paul McCartney.

Moderately, with a beat

She loves you, yeh, yeh, yeh, __ she loves you, yeh, yeh, yeh, __ she

loves you, yeh, yeh, yeh, __ yeh! _____ 1. You

1. think you've lost your love, __   Well, I saw her yes - ter - day - yi - yay.   It's
2. said you hurt her so, __   She al - most lost her mind, __   And
3. know it's up to you, __   I think it's on - ly fair, __

I Want To Hold Your Hand.

John Lennon and Paul McCartney.

19

Can't Buy Me Love.

John Lennon and Paul McCartney.

A Hard Day's Night.

John Lennon and Paul McCartney.

ev-'ry-thing seems__ to be al-right.   When I'm home__

feel-ing you hold- ing me tight,   tight.   Yeah,__ 3. It's been a

D. S. al ⊕ Coda 𝄋

⊕ *Coda*

right.   You know I feel___ al - right ___   You know I

feel al - right.__

I Feel Fine.

John Lennon and Paul McCartney.

Ticket To Ride.

John Lennon and Paul McCartney.

Help.

John Lennon and Paul McCartney.

© Copyright 1965 Northern Songs Limited, 24 Bruton Street, London W1.

Now I find   I've changed my mind,   I've o-pened up the doors. ⎫
I know that I just need you like I've nev - er done be-fore. ⎭

Help me if you

can. I'm feel - ing down _____   And I   do - ap - pre - ci - ate ___ you be-ing 'round. ___

Help me get ___ my feet back on the ground. _____

___ ___ Won't you please,   please ___ help ___ me? ___

please ___ help ___ me? ___   Help   me!   Help   me! ___   Oo.

Day Tripper.

John Lennon and Paul McCartney.

so _____ long _____ to find out, _____ and I found out.

Ah _____

Ah _____

Day Trip-per,

Day Trip-per, Yeh. _____

33

We Can Work It Out.

John Lennon and Paul McCartney.

Paperback Writer.

John Lennon and Paul McCartney.

dirt - y sto - ry of a dirt - y man,___ and his cling - ing wife does-n't un-der-stand. His
real - ly like it you can have the rights,___ It could make a mil - lion for you ov - er - night. If you

son is work-ing for the Dail - y Mail;___ It's a stead - y job___ But he wants to be a pa-per-back
must re - turn it you can send it here,___ But I need a break___ and I want to be a pa-per-back

writ - er,_____ pa - per-back writ - er._____
writ - er,_____ pa - per-back writ - er._____

2nd time
D.C. al ⬧ Coda

⬧ *Coda*

Pa - per-back writ - er,_____

Fade

Yellow Submarine.

John Lennon and Paul McCartney.

Eleanor Rigby.

John Lennon and Paul McCartney.

Moderately, with a steady beat

lower notes optional

Ah _____ look at all ___ the lone - ly peo - ple! _____

Ah _____ look at all ___ the lone - ly peo - ple! _____

1. E - lea - nor Rig - by, picks up the rice ___ in the church where a wed - ding has been, ___
2. Fath - er Mc Ken - zie, writ - ing the words ___ of a ser - mon that no - one will hear, ___
3. E - lea - nor Rig - by, died in the church ___ and was bur - ied a - long ___ with her name, ___

lives in a dream. _____ Waits at the win - dow,
no one comes near. _____ 'Look at him work - ing,
no - bod - y came. _____ Fa - ther Mc Ken - zie,

wear-ing the face ___ that she keeps ___ in a jar ___ by the door, ___
darn-ing his socks ___ in the night ___ when there's no - bod - y there, ___
wip-ing the dirt ___ from his hands ___ as he walks ___ from the grave, ___

who is it for? ___
what does he care? ___ } All the lone - ly peo - ple, where do ___ they all ___ come from? ___
no one was saved. ___

All the lone - ly peo - ple, where do ___ they all ___ be - long? ___

To Coda ⊕

1.

2.

D.C. al ⊕ *Coda*

⊕ *Coda*

All You Need Is Love.

John Lennon and Paul McCartney.

Hello Goodbye.

John Lennon and Paul McCartney.

48

49

Lady Madonna.

John Lennon and Paul McCartney.

Fri - day night ar - rives with - out a suit - case,
Tues - day af - ter - noon is nev - er end - ing,

Sun - day morn - ing creep - ing like a nun,— Mon - day's child has
Wednes - day morn - ing pa - pers did - n't come,— Thurs - day night your

learned to tie his shoe - lace. See how they
stock - ing need - ed mend - ing. See how they

Repeat 3 times

run.

Coda

ends meet.

opt.

51

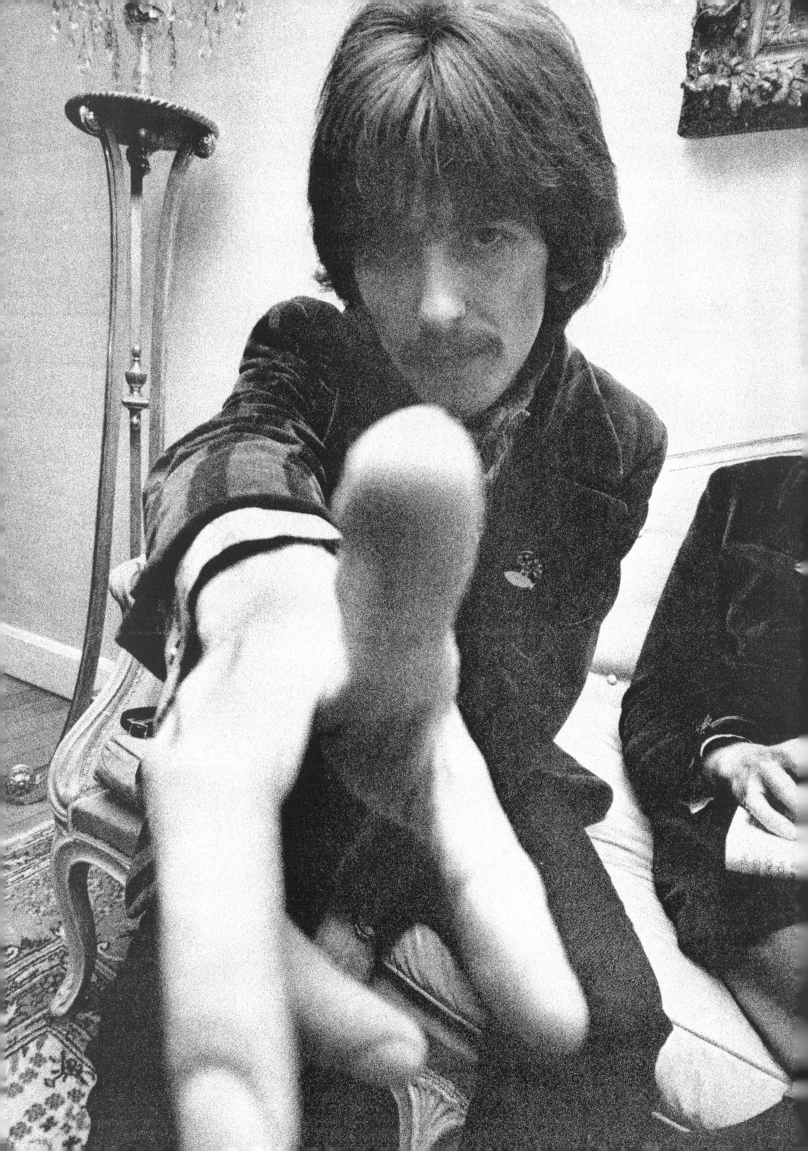

Hey Jude.

John Lennon and Paul McCartney.

© Copyright 1968 Northern Songs Limited, 24 Bruton Street, London W1.

Get Back.

John Lennon and Paul McCartney.

to where you once be-longed. _____ Get back! _____ Get back! _____ Get back _____

_____ to where you once be-longed. _____ *(Get back, Jo Jo)* Sweet Lor-et-ta Mod-ern thought she was a wo-man, but _____

_____ she was an-oth-er man. _____ All _____ the girls a-round her say _____ she's got it com-ing, But, _____

_____ she gets it while she can. _____ Get back! _____ Get back! _____ Get back _____

to where you once be-longed. _____ Get back! _____ Get back! _____ Get back _____

to where you once be-longed. _____

(Spoken:) Get back, Loretta. *Your mother is waiting for you.*

D. S. and fade out on Chorus

Wearin' her high heel shoes and her low neck sweater, Get back home, Loretta. Get back!

The Ballad Of John And Yoko.

John Lennon and Paul McCartney.

Christ! You know it ain't eas—y,———— you know how hard it can be. ————

The way things are go———ing——— they're going to cru-ci-fy—me.

To Coda ⊕

1.4. Repeat at **D.℠.** 2. Drove from 3. Sav-ing up your mo-ney for a

rain - y day, ———— giv-ing all your clothes to cha - ri - ty.

Last night the wife said, Oh boy, when you're dead you don't take no-thing with you but your

soul _____ Think!

D. S. 4th lyric
al ⊕ Coda

me.

Drums

The way things are go _____ ing _____ they're going to cru-ci-fy _____ me.

Printed and bound in Great Britain by
Caligraving Limited Thetford Norfolk

5/96 (24247)